BETWEEN DISTANT MODERNITIES

Between Distant Modernities

*Performing Exceptionality in Francoist Spain
and the Jim Crow South*

BRITTANY POWELL KENNEDY

University Press of Mississippi ❁ Jackson

www.upress.state.ms.us

Designed by Peter D. Halverson

The University Press of Mississippi is a member of the Association of American
University Presses.

Copyright © 2015 by University Press of Mississippi
All rights reserved
Manufactured in the United States of America

First printing 2015
∞
Library of Congress Cataloging-in-Publication Data

Kennedy, Brittany Powell.
Between distant modernities : performing exceptionality in Francoist Spain and the
Jim Crow South / Brittany Powell Kennedy.
pages cm
Includes bibliographical references and index.
ISBN 978-1-62846-197-8 (cloth : alk. paper) — ISBN 978-1-62674-490-5 (ebook)
1. Literature and history—Southern States—History—20th century. 2. Literature and
history—Spain—History—20th century. 3. Politics and literature—Spain—History—
20th century. 4. Comparative literature—American and Spanish. 5. Comparative
literature—Spanish and American. 6. Fascism and literature—Southern States—History—20th century. 7. Fascism and literature—Spain—History—20th century.
8. Fascism in literature. 9. Racism in literature. 10. Francoism in literature. I. Title.
PS261.K35 2015
810.9'9750904—dc23   2014031676

British Library Cataloging-in-Publication Data available

FOR TODD AND KEPA

CONTENTS

ACKNOWLEDGMENTS

This book, much like the exceptionalism it examines, has been a long process with various manifestations in the more than a decade since its seeds were planted in my undergraduate thesis. First, I must thank Steven Marsh (University of Illinois at Chicago) and Paul Allen Miller (University of South Carolina), who have been both wonderful friends and mentors who have helped me develop some very ambitious ideas into a tight and theoretically sophisticated project.

I also owe a great deal to the many scholars who have given me feedback on these ideas over the years. First, the readers of this manuscript gave me rigorous and detailed feedback that helped me tremendously in this process. In addition, Sandy Crooms was indispensable in helping me place this manuscript, and Vijay Shah has been a wonderful editor. Meanwhile, at the University of South Carolina, María Mabrey, Alexander Ogden, Robert Brinkmeyer Jr., and Lucile Charlebois were both generous and kind with comments and ideas. Keen Butterworth was particularly helpful in helping me formulate and fine-tune the many manifestations of the South in the twentieth century, and I will be forever grateful to him for that. In this project's earliest manifestation as an undergraduate thesis exploring Don Quijote's influence on twentieth-century Southern writers, J. Bainard Cowan made a major mark on this project, and Peggy Whitman Prenshaw and Yvonne Fuentes were great supporters of my work in ways that I still think about to this day.

Back home in New Orleans, my colleagues at Tulane University have been incredibly supportive of my work, particularly my chairs while there, Chris Dunn, Marilyn Miller, and Jean Dangler, and School of Liberal Arts dean Carole Haber. Last, I owe a great debt of gratitude to my family, particularly my husband, Todd Kennedy, who has had to talk about Spain, the South, and exceptionalism much more than he would have likely wanted to in the last several years, and my son, Kepa, whose consistent sleep patterns and sweet disposition helped bring this book to press much sooner than I anticipated.

BETWEEN DISTANT MODERNITIES

INTRODUCTION

Constructing Spanish and Southern Exceptionality

It is ironic that perhaps the greatest blow to Spain's perceived national consciousness—the 1898 loss of Cuba, Puerto Rico, Guam, and the Philippines—occurred as a consequence of maybe the most forgotten and ignored war in U.S. history. Yet the power-shift between one of the oldest European empires and an emergent nation-state of the "New World" involves a modern narrative that has attracted significant attention from scholars on both sides of the Atlantic. This study expands upon such transatlantic visions of national boundaries by exploring the precise manner in which two self-proclaimed "nations"—Spain and the U.S. South—defined themselves by asserting an authenticity seen as exceptional—that is, a self-invented narrative defining their cultures as "different," and sometimes better, when compared to a larger political entity, in this case, Europe and America. Thus the War of 1898—a name for the Spanish-American War whose use I will explain shortly—provides a key starting point for this project for several reasons: it marks a period when the South tried both to extract itself from and be implicated in U.S. imperial expansion and nation-building; simultaneously, it points to the end of Spain—and the beginning of the end for Europe—as an imperial power, leading to a crisis of defining what it means to be "Spanish" in a "new" and, I posit, modern world.

Calling Spain and particularly the U.S. South "nations" denotes an idea of nationalism as a linguistic system in which we are "Spanish" or "Southern" because we identify with a predetermined group of people. My discussion of nationhood as a performed entity coincides with the image in Benedict Anderson's idea of "communities" that are "distinguished, not by their falsity/genuineness, but by the style in which they are imagined" (6). While calling Spain a "nation" seems more than logical, doing the same for the South seems to involve a revisionist and racist enterprise. However, this idea of nationhood is one that is not just in line with Anderson's "communities" but one that sees national identity as a performed entity. That is, it relies on a constructed and imagined homogeneity, even if—and particularly when—that homogeneity does not exist. For example, the South's present-day notion of imagined nationhood comes from the fact that, at one point, it declared itself independent from the United States. That rupture still compels a need to "act" Southern (represented by Confederate flags, "Dixie," and so forth) even as the South tries to implicate itself in an "American" ideal. In so doing, entities like states, races, or ethnicities can be observable markers of nationhood that, in effect, become props in the performance—hence arguments, for example, that Texas and Florida are not really in the South or that the Basque Country or Cataluña are not Spanish. Examples like these suggest that nationhood must constantly be enacted both for those it seeks to include, but, more important, for those seen as separate. For Spain and the South, the history of civil war means that each has relied heavily on enacted nationhood. For example, while varying organizations of power argued that one could look Spanish or Southern, in the end it was how one acted in relation to a community of peers that determined nationality.

While national exceptionality itself seems emblematic of late-nineteenth and early twentieth-century culture, particularly in the context of fascism, my focus on Spain and the U.S. South stems from each one's place "in between" the transatlantic experience of modernity as both participated in yet because of civil war and long-lasting systemized oppression were also exceptions to U.S. and European claims to "progress." Specifically, for both Spain and the U.S. South, the idea of cultural and military defeat and the need for regeneration were, and still sometimes are, at the heart of each community's self-proclaimed exceptionality. Within these claims to exceptionalism, furthermore, exists the political and social repression each enacted for a large part of the twentieth century in the experiences of Francoism and Jim Crow. I should make clear that my purpose is not a full-scale historical comparison of these two time periods, as my study veers beyond these periods at times. Instead, I trace two specific models of performative nationalism—manifested aesthetically in various modes of cultural production—that seem exceptional during the period within which both the United States and Europe saw competing models of national authenticity coupled with the rise of fascism and the perceived threat of communism. Yet what stands out about the Francoist and Jim Crow periods is the degree to which each respectively put Spain and the South in a position to contest—and also violently confirm—different aspects of national identity throughout, and across, Europe and the United States. For example, part of Francisco Franco's success as a dictator came from his ability to construct a national vision by uniting the fascist Falange and the Catholic monarchists. Meanwhile, although William Faulkner donated money to the Republican cause during the Spanish Civil War and denounced Franco, the author's portrayal of his home region would cause many to label him a "gothic fascist" throughout his career. Examples such as these demonstrate the degree to which Francoist Spain and the Jim Crow South occupied spaces that existed in between the transatlantic engagement with fascism and communism during the early twentieth century. This very in-betweenness, coupled with each one's claims to exceptionalism, drives contemporary scholarship on these spaces as Hispanists like Jo Labanyi focus on the myths inherent in Spanish memory of the past and Southernists like Robert Brinkmeyer Jr. and Deborah Cohn locate the South's self-perceived exceptionalism in the face of fascist Europe and a sociopolitically similar Latin America, respectively. This project engages and expands upon such work and uses the comparison between Spain and the South as a means of constructing a model of performativity inherent in the relationship between "self" and "other" by looking at two cultures that, under very similar circumstances, have played both roles. In so doing, we gain a transatlantic image of modernity that questions the very distinctions it purports to perform—not just Spanishness and Southernness but also Europeanness and Americanness—and how those distinctions engage questions of national tradition in the face of impending modernity.

The fact that both Francoist Spain and the Jim Crow South relied heavily on violence to enforce their ideas of essential identity speaks to the degree to which images of Spanishness and Southernness were enacted and performed during this period. For this reason, furthermore, scholars like Mary Ann Frese Witt have noted a reliance upon theater and spectacle within Franco-Italian fascism, pointing to a "high confluence of aesthetic and political discourse, mingling the two so that they are at times indistinguishable" in turn-of-the-century France and Italy (6). The merging of the political and the aesthetic was no different in Spain and the South during this period, as political engagement found its expression in modernist literature and art. For this reason, my study focuses heavily on this material as it uses the artistic aesthetics to reveal the liminality of Spanish and Southern political discourse in the early to mid-twentieth century. No doubt part of the reason that Francoist and Jim Crow discourses seem so disparate has to do with what Frese Witt describes as the "heterogeneity of fascism" in which the ideological tenets are by no means essential, fixed, or coherent among different nations. Nonetheless, Frese Witt compiles a general list of fascism's main aspects, and most are observable in Spain and the South from the 1910s to the era following World War II: moral and philosophical relativism, a rejection of rationalism and the bourgeoisie, a disavowal of certain aspects of modernity (specifically technology), and a nostalgia for an agrarian existence (4–5). While linking fascism and the U.S. South seems more challenging, Robert Brinkmeyer Jr.'s *The Fourth Ghost: White Southern Writers and European Fascism, 1930–1950* makes that very connection by showing how commentators from both the North and the South were quick to compare fascist Italy and Nazi Germany with Southern politics of the period (3). What resulted was a crisis of conscious among many white Southern writers since it posited their Southernness as an exception to U.S. citizenry at a moment when patriotism was at an all-time high. Although Brinkmeyer's study does not directly engage Francoism and is more bio-historical in scope, such a comparison demonstrates how competing claims to national authority must be performed in order to gain, and maintain, power, hence the reason European fascism could cause the very crisis of conscious Brinkmeyer identifies in modernist Southern writers.

My idea of nationhood as a performed entity—particularly within the specific cases of Francoist Spain and the Jim Crow South—sees performativity as linked to a perceived loss of national authenticity producing a need to code, or create a new model of, lost nationhood as a means of recouping it. Perceived loss, as I show, is the reason U.S. Southerners were so eager to be part of a successful military campaign in 1898 following defeat in the Civil War only decades earlier. Meanwhile, Spain already was nearing the end of its colonial dominance, and it spent decades trying to "regenerate" itself as an empire. While the parameters of my study seem to promote an exclusive definition of performativity, it is Spain's and the South's aforementioned "in-betweenness" that actually creates an inclusive definition of performativity in a theoretical field that often sees itself divided between two dominating and, at times, competing modes of performance: that of theater and dance and that of ritual and speech act theory. My ideas on performance, at their most basic level, follow Henry Bial's assertion in the introduction to *The Performance Studies Reader* that all definitions of performance studies are themselves performed since "they are not descriptions of an already-existing body of knowledge, but attempts to create a knowledge-formation by defining, explaining, and discussing it" (1). For this reason, while my discussion of performativity falls well within the realm of contemporary work in the field, my definition of performance entails a global idea that exposes efforts to enact one image—be it of nationhood, gender, race, and so forth—in place of another, creating a dynamic in which identities are never fixed but only manifested as images that are constantly contested.

While my definition of performance implies that identities are never fixed, its does rely on the idea that the image that performance means to replace is coded, that is, marked by an organizing structure that identifies it. The idea of coded identities works within my definition of performance in that it exploits the arbitrary linguistic bond between identity and its performative while pointing to the established modes of dance and drama. The medium of theater and dance within performance studies often is seen as a natural opposition to the performatives of speech—instead of speech acting, acting becomes a kind of speech. The idea of performance producing an image that is meant to replace a coded one suggests an unstable relationship between an idea and its enactment, which manifests itself both in speech acts and ritual. Because of this instability, scholars like Jon McKenzie have sought to link the theoretical divide in performance studies by defining performance in terms of its "liminality," or as he puts it, "a mode of activity whose spatial, temporal, and symbolic 'in-betweenness' allows for social norms to be suspended, challenged, played with, and perhaps even transformed" (27). McKenzie's idea of performance as "liminal" works within a paradigm of performance in which there is a natural slippage between what is imagined (national identity, for example) and what is performed. This difference between idea and act has its origins in Jacques Derrida's idea of language when, in his essay "Signature Event Context," he distinguishes between intent and reception in speech, asserting that all language is performance. For this project, this difference between an idea and its enactment—or the process by which "Spain" and the "South" both are embodied and contested by visual representations of "Spanishness" and "Southernness"—drives my depiction of performance. Again, I am not adhering to one mode, or one resulting embodiment, of Spanish and Southern performance; instead, I explore two cultures that were simultaneously implicated in, but in other ways excluded from, U.S. and European ideas of nationalism. Removing Spain and the South from this self/other dichotomy, I show how the various performances of Spanishness and Southernness reveal a liminality that remaps these spaces: instead of being inside state, regional, and even national boundaries, they extend beyond them by both embodying and challenging the borders that contain them. In that vein, my image of performance takes McKenzie's idea one step further—instead of seeing "performance" as in-between boundaries, it sees an exploration of the performative as capable of taking us beyond imagined borders to a mode in which we are no longer defined by how we "act" but instead aware of how acting defines us.

Within the idea that performance contests and replaces coded images is a linguistic relationship in which an object is coded with a specific meaning. The definition of performance as ritualized speech finds its origins in J. L. Austin's *How to Do Things with Words*, in which he explores language not as a simple utterance of facts but as enacted speech. As Austin puts it, "to *say* something is to *do* something" (177). His most famous example of what he terms "performatives" is the act of saying "I do" in a marriage ceremony—by saying "I do," a person marries someone. Austin's work on various "speech acts" was synthesized and refined by John Searle in later years, and his own notion of speech acts constitutes, as Judith Butler claims, "verbal assurances and promises which seem not only to refer to a speaking relationship, but to constitute a moral bond between speakers" ("Performative Acts" 187). Using Austin's and Searle's model, scholars like Butler formulate speech acts as constituting social reality. As Butler argues, in saying "I am a woman," one actually performs an idea of gender that is by no means a stable identity. Instead, as she says in "Performative Acts and Gender Constitution: An Essay in Phenomenology and Feminist Theory," gender "is an identity tenuously constituted in time—an identity instituted through a *stylized repetition of acts*" (187). Taking Butler's idea of gender as a performative, one finds new meaning in Benedict Anderson's idea of nationhood as an imagined social contract. Thus when one says "I am from Spain" or "I am Southern," he or she is enacting a malleable idea of nationhood constituted in time—one that exists within coded parameters of geography, race, and gender. It was this performative quality of nationhood that was exploited during the Jim Crow and Francoist periods as organizations of power sought to define nationality not with an already-present idea of Spanishness or Southernness, but with a mode of thinking in which to be Spanish or Southern was to act a certain way, to *do* something.

Seeing nationhood as a performed act, that doing something elicits certain meaning, demonstrates again how ritual and theatricality are coded forms that are meant to elicit familiarity on the part of the audience. Joseph Roach, in *Cities of the Dead: Circum-Atlantic Performance* (1996), works within such an inclusive model of performance when he defines it as a theatricality inherent in acts of "surrogation"—that is, a process in which "culture reproduces and re[-]creates itself" as it suffers losses that it tries to replace with substitutes, or "surrogates" (2). Focusing on London and New Orleans, Roach's specific examples of performance involve multiple references to ritualized theater—for example, the Mardi Gras Indians in New Orleans and various nineteenth-century British plays. Yet while Roach no doubt sees performance related to theater, he also sees these performances as efforts to reimagine a shared cultural memory. The process of surrogation—that is, literally finding a replacement for what has "died" in society—turns memory into an act; or, to remember something is to do something that is not necessarily related to memory itself. Within Roach's model, this idea becomes apparent as efforts to substitute the past inevitably fail because, as Roach notes, "the intended substitute either cannot fulfill expectations, creating a deficit, or actually exceeds them, creating a surplus" (2). Because of this constant failure, a cyclical process occurs in which "performance" becomes an act of continuously re-remembering what has been lost. Simultaneously, however, the surrogate possesses an uncanny quality since it is meant to replace what has died, but its failure to completely do so only further highlights this failed double; as a result, the surrogate becomes a ghost from the past that haunts the present. This haunting produces an array of ambivalent emotions that incite both rampant nostalgia and an overwhelming fear that what has died will not remain within cultural memory—or the mutually agreed upon past that a nation uses to define itself. Basically, nations are either paranoid about repeating a forgotten past, or they become completely, and often blindly, reminiscent of the past.

Given these various modes of performance, this study hinges on an idea of nationality as a performative that exists in between the idea that precludes the speech act and the image that said act is meant to invoke. Furthermore, if we accept Roach's supposition that performance always "offers a substitute for something that pre-existed it" (3), then performed national identity, specifically for Spain and the South, involves the reproduction of a nationhood that twentieth-century Spanish and Southern cultural critics and artists located in a "traditional" past that they saw as more glorious, thus needing regeneration, in a "modern" environment. Following Roach's assertion that "loss" is the catalyst of surrogation, integral to my study of Spain and the South is the culture of defeat and reaction and how a military, thus a perceived cultural, defeat forced an initial reconsideration of national identity that later is reproduced via performed nationalism. For Spain and the South specifically, military defeat motivated each one's need to assert an authentic nationhood throughout the twentieth century—a fact evidenced most prominently during the Francoist and Jim Crow periods. Thus my study focuses largely on the cultural production of those eras in an effort to examine how two power structures that seemed utterly coded and monolithic were in fact multifaceted performances of a seemingly authentic Spanishness and Southernness that desired to reconstruct military defeat into a moral, and cultural, victory. The War of 1898, with its implications for shifting identities and the source of Spain's own harrowing defeat, becomes emblematic of how the past is reconstructed performatively in the present—an act that I soon discuss in more detail in order to present an early example of a phenomenon that is repeated throughout the twentieth century.

Before detailing the precise manner in which Spain and the U.S. South asserted their exceptionality, particularly in the decades before each one's civil war, it is important to note that both were places united by political circumstance. In the case of Spain, it was a space that contained diverse cultural and political divisions (including different languages) united by the marriage of Fernando II of Aragon and Isabel I of Castile in 1469. Similarly, the U.S. South, settled by a diverse group of explorers during the colonial period, did not secede from the Union with a unified gusto. Coastal states, composed of French and Spanish settlers, were politically and culturally different from, for example, the Scotch-Irish populations that settled the Appalachian states (most of whom owned few or no slaves). What set both Spain and the South apart from their European and U.S. counterparts in, particularly, the nineteenth century was a lack of industrial wealth and manpower. Both were agrarian economies leading into the twentieth century, and, while Spain as a nation is obviously much older than the U.S. South, both had a cultural diversity and an uneven economic development that, early on, set them apart from the continents that contained them. These cultural divisions in Spain and the South still exist today—despite efforts over the years to suggest otherwise—as the Basque, Catalan, and Galician populations still seek independence from Spain, and there remains sharp political and cultural divides between the coastal, urban South (in cities like New Orleans, Charleston, and Savannah) and the more rural, interior South.

For both Spain and the South, national performativity emerged out of the need to re-create a national "tradition" both in the face of military defeat and what they saw as a "modern" environment. The idea of preserving tradition in the face of modernity, at its core, represents a focus on time as both an imminent and malleable form. Eric Hobsbawm's definition of tradition sees the forms as a "set of practices" that seeks to "inculcate certain values and norms of behavior by repetition, which automatically implies continuity with the past" (Hobsbawm and Ranger 1). Such an image no doubt stands in direct contrast with modernity, a period defined by detachment from the past and, with that, freedom from fated subjectivity. The clash between "tradition" and "modernity" in many ways typifies the slippage that defines performance, or the difference between what is imagined and what is enacted. This difference becomes particularly important in the context of imagined nationhood as nations become "modern" forms only when invoking the ritualized culture of the past. In the case of Spain and the South, military defeat and civil war made this enterprise even more necessary as the "loss" of the past that typified modernity (Flatley 30–31) was compounded by defeat in war, prompting renegotiations of the past, which defined the Francoist and Jim Crow periods.

Exploring Francoism and Jim Crow within the context of performed nationalism, this project, as a logical step, shows how these specific organizations of power recall an uncanny historical past that needs constant reformulation. My definition of performance sees a connection between acts of remembering and how they recall a "familiar," coded past that is subsequently made "unfamiliar" when it is boiled down to a single idea of authenticity. Roach briefly alludes to this idea as well when he describes how the process of surrogation becomes uncanny when cultures face the "inexorable antiquation" involved in re-remembering the past, which results in emotions ranging from "incontinent sentimentalism to raging paranoia" (2) that come out of a need to cope with the presence of a familiar past in an unfamiliar present. Freud's definition of the uncanny matches how performance becomes uncanny when he makes clear that what is "*heimlich*" ("familiar") is reproduced in the "*unheimlich*" ("uncanny") ("Uncanny" 224). In other words, what is so fear inspiring about performances of an authentic sense of nation is that it *is* familiar; thus things that should belong to the past continue to haunt us in the present. Indeed, what is so frightening about Jim Crow and Francoism is that each was not a particular instance of oppression or performance of nationalism, but a very familiar one whose particular assertions of authentic identity codes are readily observable throughout Spanish and Southern history. Yet what proves most ironic about these eras is how the past was constantly reinvented to produce an image of nationhood that could be called "exceptional," thus allowing mainstream U.S. and European discourse to respectively regard Jim Crow and Francoism as "exceptional" and exclusive to Spain and the South (particularly following World War II).

The assertion of national or regional exceptionality is by no means new within cultural and political discourse. Yet a study of Spain and the South specifically shows how the assertion of a national authenticity following military defeat necessitates the assertion of exceptionality, and with it, cultural superiority, as a means of refashioning oneself into a moral and cultural victor. As such, my comparison shows how the assertion of exceptionality in Spain and the South, specifically during Francoism and Jim Crow, was, and is, a performance of an essential and authentic nationhood constructed around a very specific remembering, and forgetting, of the historical past. My grounding of performance in history, furthermore, builds upon the work of performance-studies critics like Diana Taylor, who points out that performance is by no means un- or antihistorical. Instead, as she notes in her article "Performance and/as History," it has been strategically positioned outside of history, rendered invalid as a form of cultural transmission, in short *made* un- and anti-historical by conquerors and colonists who wanted to monopolize power" (70). Taylor's point here subtly invokes the role that organizations of power play within the realm of performance and provokes the questions of who performs what for whom. Meanwhile, she is quick to point out how the realm of performances can both contest official history and also sustain "an organizational infrastructure, a practice or know-how, an episteme, and a politics that goes beyond the explicit topic" (68). This point becomes particularly important when exploring Spanish and Southern exceptionalism during Francoism and Jim Crow in that both were oppressive organizations of power that were allowed to emerge and exist for almost half a century without major political or military intervention from the "audience" to whom their performance was directed, namely, Europe and the United States, but also the international community. How both periods lasted so long is, in tandem with the use of brute force and violent oppression, a testament both to the creativity employed in the careful reconstruction of the past to assert an authentic and exceptional present and to the degree to which their "audience" relied on these assertions of exceptionality as a means of fueling their own "differing" nationalisms.

The idea of the "audience" within performance studies is a key concept when we realize that national exceptionality, particularly in the Spanish and Southern contexts, is a concept external to nationality. After all, Spain and the South did not become "othered" on their own; instead, such a distinction has been present in writings about Spain and the South for centuries. Specifically, nineteenth-century French travel writings clearly sought to exoticize and orientalize Spain and its Muslim influence. For example, in Théophile

Gautier's influential travel guide, *Voyage en Espagne* [*Travel to Spain*] (1845), he says, "La Siéra Morena franchie, l'aspect du pays change totalement; c'est comme si l'on passait tout à coup de l'Europe à l'Afrique" ["The Sierra Morena crossed, the country's aspect changes completely, as if one passed suddenly from Europe to Africa"] (168). The image of Spain as savage and African appears throughout travel writings during the nineteenth century; thus Spanish difference becomes "un-European" as it is configured outside of Spain. In a similar vein, Southern exceptionality, primarily in terms of climate and geography, was something that had been identified by early settlers in the colonial era. Meanwhile by the nineteenth century this early difference became the marker of an opposing national ideal within a nation composed of immigrants seeking common roots. Yet as Susan-Mary Grant writes in her book *North Over South: Northern Nationalism and American Identity in the Antebellum Era*, the propensity during the period was to "invent a *uncommon* descent, a process summed up by the stereotypical images of the southern Cavalier and northern Yankee" (58). While the Cavalier suggested a gentlemanly, chivalrous soldier, the New England Yankee was linked to ideas of Puritan frontierism. The fundamental difference that can be drawn from the far-reaching stereotypes here is that between "old" world—Southerners were often compared to feudal Englishman by northern travel writers—and ideas of a "new" nation. As Grant makes clear in her book, such a division was not just the self-mythologizing of a romantic South but also was a clear stereotyping, sometimes romantic and sometimes hostile, by the North as a means of asserting its own cultural superiority. Thus for both Spain and the South, the association of both cultures with an older, somehow more primal, culture illustrates not just how both cultures came to conceptualize themselves as different, but how that exceptionality came from the outside as well as from within.

My citation of French and Northern travel writings on Spain and the South is not to make either a victim of the "orientalist" gaze; quite the opposite, such depictions show how formulations of "exceptional" nationalism are often developed externally. How they get appropriated by the nation occurs during a process similar to Homi Bhabha's definition of colonial mimicry, which is an enactment coming out of "the desire for a reformed, recognizable Other, *as a subject of difference that is almost the same but not quite*" (122). As a result of this difference, Bhabha notes, "the discourse of mimicry is constructed around an *ambivalence*; in order to be effective, mimicry must continually produce its slippage, its excess, its difference" (122). While Spain and the South are clearly not colonial objects, their role as an "other," making them almost European and American, respectively, but not quite, presents an opportunity to explore exactly how the mimicry of projected exceptionality produces "slippage," "excess," and "difference," in various forms. Deborah Cohn and Jon Smith make this observation about the South in their book *Look Away!: The U.S. South in New World Studies*: "The potential for Southern distinctiveness consists in what might be called the South's literally uncanny (*unheimlich*) hybridity. To critics who imagine themselves, more or less unproblematically, as either Third World or First World, the U.S. South has appeared compellingly as familiar and exotic, both Self and Other" (9). Not only can this same kind of uncanniness be applied to Spain—whose self-image has relied on many of the Self/Other contradictions often applied to the South, that is, exotic and traditional, hospitable yet intolerant—but it is an uncanniness that is revealed specifically through the realm of performance, that is, an embodiment of exactly how the past becomes so hauntingly reproduced in the present. In my examination of the very uncanniness of Spanish and Southern assertions of an exceptional, and authentic, national identity, my goal is not to draw a direct connection between two "similar" nations, but instead, following Taylor's own work on "Americanness," to use the mode of performance to allow what she describes as "alternative mappings, providing a set of strategies and conventions that allow scholars to see practices that narrative, poetry, or even drama as a scripted genre might occlude" ("Remapping Genre" 1417). In so doing, the comparison between Spain and the South charts a transatlantic connection that does not just show the move from an "old" empire to a "new" conception of nationality, but instead shows how the old and the new exist simultaneously as they are constructed, and performed, for a global community that often looks to an "exotic" other as a means of asserting its own performed identity.

In my effort to reposition the performance of a national authenticity between Europe and America, the short War of 1898 represents a single moment when Spain, the United States, and Cuba were all asserting competing national identities for their citizens, their opponents, and the rest of the world. Even at the level of naming the war, memory and nationhood have been constructed since a country is allowed to "own" the conflict by having its name define it. For example, I utilize the decidedly nonnational "War of 1898"—a term that would cause the average U.S. citizen who learned about the Spanish-American War in school to draw a blank. In Spanish, the war has several names as well, among them, "la Guerra Hispana-Cubana-Norteamericana" ["The Hispanic-Cuban-North American War"], or simply "la Guerra de Cuba" ["the Cuban War"]. Yet the most interesting of these names is Spain's appellation of "el desastre del '98" ["the disaster of '98"], which began as a serious appraisal of Spain's loss of imperial glory but continues in usage today as an ironic view of Spain's crisis of nationhood at the turn of the twentieth century. The moldable nature of this war's identification over time suggests the very constructed sense of national memory I describe. What these differences should suggest, furthermore, is that the War of 1898 was less a direct political and military clash between the nation-states of Spain and the United States and more a posturing of two global forces—one trying to convince its public that it was still an imperial power and the other trying to convince its people that it had the constitutional and moral right to become one. What ensued during what U.S. ambassador John Hay called a "splendid little War" influenced the economic and political policies of both countries for several decades (Rosenfeld 1), marking the moment at which the United States acted for the first time as the world's police force and the moment at which Spain was thrown into a political divide that culminated in its civil war and a lengthy dictatorship.

Demystifying the War of 1898 involves a reexamination of both parties' motives, in particular the fact that neither Spanish nor U.S. leaders really wanted to declare war. The conflict itself initially involved open rebellion that was developing in Spain's remaining colonies, particularly Cuba. These struggles in Cuba began as early as 1868 and became known as the Ten Years War. As Spanish attempts to squash rebellion became increasingly brutal, the United States, which had previously offered to buy Cuba from Spain, saw its heavy economic investment in the country increasingly jeopardized (Rosenfeld 3). As a result, President William McKinley, eager to avoid war and heavily influenced by a U.S. population reading sensationalist accounts of Spanish brutality in William Randolph Hearst's *New York Journal* and Joseph Pulitzer's *New York World*, urged Spain to grant Cuban independence. Spain, for reasons I explore later and the least of which included a desire to maintain its last vestige of empire, adamantly refused. As conflict seemed imminent, McKinley dispatched the USS *Maine* to sail to Havana harbor under the guise of protecting U.S. citizens in the volatile country but with the real intention of protecting U.S. financial and military interests as well. While the United States made a posturing of peace keeping, in reality it was preparing for an "unavoidable" war.

On February 15, 1898, an explosion ripped through the hull of the *Maine*, killing 266 men aboard. McKinley quickly organized an investigation into the explosion, which concluded that an external mine had instigated a series of blasts within the ship. Despite several inquiries in recent years, the exact cause of the *Maine* explosion is still clouded in doubt. Yet Hearst's "yellow journalism" aroused U.S. popular opinion in such a manner that it became impossible to not declare war. Thus U.S. citizens became embroiled in a call to arms, repeating the popular refrain, "Remember the *Maine*! To hell with Spain!" (Pérez 57). While it appeared that the U.S. decision to declare war sprung from a humanitarian urge to free Cuba or a desire to politically defeat an antiquated empire, the United States actually engaged in a posturing to its own population about its right to increase its land holdings and do its own empire-building. Although many disapproved of U.S. imperial pursuits—the most famous opposition coming from Mark Twain—war with the Spanish was portrayed as unavoidable, thus putting the United States in the politically advantageous position of defensive player. Louis A. Pérez Jr. points to the manipulated image of the *Maine* incident when he notes, "That the *Maine* has enjoyed enduring historiographical preeminence underscores the conceptual appeal of treating the war as a function of chance, not choice" (59). Thus when the United States defeated the Spanish 109 days after declaring war, it had not done so as the founding pillar of a new empire, per public opinion, but as an international savior acting in defense of freedom.

While the constructed image of the War of 1898 from the U.S. angle also entailed the masculine frontier-spirit of Teddy Roosevelt leading his "Rough Riders" up San Juan Hill, the Spanish built a different narrative as military leaders unsuccessfully combated a very organized rebel movement, which resorted to brutal oppression that, ultimately, legitimized U.S. intervention in Cuba (Harrison 3). Following the explosion of the *Maine*, Spanish military officials believed that war was the only way to retain Spain's imperial, and national, identity, but they knew taking on a major naval power without allied support meant certain defeat. Yet much like the U.S. population, Spanish citizens were fueled by patriotic news reports and demonstrations that failed to acknowledge the country's unpreparedness (Harrison 4). In addition, in a nation that had only recently ended a series of civil wars between two competing monarchs representing the bitter divide between a traditional, absolute monarchy and a more liberal government, the Spanish military had no intention of letting a complete recapitulation to the United States propel opportunistic apportioning of blame between the Carlists and the Republicans. Thus instead of cowering as a political power, Spain was determined to be defeated honorably as a military one. Although the consequences would be no different in terms of the nation being thrown into crisis, such a desire to determine—and imagine—its own fate as this war's loser demonstrates how Spain engaged in a construction of national identity that matches the United States's depiction of itself as savior/winner.

Within the narrative of U.S. expansion at the dawn of the twentieth century there are ghosts of its own civil strife, which also involved a philosophical battle between a perceived tradition faced with an industrial modernity. Indeed, the South is unique to the U.S. military experience in the sense that, despite a very long military tradition, it was the first group of U.S. citizens to experience defeat in war. In fact, the banding together of the Southern states was a result of its secession from the Union and primarily occurred so that a semi-united military force could be formed during the Civil War. Indeed, the South only became an imagined community really upon its military defeat as it united culturally because the defeated Virginian and the defeated Mississippian suddenly fell under the same category. In addition, Spain, which had a long tradition of military and, in particular, naval power also had to reconstruct its sense of nationhood as it suffered a military defeat that, as in the South, caused a serious blow to its national consciousness. The result, in Spain, was a spirit of "regenerationism" that became a means of re-remembering a glorious imperial past—which never really existed—as a model for reconstructing its future. Such efforts prove strikingly similar to the "Lost Cause" movement in the South, which sought to reinstate elements of "traditional" Southern society in its post–Civil War environment. Both Spanish and Southern efforts to reconstruct their national identity become ironic when considering that both regions had become known for their economic and cultural backwardness during the late nineteenth century. Thus while it seems that these nations were merely nostalgic, in reality what occurred was a reimagining of nationhood that attempted to use the eternal image of "traditional" society to construct a mythic exceptionality to the "modern" and "progressive" U.S. and European nations.

The War of 1898, in the cultural memory of both the U.S. South and Spain, involves the very kind of performativity that we observe in each one's effort to construct a unified sense of nation earlier in the nineteenth century. While the War of 1898 invariably marks a power shift between Europe and America and an overall move toward a postcolonial world, the "othered" regions of these continents saw this war as a moment of reckoning for their own sense of nationhood. Before examining this moment in history in detail, however, it seems prudent to illustrate that it was not the first time that Spain and the South had engaged in such similar forms of nation-building. Indeed, it becomes easy to forget that the first explorers to what is now the coastal southeastern United States were, in fact, Spanish, and that their approach toward colonizing the New World derived from the vigorous effort to build a "Spanish" nation—that heretofore did not exist—by fifteenth-century Catholic monarchs Isabel and Fernando. Such nation building is observable, furthermore, as early as their 1492 expulsion of the Moors from Granada. It is no coincidence that Columbus's arrival in the Caribbean and the end of the *Reconquista* share this date, and as Henry Kamen notes in his book *Empire: How Spain Became a World Power 1492–1763*, "The Granada war, with its histories of suffering and heroism, was—even more than the expedition of the Canary islands—the prototype of Castile's imperial experience" (21). Although Spanish influence over the South waned as threats from the French and British pushed the Spanish closer to their colonies in present-day Texas and New Mexico, the Spanish, as Kamen details, left perhaps the greatest mark on the formation of Southern culture by providing the prevailing and the most adhered to model for the purchasing, transporting, and selling of African slaves to the colonies, beginning with their transport of slaves to Hispañola (136). It goes without saying that the practice of slavery marked the South's economic and social development well into the nineteenth and even twentieth centuries. As a result, it has been suggested in criticism that the U.S. South should be regarded less as the "other" cast into the lower stratum of the United States and instead be regarded as the northernmost point of plantation America. In such an effort to reposition the South geographically and historically within any sense of national consciousness, we again observe the very construction of nationhood described by Anderson. Even more important, we also observe the manner in which a regional "exceptionality" can be extracted from a dominant discourse—be it the North, just New England, or the United States in general. As a result, "exceptionality" becomes part of a global dialogue that fits within any malleable sense of nation, producing productive models for examining culture instead of ones that seek comparison purely in terms of opposition (North-South, Spain-Europe).

Because of this connection between the South, the Caribbean, and Central and South America, the dominant critical approach to comparative Southern studies has been to explore the relationship between the region and other colonies of the "New World." There is in fact a historical basis for this comparison when one considers the nineteenth-century Southern-born filibusters—the most famous being Tennessean William Walker—who tried to take over several areas in South America during the mid-nineteenth century. In fact, the word "filibuster" comes to English from the Spanish "*filibustero*" (pirate), and it came to specifically entail the military conquest of land without U.S. government sanction. One can see why U.S. Southerners saw great promise in the region to their south: it was geographically similar and also lived under a plantation economy. Meanwhile, as the Spanish colonies became more politically unstable, filibusters like Walker could seize control, as he did in Nicaragua, serving as its president from 1856 to 1857. Although Creole landowners sought to forge a union with the South, the U.S. Civil War put an end to such negotiations, and landowners continued to submit to Spanish rule in an effort to prevent slave uprisings (Bretz, *Encounters Across Borders*, 72). Although Walker's "Southern dream of a Caribbean empire" was brief, in reality it reflects the legacy left on the South by Spain in the sense that both—albeit at different points in history—attempted to nation-build through a plantation empire. Thus although geographical and economic connections do exist between the South, the Caribbean, and Central and South America, there still exists a performed nationhood within this communal desire to reinstate a glorious past in the face of a present defeat. It was for this reason that many defeated Southerners returned to the western frontier and South America after the Civil War. Yet such performance turns dark when realizing how reconceptualizing the past involves the conquest of land and people through military force and agrarian ideals. This "traditional" image of the past, moreover, made both Spain and the South "exceptions" to the rule of modern progress during the early twentieth century. As a result of such "othering," each was seen as backward and uncultured in the face of a progressive industrial capitalism that marked the arrival of modernity.

The kind of nationalism seen in Spain during colonization and in the U.S. South during the filibuster tradition came to a startling halt as each perceived a need for regeneration. The War of 1898—with its political and economic implications of an emergent globalized culture—provides an interesting moment to examine the interaction between two defeated "nations" of Europe and America. The nature of that defeat, furthermore, has led Peninsularists like Jo Labanyi and Southernists like C. Vann Woodward to point to both regions' admiration for a figure I call the "lovable loser," namely, someone who prefers glorious defeat rather than submission to another, opposing national will—whom Labanyi describes in *Constructing Identity in Contemporary Spain: Theoretical Debates and Cultural Practice* as those who "refuse to 'sellout' to history's (foreign, capitalist) winners." She adds, "This glorification of heroic losers can be read not just as a 'making a virtue of necessity' in the absence of a gallery of victors, but, more positively, as a strategy of ensuring that those who were not allowed to leave a trace on the historical stage do leave their trace on the cultural arena" (6). Thus Spain and the South consistently tried, albeit at different moments, to make themselves into historical winners by remembering the past in a manner that justified and legitimized further military action or simply resulted in propagandistic efforts to glorify an inglorious past. These efforts involved a specific manipulation of the historical past as Southerners tried to re-create a new myth for their Civil War loss within the confines of the U.S. 1898 victory, thus defining themselves as the valiant warriors they thought themselves to be—even if it was for the wrong war. Meanwhile, Spain translated its loss into an urgent need to redefine its nationhood, and the subsequent, competing definitions of this "nation" plunged it into civil war, resulting in a dictatorship famous for its own prevailing ideas of national identity. What the War of 1898 produced was a moment in history when these two nations engaged in an almost dialogic path of self-destruction and self-reconciliation. As Spain suffered defeat at the hands of the United States and plunged itself into a existential nationalist doubt, the U.S. South—which had suffered a similar defeat at the hands of the Union only a few decades earlier—tried to implicate itself in U.S. military achievement. Such an effort reflects a desire to forget defeat in a manner that refashions oneself into a historical winner.

For the U.S. South, the War of 1898 was a moment of reckoning. Having been defeated in a civil war that it envisioned as a second American Revolution (1861–65), occupied during Reconstruction (1865–77), and still clinging to Confederate sympathies, Southerners did not initially enlist in the military with quite the gusto of their Northern compatriots. Yet they did fight in relatively large numbers, and as Nina Silber notes in her book *The Romance of Reunion: Northerners and the South, 1865–1900,* "Southerners again won the praise of writers and speakers who acknowledged the strong, though ill-defined, commitment that has guided the Confederacy and now motivated the South to fight the Spanish" (180). In other words, the once very Southern refusal to, using Labanyi's phrasing, "sell-out to history's . . . winners," and instead try and defeat them, had become a U.S. ideal, and the South was poised to make a name for itself in that enterprise. In addition, the sinking of the USS *Maine* had more than aroused the emotions of all U.S. citizens. Thus the war began to appear as an opportunity for natural reconciliation between the once-divided North and South—to such a degree that when war was officially declared, both "Dixie" and "The Battle Hymn of the Republic" were played during the congressional vote.

The ambivalent tone of Southern participation in the War of 1898 suggests a slightly more subversive goal. Indeed, as Silber notes, the male

Southerner's successful participation in the war caused him to emerge "in an invigorated light after the conflict with Spain, assuming a new and prominent position in American culture. White southern men who for years had been conscious of trying to reignite their sense of virility, lost little time in helping to promote their regional manliness to both southern and national audiences" (185). In addition, in his essay "Remembering the *Maine*: The United States, 1898 and Sectional Reconciliation," John Oldfield makes a compelling argument that the design and placement of memorials to the USS *Maine* throughout the South suggest a desire to implicate itself in the "successful" narrative of U.S. military achievement. For example, the most convincing examples include a gun from the *Maine* given to South Carolina that, during the First World War, was pointedly moved near a monument to the Confederate dead.¹ In addition, Oldfield notes that a similar monument to the *Maine* faces Fort Sumter in Charleston—the place where the first shots of the Civil War were fired—while it is surrounded by both Confederate cannons and other guns from World War I. Quoting Catherine Bishir, who describes these spaces as a "continuum of patrician patriotism," Oldfield makes a singular point by describing similar examples of monuments to the *Maine* in both Raleigh, North Carolina, and Atlanta, Georgia—many of which have similar styles and phrases as Civil War monuments. Thus he posits, "The spirit of the Confederacy blended easily with American nationalism and dreams of empire. That it did so was a measure of the difference that the Spanish-American War had made" (57). Faced with the eradication of its Confederate past under a U.S. national blanket, the South would use monuments to creatively perform its past in a way that transforms Southerners' own self-conception of a "defeated nation" into a historical victory.

Of course, the South's vision of itself as champion came fundamentally at the expense of Spain, whose crippling loss created a similar desire to transform itself into a historical winner. Aside from calling the war "el desastre" (the disaster), a series of intellectuals of the time—controversially and somewhat unfairly grouped under the guise of the Generation of '98—began to question elements of Spanish culture and seek answers to it in metaphorical terms, most notably with the image of Don Quijote. The figure of Don Quijote has a specifically performative and transatlantic function within early twentieth-century culture, which Christopher Britt-Arredondo explains in his book *Quixotism: The Imaginative Denial of Spain's Loss of Empire*: "By seizing on the imaginative and suggestive powers of literature, in their essays they represented the events of 1898 as an encounter between a Spanish Don Quixote and his Anglo-Saxon nemesis, Robinson Crusoe" (2). Indeed, the image of Don Quijote versus Robinson Crusoe suggests a degree to which Spain performed its "traditional" culture for the rest of "modern" Europe by contrasting Britain's new brand of picaresque hero—one who represented the sort of ingenuity and work ethic espoused by industrial modernity. Yet simultaneously, Spanish intellectuals were in a torn situation of wanting to preserve Spanish identity while advocating a modernization in the country via greater union with European ideals (Pinedo 133).[2] Thus the figure of Don Quijote himself was reimagined by artists throughout the twentieth century as his defeat at the end of Cervantes's novel was reinterpreted by artists as varying as Miguel de Unamuno and Pablo Picasso to serve as both an example of and an alternative to an industrial modernity they saw as destructive and homogenizing.

The conflict inherent in the impulse to modernize while preserving tradition prevailed throughout the twentieth century and came to a head when the Proclamation of the Second Republic compelled King Alfonso XIII to leave Spain and instigated some of the most radical constitutional changes seen in the history of constitutional democracy. Yet this period marked a similarly precarious moment in Spanish history. As Sandie Holguin notes in her book *Creating Spaniards: Culture and National Identity in Republican Spain*, the Second Republic, much like the monument-wielding South, "tried to reconfigure an official culture and make it accessible to a popular audience, in the process turning one of the oldest European states into a modern nation" (10). The emphasis here on a "popular" audience again points to the performed aspect of this reconfiguration that is not very different from the South's reworking of its own Confederate myth in the public sphere. Of course, such radical changes were challenged by an array of factions—including monarchists, fascists, landed gentry, and the Catholic Church, to name a few—whose own image of nation differed dramatically. Thus the difference between tradition and modernity mirrors a political division of how to engage the Spanish masses. In the end, it was the slippage, or the difference, between the arrival of modernity and capitalist progress and a traditional, agrarian culture that caused the Second Republic's failure. It was a conflict, furthermore, that reached its fruition with Spain's Civil War. The Spanish Civil War's very public presence in global consciousness—represented by the numerous foreign brigades that volunteered to fight in it—represents how this division between "tradition" and "modernity" was not only a difference manufactured by competing ideas of Spanish exceptionalism: it was also a difference effected by this uneven arrival of modernity in

Spain as its economy began to mimic that of Europe—when labor moved from farms to factories—while the cultural mind-set was still dominated by rural towns in Castilla y León, not Madrid and Barcelona. For the international community, the slippage between a traditional and a modern Spain was a difference that, on both sides, came to represent a "loss": either one would lose the comfort and assuredness of a concrete past and tradition, or, one would be betrayed by the promise of self-determination that modern "progress" promised to the individual. What side one chose to fight on, in many ways, represented not just what one hoped to gain, but what one was willing to lose.

Once the Spanish Civil War was over, the Spanish populace fragmented into groups of winners and losers, prompting a renegotiation of national identity that persisted for most of the twentieth century and, some would argue, to this day. Yet while Spain's path toward dictatorship seemed to involve a monolithic imagining of nationhood, in reality the ideal of nation promoted by Francoism is as multifaceted and conflicted as the image of the Caudillo himself. As Gabrielle Ashford Hodges describes in her biography of Franco, the 1898 loss loomed heavy on the consciousness of a young boy who suffered under the fierce authority of a liberal-thinking father. As Ashford Hodges notes, Franco "in due course, seize[d] upon the loss of Cuba o validate his conviction that he—like Spain itself—was under attack from everything he associated with his left-wing, anti-clerical, Freemason father" (16). Franco's determination to save Spain from liberalism slowly became a maniacal desire to renew Spain as an imperial power. The result of this determination, moreover, proves similar to the South's desire to refashion its Confederate past into a part of a useful U.S. historical narrative. As Labanyi best explains it, "In this sense Francoism, which historians are now starting to rethink not as a rejection of modernity but rather as a form of conservative modernity (Richards 1998), subscribed just as much as its liberal and socialist antagonists to the modern capitalist ethos of progress—that is, put crudely, a view of history based on the notion that those who triumph are by definition the best" (*Constructing Identity* 7). To this end, "traditional" Spanish values (if they could be said to exist in the first place) became an effort to participate in European "progress." For example, throughout the process of positing itself as "exceptional," Spain, per Bhabha's model, mimicked the very ideas of European progress Francoism supposedly rejected. By acting uniquely "Spanish," Spain was just European enough that its excesses, its difference, succeeded in making Spain into both self and other. Throughout its history, this mimicry has become a tool not just for Spain, but for a European, and international, community whose ideas of "self" relied on such performativity. Such a process becomes apparent throughout Spain's history when, despite a three-decade-long oppressive dictatorship, nations as varied as Nazi Germany and the United States during the Cold War sought Spain out as a political ally. What both of these political relationships illustrate is the fact that Spain's "difference" meant that these power structures could both accept Spain as an ally but still assert an opposing image of exceptionality that relied on an image of Spain as "other." Clear evidence for such a dichotomy emerges in photos from President Dwight D. Eisenhower's visit to Spain in 1959, where the president, still regarded as a military hero, embraces a uniformed Francisco Franco while dressed in civilian clothes. Eisenhower's dark black coat contrasts with the sea of brown worn by Franco and his ministers. Even more, Eisenhower seemed to rely on the image of Spain as a dictatorship, seeing his nation as clearly "different" from Spain. He remarked after his trip, "There was no discernible mannerism or characteristic that would lead an unknowing visitor to conclude that he was in the presence of a dictator" (quoted in Ashford Hodges 233).

Within the process of reconfiguring loss into victory, the uncanniness of such a performed act becomes strikingly apparent as Spain's and the South's devotion to the "lovable loser" figure, identified by Labanyi and Woodward, recalls the very loss that narratives of victory aim to forget. The result is an ambivalent view of nationalism, as the need to cope with a "loss" in the past is subsumed by the impulse to forget that loss and make oneself into a winner. Not surprisingly, that loss haunts the individual, and this very uncanny sense of nationalism typifies Spain's and the South's engagement with modernity, especially if we see Francoism and Jim Crow as expressions of a conservative modernity. While Spanish and Southern claims to exceptionality appear to place them outside of the modernist milieu, critics like C. Christopher Soufas in his book *The Subject in Question: Early Contemporary Spanish Literature and Modernism* lay out a literary history that sees Spain as a full-fledged participant in the modernist questioning of subjectivity that dominated the first half of the twentieth century. For both Spain and the South, such an engagement becomes clear when observing how, within the performance of an authentic and exceptional nationhood, the past haunts any present sense of self or nation, thus prompting the very questions about personal and national identity witnessed throughout modernity. What proves most striking about the desire to create, and perform, a new, "progressive" sense of nation is that these performances invariably fail since they never reconcile the past that haunts them with a present that confounds them. What is left when these performances fail, furthermore, are the very ghosts of the past that a progressive modernity seeks to remove from memory.

What this study purports is a narrative of these ghosts that are left behind. Thus instead of a chronological study of "master" texts, I trace a pattern of loss and coping that compels the modern subject to perform in a modern Spain and South. Chapter 1 seeks to explain the philosophical underpinnings of this loss, looking at the "lovable loser" Don Quijote, whose idealism and devotion to a perceived loss of "tradition" become a philosophical and aesthetic model for performativity in Spain and the South as the so-called Generation of '98 writers in Spain and the Fugitive poets and Nashville Agrarians in the South write poetry and philosophy that conceptualize a perceived loss of a performed Spanish and Southern tradition as they cope with said loss within modernity. The performativity inherent in such a loss becomes echoed throughout the century as the modern, autonomous thinking subject struggles to enact a coded Southernness and Spanishness. Chapter 2 focuses on this struggle, as main characters in William Faulkner's *Absalom, Absalom!* and Camilo José Cela's *La familia de Pascual Duarte* attempt to reconcile a past haunted by civil war. Their main characters' melancholic relationship with that past weaves a path toward self-destruction that allows Faulkner and Cela to expose the South's and Spain's own inability to "let go" of their "traditional" past as defended in each one's civil war. While there are no doubt countless examples of main characters from both traditions that mirror the examples found in Faulkner's and Cela's novels, chapter 3 looks forward in the South and backward in Spain to find two modern subjects that move from the melancholia experienced by Faulkner's and Cela's main characters to a place of mourning. Indeed, while Pío Baroja's *El árbol de la ciencia* [*The Tree of Knowledge*] (1911) and Walker Percy's *The Moviegoer* (1961) seem disparate in time, both authors find themselves on the periphery of Spanish and Southern letters because of Baroja's Basque and Percy's Catholic heritage as well as each writer's use of a suicidal, autobiographical main character influenced by existential philosophy. This link shows the ambivalence inherent in performativity when the modern subject attempts to renew a traditional past in the modern present. While both characters' decisions to "let go" of the past and reach a state of mourning seem disparate as one commits suicide and one does not, both subjects' constant search for "truth"—and subsequent acceptance that such a thing does not exist—provides a means by which we can not only critique concrete ideas of coded nationalism but show how they can be productively remembered as the ghosts they harbor are let go by the modern subject.

The degree to which performance allows the modern subject to cling violently to national exceptionality while also giving him or her the means to reject it speaks not just to the existential pliability that performativity provides but also to the degree to which Spain and the South represent specific examples of performance where seemingly rigid binaries of "self" and "other"—inherent in contrasts "Southern" and "Northern," "Spanish" and "European"—are experienced simultaneously by the modern subject. With that in mind, Spain and the South during Francoism and Jim Crow also present particular instances where racial and gender codes are affirmed and rejected simultaneously via performance. Chapter 4, therefore, takes what Paul Gilroy identifies as an inherent "double-consciousness" within modernity and exposes the performativity inherent in that experience, particularly within the racial and biological "purity" that was so violently affirmed in Francoist Spain and the Jim Crow South. Framing this chapter with African American writer Richard Wright's experience in what he describes as Franco's "pagan" Spain, I examine how Spain and the South provide specific examples where racial indeterminacy compels the subject to embrace performativity as a means of shirking the expectations of "race" and "biology" thrust upon them by those perceived as "pure." This acceptance highlights the performativity inherent in images of purity to begin with, which simultaneously highlights the performativity inherent in another seemingly biological determiner: gender. Thus chapter 5 attempts to locate the Butlerian model of gender performance within a conception of performativity as a nationalist act of memory. My goal, however, is not to discuss the stereotypes of Spanish and Southern womanhood: the Southern "belle" and the "sencilla" ("simple") Spanish mother. Instead, exploring the performativity of these images, I expose the slippage and excess that occurs when that performance fails, creating the "bad" woman—whom I describe as the "picarona" in Spanish and whom Betina Entzminger has termed the "bad belle" in the Southern tradition. In Spain and the South, that figure becomes a heroine precisely because she is masculine while ambivalently adhering to and subverting the image from the past meant to define her. In so doing, the "bad" woman becomes another form that reminds us of the ghosts that get left behind in the effort to construct, and perform, new and "progressive" narratives of gender and nation. These "new" images of nation—and the degree to which they still perform the old—drive the sixth and final chapter examining tourism in democratic Spain and the "new"

South. By examining tourist culture, chapter 6 shows how the commodification of the "old world" Spain and South is performed via its construction of seemingly "new" urban spaces, in particular, the Olympic cities of Barcelona and Atlanta. Meanwhile, films like José Luis Guerín's *En construcción* [*Work in Progress*] (2001) and John Sayles's *Sunshine State* (2002), though very different, directly address the issue of urban renewal in Barcelona and along the Florida coastline, respectively, demonstrating the "construction" that making the old into something new is a performance that involves constructing it as "authentically" old, thus making it worthy—and interesting—for renewal. What Guerín and Sayles critique, therefore, is not the altering of the landscape itself, but the performativity inherent in constructing space around binary opposites, specifically those of new and old as well as foreigner (or tourist) and native.

In identifying the weaving path toward myth and nation, what this project ultimately entails is not a transatlantic anxiety of influence, but instead a narrative of preserving and questioning ghosts of the past and performing this conflict for the masses. While this narrative has been presented independently at times by scholars on both sides of the Atlantic, what I hope to show is how such a comparison creates not a reductive, but a constructive view of memory. As it stands, the act of relegating Spain and the South to peripheral regions that participate in a national discourse but still remain on the outside only serves to enable the kind of national mythmaking that consigned them to the position of "other" in the first place. Yet again we are faced with what Cohn and Smith term as the South's "uncanny hybridity" in the sense that it has been the object of and a major participant in postcolonial subjugation—something that can also be said of Spain. As a result, both of these spaces occupy a contested space within an imagined globalized community, thus possessing both the fortunate and unfortunate ability of reminding the world of its own hybrid-participation in subjugation and oppression. Such a space is by no means unique to Spain and the South, but my discussion of these regions does serve to highlight the degree to which a discourse of exceptionality becomes revealed via a performative mode that implicates the self, the "performer," just as much as it does the other, that is, the "audience." In so doing, it allows us to rethink, and reposition, who benefits from this performance as a means of showing that these "othered" nations, which admittedly "othered" themselves, were complicit in a transatlantic modernity in which Europe and America were vying for political and cultural authority—a fight that, given the current economic crisis and differing models of education, health care, and currency, continues to this day. In the end, there are many Spains and many Souths throughout the world, but upon encountering these exceptions to a global imagined community, our propensity has been, and continues to be, either to exoticize or obliterate that which we love and hate within our romantic image of the world—when our pursuit should instead be to explore how these exceptions contest such a "global" image in the first place.

Chapter 1

BREATHING MODERN LIFE INTO THE QUIJOTE

Spanish and Southern Regeneration in the New Century

———————————————⊃⟩◯⟨⊂———————————————

When Miguel de Cervantes addressed his "leisurely reader" in the prologue to *The Ingenious Gentleman Don Quijote de la Mancha*, he had no idea just how much his character later loomed over modernity. One need only remember the imagined adventure of Mark Twain's Tom Sawyer and Huck Finn or Picasso's paintings of the knight and his squire to find evidence for his influence in the nineteenth and twentieth centuries. But this chapter is not about Don Quijote, nor is it about his direct influence on a series of Spanish and Southern writers from the early twentieth century, despite its existence. Instead, this chapter uses the *Quijote* to highlight a particular kind of performativity in which a glorious, but defeated, past is willfully reproduced to pass for a grim present—an act echoed in the "regenerationist" efforts among Spanish writers like Miguel de Unamuno, José Ortega y Gasset, and Antonio Machado as well as John Crowe Ransom, Allen Tate, and Robert Penn Warren in the South. While these movements and their implications were, in many ways, reactionary, elitist, and tinged with racism, these qualities have caused critics to "group" these writers away from the ideological and aesthetic implications of high modernism. Yet much like Cervantes's knight-errant, the writers placed into the respective categories of Nashville Agrarian or the Generation of '98 define Southern and Spanish nationhood within a traditional ideology—a code of honor and homogeneity rooted in the historical past—as an ethos that emerges organically from the modern, autonomous thinking subject. While such definitions of nationhood seem contradictory, or ambivalent at best, this dichotomy also demonstrates exactly how Spain and the South came to exist as both "self" and "other"—how each imagined a past that was exceptional as a means of simultaneously engaging and challenging ideas of U.S. and European promises of modern progress. The methods by which these writers defend Spanish and Southern tradition while employing a high modernist aesthetic speak to the quixotism inherent in such a performance. That performativity, meanwhile, typifies Spanish and Southern encounters with fascism, as scholars and critics on both sides of the Atlantic grappled with tradition and modernity during the early manifestations of Francoism and Jim Crow.

The degree to which early twentieth-century thought in both Europe and America was defined by shifting ideologies and allegiances exists in various biographies of writers who found themselves on opposite sides of whatever political affiliation they had subscribed to. Among the Generation of '98 and the Fugitive-Agrarians, the particular cases of Miguel de Unamuno and Robert Penn Warren stand out from both a philosophical and bio-historical standpoint. Unamuno, as evidenced by various essays throughout his career, appeared a champion of Spanish nationalism. Following the "disaster" of 1898, he promoted the regeneration of Spanish ideals that involved a vision of Spain with a Castilian base, and his initial support of Francisco Franco came as he saw Spain in need of a unifying force. Yet within Unamuno's philosophical works there was a persistent agony and conflict that drove his desire to "Europeanize" while simultaneously "nationalize" Spain—a conflict between self and other that he promotes in *En torno al casticismo* (1902) when he says that it is better "hacer resaltar la fuerza de los extremos en el alma del lector para que el medio tome en ella vida, que es resultante de lucha" ["to facilitate bringing out of the force of extremes in the reader's soul so that a middle ground takes life in that force, which is the result of the fight"] (784). Yet in his final years Unamuno did not seek a balance, and at one point Spain's most famous promoter of a national selfhood addressed the horror of the fact that his conceptualization of Spain had become a haunting reminder of an "other," inhospitable past.

That moment arrived Columbus Day, 1936, at the University of Salamanca, where Unamuno served as rector. He was participating in a celebration in place of General Francisco Franco, who could not attend, with Franco's wife, Doña Carmen, Foreign Legion General José Millán Astray, and Bishop Enrique Plá y Deniel all in attendance. While Falangists gave several speeches on Spain's lost imperial glory, Unamuno reached a breaking point when Professor Francisco Maldonado delivered a diatribe entailing how the communists, the Basques, and the Catalans were fighting to ruin "traditional" Spain. His talk elicited cries of the Foreign Legion slogan, "¡Viva la muerte!" ["Long live death!"], and as the room fell silent following an eruption of fascist cries and salutes, it fell to Unamuno to close the meeting. His remarks, which have taken on a performative quality themselves in how they have been remembered and re-remembered over time,[1] were a twofold rejection of fascism: admitting his Basque heritage (and coyly pointing to the fact that the bishop in attendance, whether he liked it or not, was Catalan) and adamantly denying the Legion cry, "Long live death!," telling the audience, "Venceréis porque tenéis sobra de fuerza; pero no convenceréis" ["You will win because you have more than enough force; but you will not convince"]. Noting how the men in the audience did not possess "reason" in the "struggle," Unamuno, a man whose philosophy celebrated paradoxes and whose work enacted the struggle of incorporating Spanish tradition into European modernity, dismissed Millán Astray's salute to "death" that is "long living." He called the general a cripple like Cervantes, but without the wisdom of Don Quijote's creator. As the tension in the room mounted, Unamuno had to be quickly ushered out by Franco's wife. He soon lost his position as rector of the University of Salamanca, rarely leaving his home and dying somewhat mysteriously that December. For a man who had spent so much of his career promoting his vision of Spain, in the end it was not a static, monolithic image of nation that dominated his thought, but instead a hybrid one that showed how the preservation of a national selfhood had not breathed new life into the Spanish nation, but instead reproduced a "tradition" that haunted its citizenry with images of death.

The paradoxical nature of Unamuno's political and philosophical beliefs echoes a similar duality in Robert Penn Warren's writings. The most famous of the Fugitive-Agrarians, Warren's contribution to *I'll Take My Stand*, "The Briar Patch," defends racial segregation and rejects higher education for African Americans. Like most of the essays in the collection, Warren's stands as the cornerstone for present-day Southern conservatism, yet Warren later admitted that his image of segregation, which blindly adopted the idea of separate yet still equal, had been one that was completely detached from actual Jim Crow politics that existed in the 1950s and 1960s. Indeed, Warren, despite a fairly distinguished career as a writer, spent most of his life explaining his position, even after he reversed these opinions in *Segregation: The Inner Conflict in the South* (1956). Throughout this book, Warren saw the issue of race in the South as being one of both inter- and intrasubjectivity. In other words, he believed Southern whites needed to come to terms with their own tradition—and guilt—as individuals before they could understand the African American experience (Cobb 210). Like Unamuno, Warren reached his breaking point at the peak of his academic career. During his tenure at Louisiana State University (LSU) Warren came face to face with the uncanniness of his own attempts to preserve Southern tradition, and it marked him both as an individual and a writer. In the book *Away Down South: A History of Southern Identity*, James C. Cobb describes this moment in 1939 when Warren observed a white man beating a black teenager in Baton Rouge, Louisiana, and found himself frozen, completely unable to intervene. Warren describes that it was not fear that kept him from stepping in—which, thanks to an LSU football player, he did not have to do—but instead a sense of utter "aloneness" (quoted in Cobb 211). Here Warren identifies a feeling that Cobb sees in many Southerners of that era: a sense of being outside the Southern community they seemed to know and belong to but clearly did not. Thus much like Unamuno, who supported a brand of nationalism that later repulsed him, Warren left LSU in 1942 to take a position at Yale and never returned to live in the region that he spent a career trying to define.

The manner in which regenerationist movements among writers like Warren and Unamuno begin as idealistic defenses of national and regional identity that later cause them to recoil in horror speaks to both the heterogeneity of fascist movements in this period as well as both writers' struggle with Spain and the South as "other" within a European and U.S "self." While it is easy to simply call them "quixotic" (as countless have done), a closer examination of Cervantes's knight-errant—and his own defense of Spanish honor—shows how Don Quijote is a figure that also embodies Spanish nationalism as both self and other: by taking on adventures to defend a "traditional" Spain, he plays a role that completely alienates him from his community. In such a light, Cervantes's novel has a great deal to say about the performance of national identity, particularly if we define "performance" as a mode that can both reflect but also contest claims to cohesive identity. Such an image of both the *Quijote* and performativity stems from Barbara Fuch's work in her book *Passing for Spain: Cervantes and the Fictions of Identity*, when she describes how Cervantes's multiple characters who adopt alternate identities through disguise—from the cross-dressing Dorotea and the Moorish captive Zoraida to the knight-errant himself—question any kind of essential national identity in seventeenth-century Spain. Fuchs makes it clear that she is not trying to paint a picture of Cervantes as a "philosemite," but instead trying to show how "his texts constantly de-emphasize and problematize essence, suggesting an openness toward the convincing *performance* of Spanish identity instead of an obsession with transparency and genealogy" (9). Don Quijote himself represents such performativity when he imagines a chivalric past and adopts that image by trying, and often failing (think of the windmills), to "pass" as a knight who can save Spain from the perils of what he calls the "Age of Iron." Seeing Don Quijote as a model of fluid subjectivity—for both the individual and the nation he symbolizes—one can readily observe how the mad hidalgo's efforts to effectively "play" his role of cultural savior becomes an attractive performance to cultures that, in the twentieth century, had become defined by loss.

The image of Don Quijote as a figure whose idea of Spanish tradition is bound up in his own fluid subjectivity is part of the reason he was so attractive to modernist artists. Yet central to Don Quijote's self-conceptualization is his honor as it drives Alonso Quijano's desire to take up arms early in Cervantes's novel when "le pareció convenible y necesario, así para el aumento de su honra como para el servicio de su república, hacerse caballero andante" ["it seemed convenient and necessary, as much for the sake of his honor as for the duty to his nation, to turn himself into a knight errant"] (72). In the context of Cervantes's novel, "honor" is an integral part of a chivalric code that dominated much writing of the period. Yet this same conception of honor dominated U.S. Southern culture in the nineteenth and twentieth centuries as antebellum Southerners voraciously read Sir Walter Scott and as postbellum Southern culture conceptualized the South's defeat in the Civil War as a stain on the South's honor. In his seminal work on the topic, Bertram Wyatt Brown defines honor not just culturally in the South but theoretically as a form, pointing to its two main components: "the inner conviction of self-worth" coupled with "the evaluation of the public" (14). What Brown highlights as integral to the idea of honor is its performativity as he shows how it is "both internal to the claimant, so that it motivates him toward behavior socially approved, and external to him, because only by the response of observers can he ordinarily understand himself. The internal and external aspects of honor are inalienably connected because honor serves as ethical mediator between the individual and the community by which he is assessed and in which he must also locate himself to others" (14). Part of the reason that honor often becomes the means to code nationhood is its role as an "ethical mediator" between the individual and his or her community. For the writers discussed in this chapter, "traditional" images of Spain and the South are enacted and contested by a modern world and their own modern subjectivity. This quality is what allows Warren and Unamuno to react so strongly, and divergently, to seemingly homogenous ideas of Spanishness and Southernness. That divergence comes not from a change in Southern or Spanish "tradition" per se, but a shift in how they code it; thus while their concern is not always "honor," the honor code it-self—particularly its link between an individual's self-worth versus commu-nity expectations—becomes the dominating model of performativity and the source of these writers' "quixotism" in the early twentieth century.

The degree to which national tradition becomes bound up in a per-formed honor code speaks specifically to the extreme confluence of aes-thetic and political discourse within fascism, which Mary Ann Frese Witt discusses in her book on fascism (6). While she focuses on France and Italy, the ways in which Spanish and Southern "tradition" are bound up in an honor code that values individual self-worth speaks to its placement within a modern aesthetic, what Brown calls a "sense of personal completeness" that complies "with modern notions of individuality" (14). Don Quijote certainly embodies that brand of honor, and his self-worth allows him to change, blend, and/or ignore various elements of traditional, chivalric honor depending upon his personal circumstances and own "insanity." This ability to recode honor on the part of the individual, in many ways, explains the heterogeneity of not just fascism but also the movements founded in reaction to it. No doubt a similar plurality emerges in Spain and the South. Indeed, the idea of fascism evolved dramatically over the course of Franco's forty-year dictatorship, particularly as he sought to make Spain more capi-talist and less agrarian in the 1950s and 1960s. Meanwhile, the Agrarians, though unfairly accused of fascism,[2] promoted an ideology that, evidenced by Warren's ideas, demanded constant reformulation both as the United States entered World War II and, even more specifically, as Jim Crow poli-tics became equated with fascist movements because of its oppressive and increasingly violent repercussions. While it seems easy to posit these shifts as changing politics, in reality they represent the consequences of trying to mimic a "progressive" modernity, represented by industrial capitalism, while trying to regenerate a defeated "tradition" that lay in opposition to a modern Europe and United States. The result is not simply a move from one idea of Spain or the South to another, but competing ideas of national identity that are ambivalent and that produce a slippage in which Spain and the South *want* to be European and American—just not enough to lose their claims to exceptionality.

Instead, as Spain and the South attempted to reconstruct a defeated na-tional identity in the early twentieth century, each reproduced an uncanny "double" of their defeated selves that Freud describes as a "preservation against extinction" ("Uncanny" 235) or, in a national context, a preservation of "Spanishness" and "Southernness" that selectively incorporates elements of so-called European and American culture. For Freud, this double emerges out of a "primary narcissism," a self-love that demands the reproduction of the self. Yet Freud also makes clear that, when this self-love is overcome, "the 'double' reverses its aspect. From having been an assurance of immortality, it becomes an uncanny harbinger of death" ("Uncanny" 235). For Spain and the South, the traditional idea of culture espoused by Unamuno, Ortega, and Ransom is one that creatively reproduces a "self" located in the past. Yet when that "double" attempts to inculcate itself in a U.S. or European collective—when the self-love is overcome—exceptionality becomes a haunting reminder of worlds that these writers think they have left behind, thus making the reproduced self into an uncanny other that recalls a traumatic and oppressive past that has not been laid to rest, despite the fact that it has been "defeated" in war.

Given that writers like the ones described above represent regenerationist movements that are reactionary and characteristic of the very narcissism that produces an uncanny double, they have been misguidedly "grouped" away from the modernist artists and thinkers that follow them by being placed, in Spanish criticism, into the "Generations" of "1898" and "1927" or, in the South, characterized as "Fugitives" or "Agrarians." While many of the writers discussed here accepted these distinctions at various stages of their careers, the "othering" of these writers to the margins of modernist expression prescribes them to a "backward" viewpoint that actually is contested by the ambivalent nature of their thought. Indeed, if one examines the uncanny doubles that emerge from attempts to preserve Spanish and Southern tradition, one finds a possibility that Freud describes when he says, "The idea of the 'double' does not necessarily disappear with the passing of primary narcissism, for it can receive fresh meaning from the later stages of the ego's development. A special agency is slowly formed there, which is able to stand over against the rest of the ego, which has the function of observing and criticizing the self and of exercising a censorship within the mind, which we become aware of as our conscience" ("Uncanny" 235). Freud's vision of the double finds itself in line with Homi Bhabha's idea of colonial mimicry when he describes that its menace is "its *double* vision which in disclosing the ambivalence of colonial discourse also disrupts its authority" (88). While it is an oversimplification to say that various members of the Generation of '98, the Fugitives, and the Agrarians develop a conscience about their problematic ideas (although Warren and Unamuno suggest it), this uncanny adoption of a "Spanish" identity that is not quite European or a "Southern" identity that is almost American has the ability to "disrupt the authority" or "stand over against" the ego as a means of questioning how exceptionality is projected onto the other as a means of asserting, and performing, an authentic nationhood.

In many ways, the perceived loss of tradition, via defeat in war, prompted Spain and the South to perform an authentic nationhood—what Joseph Roach aptly calls "the doomed search for originals by continuously auditioning stand-ins" (3). While these defeats in the U.S. Civil War and the War of 1898 no doubt scarred these cultures, particularly because they signaled the end of their supposed imperial glory, it seems only fair to note that the South slowly recovered by the mid-twentieth century while Spain plunged itself into civil war and a lengthy dictatorship. In addition, Spain and the South are not the only nations to experience, and try to compensate for, military defeat in this period—Nazi Germany is an obvious parallel. Yet what is interesting is that both Spain and the South were defeated by a "modern" United States with better guns, faster ships, and more troops. Thus as Spain and the South attempted to reinvoke a traditional nation, they simultaneously mimicked images of "successful" nationhood while clinging to a defeated ideal. In so doing, both cultures unconsciously reproduced an uncanny "other" that was capable of destabilizing all forms of exceptionality, including their own. This process becomes the essence of quixotic performativity as efforts to "pass" for a national self and the inability to do so is how we realize the ambivalence inherent in this very process. My calling this performativity quixotic stems from critics like Jo Labanyi identifying a key difference between Latin and Anglo-American cultures in that the former tends to choose as national heroes and heroines "not those who triumphed but those who lost spectacularly because of their refusal to compromise: that is, using the modern language of the market, those who refuse to 'sellout' to history's (foreign, capitalist) winners" (*Constructing Identity* 6). It is for this reason that Don Quijote figures quite prominently in essays and literature of the early twentieth century as a counterpoint to an Anglo-Saxon nemesis, Robinson Crusoe (Britt-Arredondo 2). Although it seems that the South should be a participant in such Anglo-Saxon success, defeat in the Civil War ensured that it too embraced the lovable loser; thus Mark Twain's Tom Sawyer finds inspiration for his adventures in those of Cervantes's mad hidalgo,[3] an inspiration that persists in several Southern Quijotes that appear throughout the twentieth century, from Faulkner's Quentin Compson and Gavin Stevens to Walker Percy's Binx Bolling.

The perceived loss of a coded tradition is very much what Unamuno and Warren experienced, and that "loss" drives them to find a surrogate selfhood embodied not by one idea of nationhood but by the autonomous thinking subject—one that can negotiate the various Spains and Souths that exist in the years leading to the Spanish Civil War and World War II. This emphasis on individual will becomes the basis for a quixotic performativity that attempts, like Cervantes's knight-errant, to selectively invoke a past honor code in a grim present. Throughout essays by Unamuno, Ortega, and the Nashville Agrarians, this very performativity becomes the means of negotiating "tradition" and "modernity." While critics have tended to see these writers and their ideas as backward-looking, such quixotic performativity places them firmly within the confines of high modernism as they make Spanish and Southern tradition try to pass for a European and American modernity. For the Nashville Agrarians, the quixotic figure emerges in their desire to find a modern value in the defeated Southerner who renegotiates his or her past as a means of participating—or at least passing—within an "American" modernity. Even more specifically, Unamuno's and Ortega's ideas exhibit this performativity within their efforts to breath modern life into the Quijote, that is, to see a figure firmly entrenched in a traditional, Golden Age past as a modern figure that can mold his own subjectivity by enacting a constantly changing role in his environment. Ortega's famous mantra "Yo soy yo y mi circunstancia" ["I am I and my circumstance"] and the philosophical perspectivism it implies, as well as Unamuno's collective sense of *intrahistoria*, function within the realm of modernity in which the individual is compelled to free himself or herself from external definitions—even if the performativity inherent in that process causes him or her to reproduce that which he or she is escaping.

For both Unamuno and Ortega, Don Quijote possesses a spiritual quality that suspends him between the confines of the past and the seemingly grim confines of an industrial present. In his *Meditaciones del Quijote* (1914), Ortega praises Don Quijote's will and sees him as heroic precisely because he refuses to bend to the fated subjectivity of the epic hero (142). Unamuno in particular references Cervantes's knight-errant in countless essays, and he sees Don Quijote's story as a tragedy analogous to that of Spain itself. In *Del sentimiento trágico de la vida* [*Of Life's Tragic Sentiment*] (1913), he describes this tragedy as a fight "entre lo que el mundo es, según la razón de la ciencia nos lo muestra, y lo que queramos que sea, según la fe de nuestra religión nos lo dice. Y en esta filosofía está el secreto de eso que suele decirse de que somos en el fondo irreductibles a la Cultura, es decir, que no nos resignamos a ella. No, Don Quijote no se resigna ni al mundo ni a su verdad, ni a la ciencia o lógica, ni arte o estética, ni a la moral o ética" ["between what the world is, according to the reason that science shows us, and what we want it to be, according to the faith that our religion tells us. And in this philosophy lies the secret that normally tells us that we are, at our depths, irreducible to Culture, that is to say, that we do not resign ourselves to it. No, Don Quijote does not resign himself to the world or to truth, to science or logic, to art or aesthetic, to moral or ethic"] (314). In an earlier collection, *En torno al casticismo* [*On Castilianism*] (1902), Unamuno describes the end of Cervantes's novel as an allegory of Spain itself, citing the moment when the knight renounces his life of chivalry and dies surrounded by a community insisting that he is, indeed, a knight-errant who has saved Spain. For Unamuno, Don Quijote's final moments represent a fluidity of identity as the don constantly wills his own existence, changing identities and roles when it suits him. In other words, it is Don Quijote's performativity that is most attractive—and most universal—to Unamuno when he compares the knight's "path" to that of Spain and says, "a ése pertenece porque de puro español llegó a una como renuncia de su españolismo, llegó al espíritu universal, al *hombre* que duerme dentro de todos nosotros" ["it follows that path because the pure Spaniard arrived at a renunciation of his Spanishness, thus arrived at a universal spirit, to the *man* that sleeps inside of all of us"] (791). Much like Unamuno imagines Spain as both "self" and "other," he does the same with Don Quijote: he is an exceptional hero who represents the "universal spirit" in us all. Even more, Unamuno, and many of the writers in this chapter, do not admire the insane don for his success, but for his ability to maintain his identity in the face of failure.

In their affirmation of the quixotic figure, it becomes clear in Unamuno's and Ortega's writings how Don Quijote becomes a narcissistic double for Spanish identity as each attempts to reclaim, and reproduce, a national past as a referent for a modern present. For Unamuno, this effort is best encapsulated by his concept of *intrahistoria*, an image of history centered not around large-scale events but on the realities and experiences of everyday people. While quite obviously more populist, the concept of *intrahistoria* carries with it a new conception of time and individual subjectivity that sees both as fluid and evolving. With this in mind, the concept of Spanish "tradition" becomes a coded form that is reproduced to play a modern European role. Unamuno makes this idea clear in *En torno* when he says that the intrahistoric life, "silenciosa y continua como el fondo mismo del mar, es la sustancia del progreso, la verdadera tradición, la tradición eterna, no la tradición mentira que se suele ir a buscar al pasado enterrado en libros y papeles y monumentos y piedras" ["silent and continuous like the same fold of the sea, is the sustenance of progress, the true tradition, the eternal tradition, not the lie that normally goes in search of the entombed past in books and papers and monuments and stones"] (793). Unamuno's desire to seek a universalizing tradition while praising individual will becomes a central paradox within his work as he promotes a Spanish nationality that can be regenerated within a modern European ideal. Yet for Christopher Britt-Arredondo, Unamuno's work by 1913 centered exclusively on Spanish exceptionality and national identity, and his "struggle" now was not between a modern Europe and a decadent Spain. Instead, as Britt-Arredondo posits in his book *Quixotism: The Imaginative Denial of Spain's Loss of Empire*, Unamuno's struggle was "between irrational faith and reasonable doubt, a 'tragic' affirmation of faith-in-doubt. In a word, regeneration had become, for Unamuno, a matter of affirming the Spanish nation's irrational spirituality, its Quixotism" (77). What Britt-Arredondo observes in "Quixotism" is a "spirituality" that never reconciles the presence of tradition and modernity, the old and the new, but one that affirms an almost essential exceptionality to these forms. In other words, Unamuno's "struggle" becomes outright contradiction that aims to "pluck a moral victory from the perennial secular 'backwardness' of his defeated nation" (77). While Britt-Arredondo sees "Quixotism" as the foundation for Unamuno's and Ortega's ideology, I instead see it as the model for their performativity, that is, the way they creatively link past and present, tradition and modernity—a paradox that I do not think, at an ideological level, Unamuno ever reconciles. Instead, as Carlos Barriuso shows in his book *Los discursos de la modernidad: Nación, imperio y estética en el fin de siglo español (1895–1924)*, such a struggle becomes emblematic of modernity itself in Spain, which is why his book, as well as my comparison to the Nashville Agrarians, "se centra en las tensiones que se producen entre la mentalidad social conservadora de un sector intelectual castellano parlante. Por un lado, este sector anhela restituir melancólicamente una sociedad rural en declive para retornar a un utópico modelo de estabilidad preindustrial" ["is centered among the tensions that are produced among a conservative social mentality within an intelligentsia of Castilian speakers. On the one hand, this sector yearns to melancholically reinstate a rural society in decline to return to a utopian model of preindustrial stability"] (19). Meanwhile, these tensions constantly reappear in Unamuno's writings as he prescribes an ever-changing role for Spain that attempts to be both exceptional and universal, traditional and modern. These contradictions emerge out of Unamuno's quixotic performativity, or the desire to play an exceptional role that will fail, but that is glorious in its refusal to, quoting Labanyi, "sell-out" to mainstream society's winners. This failure, furthermore, creates a slippage between Spain as it is imagined as a double of a traditional ideal in the past and as it exists as a modern nation. While this slippage exposes how Spain became both self and other during the early modernist period, that very otherness becomes the means by which Unamuno indicts a similarly mythic Europeanness. He launches this attack in *Del sentimiento trágico de la vida:* "¡Europa! Esta noción primitiva e inmediatamente geográfica nos la han convertido por arte mágico en una categoría metafísica. ¿Quién sabe hoy ya, en España por lo menos, lo que es Europa? Yo sólo sé que es un *chibolete....* Y cuando me pongo a escudriñar lo que llaman Europa nuestros europeizantes, paréceme a las veces que queda fuera de ella mucho de lo periférico—España desde luego, Inglaterra, Italia, Escandanavia, Rusia . . . —y que se reduce a lo central, a Franco-Alemania con sus anejos y dependencias" ["Europe! This primitive and immediately geographic notion has converted us by magic art into a metaphysical category. Who knows today, in Spain especially, what is Europe? I only know that it is a *shibboleth....* And when I compel myself to scrutinize what our Europeanizers call Europe, it appears to me at times that many remain outside of it—Spain of course, England, Italy, Scandinavia, Russia . . . —and that it is reduced to its central core, to Franco-Germany with its annexes and dependencies"] (298). Unamuno's image of nationality as a performance becomes clear when he describes it as a "shibboleth," invoking the story of the defeated Ephraimites who had to perform their nationality by saying the word that identified them to their foes. In other words, for Unamuno, nationality is not an idea; it is an act embodied in speech—much like Don Quijote is not a man as much as the role he gives himself but calling himself "Don," or not, as is the case at the end of Cervantes's novel. Even more, prescribing a role to Spain allows Unamuno to understand it as an "other" within an also-mythic idea of European exceptionality.

Unamuno's vision of Spain that straddles many of the natural paradoxes dominating early twentieth-century thought—coupled with what he sees as a quixotic struggle between the world as it is and how we want it to be—means that there is an inherent difference between those two concepts. Put differently, Spain will never effectively play the role that he imagines for it because the past will never effectively pass for the present. This very slippage, however, becomes even more prominent in Ortega's work as his image of Spanish exceptionality takes on an elitist tone—one readily identified by scholars, some of whom use it to both defend and vilify the writer. Britt-Arredondo thus critiques Ortega: "The principal motivating force of [Ortega's] elitism is not, as many of Ortega's more enthusiastic apologists have tended to sustain, the so-called Europeanization of Spain. Rather, Ortega's elitism is meant to provide for the moral transformation of the decadent Spanish masses such that they might eventually rise out to a new imperial glory" (105). Again, the point here is that Ortega's work contains an ideology inherent in, and linked to, his quixotism. Instead, I view it as a model of his performance within modernity, one that creates a double of a Spanish self, following Freud's model, and when that narcissism fades, all that is left is an uncanny form. Even Freud's image of the uncanny seems quixotic when he says, "an uncanny effect is often and easily produced when the distinction between imagination and reality is effaced, as when something that we have hitherto regarded as imaginary appears before us in reality, or when a symbol takes over the full functions of the thing it symbolizes, and so on" ("Uncanny" 244). The idea of a "symbol" taking over the full "functions" of something else is the very essence of "passing" and how, within the uncanny, that passing becomes quixotic in the attempt to synthesize imagination and reality.

Ortega's image of a "traditional" Spain is not linked to an intrahistoric past like Unamuno's. Instead, Ortega, heavily influenced by German philosophy of the period, focuses on the individual's relationship to his or her environment as a measure of his or her existence, as seen in the statement in *España invertebrada* [*Invertebrate Spain*] (1921) that "solo *debe ser* es lo que *puede ser*, y solo puede ser lo que se mueve dentro de las condiciones de lo que *es*" ["all that *should be* is what *can be*, and all that can be is what moves within the conditions of what *is*"] (113). Within Ortega's image of what *is*, there is an elitist tone, and an uncanny reminder of the past, in his desire to reform the decadent Spanish masses under the influence of a social elite who will "encourage" the masses to submit and "repent" (Britt-Arredondo 108). This language, which Britt-Arredondo quotes from Ortega's *España invertebrada*, no doubt recalls a nation constructed upon a religious zeal and political hierarchy that had ruled Spain for generations. Yet Ortega goes through a careful process of making Spain both self and other when he suggests that what makes Spain similar to say, France or Italy is its "raza autóctona" ["indigenous race"] (130); yet he asserts that it is different from its European counterparts in that it did not receive a "Germanic" feudalistic system, thus reducing it to a Roman "state of individuals" and not a "German" "community of men" (130). Ortega's nostalgic longing for a Spanish nation in the present that comes from a primal German state shows how his vision of Spanish regeneration is by no means immune to external verities or traditions. Instead, his pointing to how Spain is different from other European nations shows how exceptionality becomes a prop in the performance of an authentic nationhood by taking one's "exceptional" past and showing its emergence in present culture. In reality, however, it becomes a prop that converts the "doubled" Spanish self and its "indigenous race" into a haunting and uncanny place. Thus instead of the "community of men" that Ortega desires, what actually emerges is an uncanny "state" of fragmented individuals whose otherness, not a coherent selfhood, comes to the surface.

While the consequences of Ortega's thought seem much more problematic, in reality it represents the same kind of performance of national identity observed in Unamuno, that is, the process of making a doubled "traditional" past pass for a modern present. While this seems obvious when given his image of a Germanic "community of men," Ortega seems to contradict himself when he refutes the idea of a coherent "Spain" with a Castilian base. In fact, Ortega takes a page from Unamuno by refuting any idea of a static national past, making it clear in *España invertebrada*, "No es el ayer, el pretérito, el haber tradicional, lo decisivo para que una nación exista. Este error nace, como ya he indicado, de buscar en la familia, en la comunidad nativa, previa, ancestral, en el pasado, en suma, el origen del Estado" ["It is not yesterday, the preterit, the traditional qualities, the decisive thing that allows a nation to exist. This error is born, as I have already indicated, in searching within the family, the native community, previous, ancestral, in the past, in sum, for the origin of the State"] (41). While Ortega's move here seems to refute the historical past, his distinction between what allows the "nation" to exist versus the origins of the Spanish "state" implies that history and nationhood are malleable forms. While his description of an "autonomous race" of Europe seems to suggest otherwise, Ortega is not opposed to an exploration of the past as much as he is not interested in a monolithic understanding of it or the "state." Instead, Ortega, like Unamuno, sets up a framework in which "tradition," though originally conceptualized in the past, can be reconstituted to be nondecisive and contemporary, thus passing for a particular kind of nationhood in the present. Through this process, Ortega sees Spain playing its proper role in the history of European nationhood—one that mimics a modern, European self while recalling a traditional Spanish past that, when reproduced to create a malleable sense of time and history, actually achieves the opposite ends he imagines.

It should come as little surprise that in the face of military defeat and the crisis of "What is Spain?" Ortega and Unamuno do not come up with a coherent idea of Spanish identity but instead a method of acting so that multiple Spains—including the defeated one—could pass for a "regenerated" nation. Thus the dominant strain to their ideology is not quixotism per se but instead a quixotic performativity that looks to neither a traditional past nor a modern present, but an act of constantly renegotiating both, which has consequences for how the individual relates to his or her sense of nationhood. Central to this image of quixotic performativity, furthermore, is the role of the individual, the autonomous thinking subject who inevitably must wrestle with the ambivalent enterprise of defining nationhood. In her article "Intellectual Affinities: The Southern Fugitive-Agrarians and the Generation of '98," Montserrat Ginès compares these early twentieth-century Southern and Spanish writers by showing how they conceptualize citizen-selfhood. She says, "dramatizing the transitional conflicts that each [group] was experiencing was the only possible way for them to find their bearings in life, i.e., to define themselves" ("Intellectual Affinities" 186). Ginès's description of the "dramatization" of the relationship to self and nation among the Fugitive-Agrarians and the Generation of '98 demonstrates specifically how these writers were not coming up with a new identity per se, but instead a new method of reconfiguring identity in the face of "defeat." While Ginès sees this tendency as unique to Fugitive-Agrarians and the Generation of '98, in reality these thinkers were part of U.S. and European intelligentsia who were trying to cope with a modernity that supposedly freed the individual from fated subjectivity while simultaneously finding a place for national identity and "tradition." Again, where Spain and the South find a unique vantage point is the degree to which their coping with military defeat and the "loss" of their tradition causes them to reinvoke that past while mimicking the "progressive" nationhood that defeated them. Because this performance of nationhood creates a slippage between past and present—in which neither is effectively reproduced—this uncanny "double" that Freud identifies has a second aspect. Realizing the double's uncanniness, there can come "fresh meaning from that later stages of the ego's development," that is, the ability to "stand over" and "criticize" the ego as a means of "observing" and "criticizing" the self ("Uncanny" 235). In other words, by being suspended between two myths of past and present—of prevailing tradition and a freeing modernity—these writers give us a lens to observe how these myths weigh on individual subjectivity as it relates to national identity.

Before they would write their treatise on the South, many of the men who comprised the Nashville Agrarians began by escaping Southern exceptionality, writing poetry and holding informal meetings while at Vanderbilt University. Like Unamuno and Ortega, writers like John Crowe Ransom,

Donald Davidson, and Allen Tate saw the South's "problem" and heartily re-
treated from it, if only figuratively, through their poetry (Cowan 34). While
it seems that the escape from contemporary Southern culture espoused by
the Fugitives provides a contradiction to their work as Agrarian defenders
of Southern culture barely a decade later, in reality it only reflects the constant reformulation of the "South" and its "past" that is also observable in
Ortega's and Unamuno's contradictory ideas about the origins of "Spain." Yet
again, even in the refutation of the past, one can readily observe the willful
attempt to make it pass for the present and to envision the defeated Southerner as an autonomous self who is not irreducible to an American industrialism that steamrolls him or her. Though the Agrarians do not invoke
Don Quijote directly (despite the fact that many critics and scholars have
called them quixotic), their insistence on finding virtue in the life of the
defeated Southerner is a quixotic performance of national and individual
identity that, in some ways, wants to see the South as "American," but not
quite.

While many have been quick to identify an Agrarian "ideology," the collection of essays in *I'll Take My Stand* contains a broad range of ideas—
some more extreme than others—that constitute an agrarian "way of life"
(xxxvii). This approach, furthermore, proves radically similar to Unamuno's
image of *intrahistoria* in that it does not seek blind acceptance of the past
as fact, but merely a method of integrating the past into everyday reality.
With that in mind, I posit that, like Unamuno and Ortega, the Agrarians,
specifically John Crowe Ransom, engage in a performance of Southern nationhood in which they reclaim a traditional past that is meant to pass for a
modern present. This fusion appears by showing how the past can reemerge
via the "will" of the individual. In the same manner that Ortega and Unamuno praise the "heroic" and "universal" will of Don Quijote, the introduction to *I'll Take My Stand* invokes this same quality in the individual, saying
"Proper living is a matter of the intelligence and the will, does not depend
on the local climate and geography, and is capable of a definition which is
general and not Southern at all" (xxxix). Thus the desire to make tradition
into a form that can be regenerated in the present involves a specifically
modern, and quixotic, enterprise of self-conceptualizing, and performing,
an authenticity that actually stems from an "exceptional" past but that appears to be immune to the kind of authority represented by tradition and
history.

The exaltation of the individual for John Crowe Ransom and Unamuno stems from a perceived threat of homogenization that both saw as

an Americanization or a Europeanization, specifically linked to industrial modernity. In *I'll Take My Stand*, for example, the attack on industrialism becomes an attack on it as an "American" ideal (xlii). For the Agrarians, the nationalist implications of industrialism conflict heavily with the claims of the American Dream, the "progress" of Benjamin Franklin's idea of the self-made man. In the collection's first essay, "Reconstructed but Unregenerate," Ransom exposes this conflict, saying, "Man is boastfully declared to be a natural scientist essentially, whose strength is capable of crushing and making over to his own desires the brute materiality which is nature; but in his infinite contention with his materiality he is really capitulating to it" (8). Indeed, just as Ransom questions the relationship between the individual and his or her environment, Unamuno shows a similar skepticism for what he describes in *Del sentimiento trágico de la vida* as "una enorme actividad social, una ponderosa civilización, mucha ciencia, mucha arte" ["an enormous social activity, a ponderous civilization, much science, much art"], linking it to the "marvelous" industries and huge factories that began to dot the Spanish landscape in the early twentieth century. Yet he wonders, like Ransom, whom it serves, asking, "¿Se hizo el hombre para la ciencia o se hizo la ciencia para el hombre?" ["Was man made for science, or was science made for man?"] (56). For Ransom and Unamuno, the threat of the individual's Europeanization or Americanization comes as they try to regenerate a national ideal seen as the "other" to European and U.S. modernity—hence the struggle to conceptualize and perform an idea of the autonomous thinking subject as outside of those very cultural determiners. As such, the ambivalence inherent in trying to fold "tradition" into "modernity" is the source of that performance's failure. In other words, by positing the individual as a quixotic figure, a loveable loser, that resists the allure of "progress," Ransom describes a figure that, in the end, hauntingly resembles the defeated and othered Southern citizen—the Alonso Quijano who tries to pass for a successful Spanish nation by going on his own invented adventures.

Of course the reason Ransom feels the need to reconcile past and present comes from the fact that this "historical" past had already been defeated in war: the South, like Spain, was no longer an agrarian empire whose success served as an exceptional example of statehood. Indeed, Ransom acknowledges that "it is out of fashion nowadays to look backward rather than forward" (1), while the introduction makes clear that the Nashville Agrarians are not proposing "for the South, or for any other community in this country, an independent political destiny. That idea is thought to have been finished in 1865" (xlii). Yet simultaneously Ransom does seek to regenerate a Southern "tradition" perceived as exceptional and linked to a "European" ideal. In so doing, Ransom returns his audience to the antebellum division between Yankee frontierism and Cavalier chivalry, but he seeks to make Southern tradition into a modern form by illustrating how this ideal can be incorporated into contemporary society by following a model set forth by England, that is, "the stable economic system by which Englishmen are content to take their livelihood from the physical environment" (4). What Ransom reveals here, aside from the fact that he had never been to Manchester or Liverpool, is his vision of a "Southern" tradition that, by calling it "English" or "European," can be recast as a successful economic enterprise capable of resisting the industrial "progress" that the Agrarians saw as incredibly dangerous to Southern tradition—a "tradition" they attempted to locate in their contemporary, American environment.

One of the most direct discussions of "tradition" in *I'll Take My Stand* is Allen Tate's essay on religion, which is a concept that he sees as linked to the idea of tradition. As such, Tate asks, "How can Tradition, which is always embarrassing to practicality on a larger scale, be defended?" (166). His immediate answer to that question is that tradition is always defendable, but, he asserts, "a recovery and restoration is a more difficult performance" (166). The reason that Tate sees the defense of tradition as a performance is the fact that modernity no longer deems it essential. In other words, Tate claims that the contemporary view of the past reduces history to a series of equal and quantifiable "abstractions"; thus the difference between Christ and Adonis does not matter to the Christian myth since it is "a vegetation myth, varying only in some details from countless other vegetation myths" (162). Thus tradition, in order to exist, must be asserted through performance: it cannot exist as an eternal form that springs from itself. In so doing, Tate makes the ultimate claim for quixotic performativity when he asserts that the only way for a Southerner to take hold of his or her "Tradition" is "by violence." Like Cervantes's knight-errant who fights "practical" Spain in order to reclaim a gilded one, Tate understands—yet bemoans—the performativity inherent in reconstructing tradition. Thus he ends his essay with a paradox: the idea of using will, an "instrument, which is political, and so unrealistic and pretentious that he cannot believe in it," as a means of constructing a "private, self-contained, and essentially spiritual life" (175). It is a duality, however, that only creates doubt.

While Tate does not claim to know the fate of Southern "Tradition," the act of asserting it actually creates a double of Southern selfhood that attempts to seem "American" while retaining its exceptional allure. Naturally, this double fails in its efficacy because the past cannot be replicated in such a manner. Instead, that double becomes an uncanny reminder of a traumatic Southern past, which Ransom blindly recalls when he describes the "agrarian" South in what is regarded as one of the most controversial statements in the collection: "Aristocracy is not the word which defines this social organization so well as squirearchy, which I have borrowed from a recent article by Mr. William Frierson in the *Sewanee Review*. And even the squires, and the other classes, too, did not define themselves very strictly.... It was a friendly society, yet a realistic one; for it was a failure if it could not be said that people were for the most part in their right places. Slavery was a feature monstrous enough in theory, but, more often than not, humane in practice; and it is impossible to believe that its abolition alone could have effected any great revolution in society" (14). Ransom's description eerily echoes Ortega's description of the aristocracy without feudalism that created a collection of fragmented individuals who, to borrow Ransom's terms, were not in their "right places." While it seems easy to posit Ransom as a blind racist, just as we can identify Ortega's elitism, there is instead a more revealing element to these writers' desires to incorporate a "traditional" and "exceptional" nation into an American and European ideal. For Ransom, the abolition of slavery had *not* produced a great revolution—the South was still laboring under a very exploitative agricultural economy. As a result, he invokes an image of nationhood and individualism in which, like the antebellum South, people lived in a community in which all were in their "right place." Indeed, this very argument leads Robert Penn Warren in "The Briar Patch" to defend racial segregation in this South while seeming to contradict himself by arguing that "what the white working man must learn . . . is that he may respect himself as a white man, but, if he fails to concede the negro equal protection, he does not properly respect himself as a man" (260). Again, it is important to note that Ransom and Tate are not looking for a return to the pre–Civil War South—just as Ortega is not really advocating German tribal culture. Instead, what occurs is a performative doubling of the self in which the Fugitive-Agrarians try to make the "old" South pass as a "new" nation. Ultimately, the ambivalence that comes out of such performativity only reveals a traumatic past that serves not to fold the South into the United States, but instead to solidify it as the United States' uncanny, racist other.

The uncanny by-products that result from attempts to performatively inscribe a "traditional" South into a "modern" United States do not just serve to solidify the South as a U.S. backwater (though images of trailer parks and hillbillies have helped that effort over the years). Instead, they provoke a questioning of this self/other dichotomy that Freud sees as the ability to objectively observe the ego as a means of "criticizing" the self ("Uncanny" 235). This aspect explains the ambivalent and contradictory elements of many of the Fugitive-Agrarians' and Generation of '98's claims. It is a process, for example, that allows Warren to argue for racial segregation while sincerely promoting African American equality. Similarly, it is how Unamuno develops a philosophy, in *En torno al casticismo,* where he promotes the affirmation of contradiction (784), allowing him a space where "tradition can live in the folds of the present" (794). It is also the means by which the desire to celebrate Spanish "tradition" causes him to justify the conquest of Latin America. However, in the desire to have Spain and the South "pass" as members of a new European or U.S. collective is the ability to simultaneously affirm such national myths, since they exist only as a counterpoint to ideas of Spanishness or Southernness. C. Vann Woodward makes this point about the Agrarians in *The Burden of Southern History* when he describes how Southerners, at the turn of the twentieth century, were capable of debunking U.S. national myths, particularly those of its innocence, since the South had itself "writhed in the torments of its own conscience until it plunged into catastrophe to escape. The South's preoccupation was with guilt, not with innocence, with the reality of evil, not with the dream of perfection" (21). This quality, for Woodward and a generation of scholars that follow, makes the South an "other" within U.S. letters. Similarly, Spain suffered a similar fate for its own incomplete modernity that was, in reality, questioning what modernity had to offer following the defeat of its own "dreams of perfection" by the very U.S. imperial expansion for which the Southern Agrarians expressed so much skepticism.

The image of Cervantes's knight-errant as a willful, autonomously thinking subject is one that modernists re-create in a series of Spanish and Southern Quijotes throughout the century. Much as Cervantes's hero plays a role that suspends him between past and present, the novel becomes the dominant art form for the best and most detailed development of the autonomous thinking subject. With this fact in mind, I conclude by discussing this figure in the works of the authors that began this chapter. At the outset, Miguel de Unamuno's *Niebla* (*Mist,* 1914) and Robert Penn Warren's *All the King's Men* (1946) seem very different, particularly given the latter's focus on politics and its Huey Long–inspired character compared with Unamuno's tale of the privileged upper classes in an unnamed city. Yet both authors create two characters who attempt to will their own subjectivity by playing roles that seem immune to any external verity. In that sense, neither work is really "about" the modern philosophical or political underpinnings they depict, but instead they focus on their respective main characters, Augusto and Jack, both sheltered members of the upper class who seek some sort of alternative reality as a result of the same problem that plagues several characters that follow them: the bonds of modern subjectivity that renders meaningful engagement with the past impossible. Like the Quijote that prefigures them, these main characters find themselves playing a role that wrestles between the past and present—the same "self" and "other" dichotomy that typified national identity in this period. The result for these characters, however, becomes a struggle with time as a form while they face a modern world that supposedly will free them from the weight of tradition but instead only plunges them into doubt—a process that again questions the entire enterprise of national exceptionality.

The crisis of being in time becomes existential for Augusto in Unamuno's novel. Throughout various conversations with his dog, Orfeo, Augusto contemplates how he sees himself versus his projection onto the world: "¿Muchas veces se me ha ocurrido pensar, Orfeo, que yo no soy, e iba por la calle antojándose que los demás no me veían. Y otras veces he fantaseado que no me veían como me veía yo, y que mientras yo creía ir formalmente, con toda compostura, estaba, sin saberlo, haciendo el payaso, y los demás riéndose y burlándose de mí" ["Several times, it has occurred to me to wonder, Orpheus, that I am not myself, and I was walking through the street feeling as if the rest of the world didn't see me. And other times, I have fantasized that they don't see me as I see myself, and that while I believe that I am going formally with great composure, I was, without knowing it, acting like a clown, and the others are laughing at and mocking me"] (140). Not unlike Don Quijote who wanders the world, certain of himself, while everyone mocks him, Augusto is different in that he experiences a doubt so profound that only death seems certain; thus he considers ending his life. Yet before Augusto can commit suicide, he decides to go to Salamanca and discuss this option with Don Miguel de Unamuno. Here Niebla's creator plays a large game with his audience and his character by making himself into a monstrous, all-powerful creator. When Unamuno tells Augusto that he plans to kill him in the next chapter, Augusto is compelled to live, equating it with his sense of self as he begs Unamuno, "¡Quiero ser yo, ser yo! ¡Quiero vivir!" ["I want to be me, be me! I want to live!"] (284). As his creator-author describes Augusto's death as written, it appears as if Augusto's subjectivity is bound up in the confines of a pretold plot. Augusto does die, but he returns as a ghost in the dream of Unamuno, who now considers resuscitating his character. Removed from the confines of literary fate, Augusto as a ghost represents the uncanny fear of subjectivity in which Unamuno is not the all-powerful author, a point Augusto makes clear to him. Thus as Soufas points out in his reading of the novel, "The true protagonist [of this novel] is not Augusto Pérez or Miguel de Unamuno but the *niebla* itself, the structure of thought and consciousness that is always and simultaneously in forma-tion and collapse, an ultimate reality that is primordially formless" (*Subject in Question* 96). In other words, as Augusto—much like the Spanish na-tion he represents—plays two roles, one as the subjective self, defined as the character in Unamuno's *nívola*, but also the other, the ghost that haunts Unamuno by reminding him that he cannot will subjectivity, both perfor-mances are destabilized within the confines of the *niebla* that is, at its heart, "formless."

The manner in which Unamuno plays with the idea of subjectivity in *Niebla* by making himself a character-victim of subjective doubt in his non-novel finds a parallel in Warren's ability to question the confines of the self with political and historical discourse. *All the King's Men* centers around the character of Jack Burden, a Ph.D. student in history and assistant to Willie Talos,[4] a populist Southern politician largely based on the infamous 1930s Louisiana governor Huey P. Long. While the rise of an idealistic young poli-tician to the throes of power and corruption appears the central concern of a novel concerned with subjectivity, in reality it details Jack's search not just for an authentic selfhood but for an intersubjectivity—that is, a relation-ship with a person that can affirm that identity—in a world that provides no semblance of truth for him. Thus the narrator observes, "the story of Jack Burden and the story of Willie Talos are, in one sense, one story" (224). While the engagement with the past, particularly the historical past, that occurs in this novel seems to approach memory as a finite object, in reality the "one sense" that observes "one story" pointedly suggests otherwise. Jack serves as a third-person narrator for his own story, and in the chapter in which he describes a former image of himself who researches a disserta-tion chronicling his great-uncle's demise, he identifies a subjectivity that is utterly detached from his contemporary sense of self (or lack thereof): "this Jack Burden (of whom the present Jack Burden, *Me*, is a legal, biological, and perhaps even a metaphysical continuator)" (224). Jack's "first excursion" into the past (224), which he calls a "refuge" (227), entails the careful reading of his uncle Cass Mastern's journal and letters for a year and a half, at the end of which Jack surmises that "he did not know Cass Mastern. He did not have to know Cass Mastern to get the degree; he only had to know facts about Cass Mastern's world. But without knowing Cass Mastern, he could not put down the facts about Cass Mastern's world" (265). Tied up in his own sense of aimlessness, Jack feels he cannot commit his great-uncle to the bonds of language if the man is not available to him, much like Augusto does not exist other than on Unamuno's page.

Mastern's subjective self, therefore, is utterly bound to Jack's. Meanwhile, this "first excursion" into his family's history prepares him to discover a second truth about his past: the fact that Judge Irwin, a close family friend and also a political rival of Willie's, is his father. A series of disastrous events follow this discovery: Willie is assassinated by Jack's childhood friend—who also dies during the incident—and Jack finally realizes his love for Anne Stanton, who is both Willie's mistress but also the sister of his boss's assassin. Indeed, the various discoveries of "truth" in this novel all come from these characters suffering an ideological betrayal that is typified by that of Willie Talos—the good and humble public servant who wants to help his fellow men and women but who is corrupted both by power and a belief in historical determinacy. In the end, it is Jack who must come to terms with the various truths in this novel as he reaches a point at which he understands the multiplicity of both language and time as forms. For example, when he visits Willie's widow, she tells him, "'He was a great man, Jack. . . . You see, Jack, . . . I have to believe that'" (593). Jack realizes that she does have to believe that in order to "live" and that, in many ways, so does he. In realizing this quixotic "will" to believe and construct memory, furthermore, Jack can begin to write the book on Cass Mastern as he embarks on another excursion "out of history into history and the awful responsibility to Time" (609). In the end, therefore, Jack does not reject history or even myth (he still believes in Willie), but he comes to understand a new history driven by the individual where "Time" still weighs on us in capital letters, but it does so in a manner that is identifiable by the subject instead of lingering as a haunting force. Ultimately, the historical past in Warren's novel is not so unlike Unamuno's *niebla* (mist)—a structure whose facts form and collapse into discernable truths that simultaneously weigh upon us but also make us aware of our own subjectivity by revealing its very intangibility and "awful responsibility."

Warren's and Unamuno's novels provide a prophetic glance into the artists who follow them. Indeed, these new Quijotes—represented by Jack and Augusto, whose varying models of subjectivity help their authors endure the varying traumas of the twentieth century—largely stem from ways of selectively remembering and forgetting the past. Yet throughout this entire engagement with modernity and mainstream modernism, these writers still consistently employ a discourse of cultural exceptionality, as the plight of bourgeois subjectivity remains located within a geographical landscape defined as "Spanish" or "Southern." Yet if we examine the quixotic performativity these writers employ, the myth of exceptionality emerges less as a strictly defined discourse of difference and instead as an uncanny "double" that threatens to examine, and self-examine, the European and U.S. ego. Thus Louis D. Rubin looks at a controversial text like *I'll Take My Stand* as something other than a racist treatise on Southern ideals. Instead, for Rubin, it "was and still is a prophetic book. Its very 'impracticality' constituted its strength, for the refusal of the twelve southerners to be bound by what in 1930 was considered 'practical' and 'inevitable' enabled them to see beneath the surface of Progress and examine the largely unquestioned assumptions on which much of its rhetoric is based" (xxi). Ultimately, while it is easy to look at these men as Quijotes who escape to a regional myth of the past, it is instead more productive to view their efforts as willful refutations of a mythic present—one that may be uncanny but one that is most certainly modern as well.

Chapter 2

THE RELIGION OF BLOOD AND MYTH

William Faulkner's and Camilo José Cela's Modern Subjects

V. K. Ratliff, the resident observer in William Faulkner's Snopes Trilogy, sums up European fascism by indicting its three main players: "That one already in Italy and one a damned sight more dangerous in Germany because all Mussolini has to work with are Italians while this other man has Germans. And the one in Spain that all he needs is to be let alone a little longer by the rest of us who still believe that if we just keep our eyes closed long enough it will all go away" (*Snopes Trilogy* 822). V. K.'s distinction between Mussolini, Hitler, and Franco suggests that Franco's existence requires a collective denial on the part of the international community—a denial he links to the U.S. South when he veers into a discussion of the "K.K.K. . . . , Long in Louisiana . . . , not to mention our very own Senator Clarence Egglestone Snopes right here in Yoknapatawpha County" (823). Throughout Faulkner's body of work, he populates Yoknapatawpha with a series of "modern," social-climbing "Snopes"; yet he simultaneously criticizes Southern claims to exceptionality asserted by groups like the Ku Klux Klan, which V. K. compares to European fascism by seeing them as constructed by-products of the "shibboleth of the democratic lexicon and its mythology" (822). The idea of democratic "mythology" as a "shibboleth" recalls Miguel de Unamuno's image of a European collective as a "chibolete" in *Del sentimiento trágico de la vida*. Such a term prescribes an arbitrary quality to cultural exceptionality by invoking the biblical tale of disguised Ephraimite refugees killed by Gileadites who identified their foes by their inability to correctly pronounce "shibboleth." In pointing to that arbitrariness, my opening this chapter with a comparison of Francoism and Jim Crow is not an effort to draw a historical link between two monolithic and violent power structures. Rather, I see V. K. Ratliff as presenting yet another image of national authenticity as performative, comparing it to the Ephraimites, who had to enact nationality through speech. By exposing such performativity at the level of the characters and their text, however, Faulkner and Spanish counterparts like Camilo José Cela struggle to reconcile the creative renderings of the past within the present, which defined each author's ambivalent relationship with his respective culture during Francoism and Jim Crow. Like writers before them, both Faulkner and Cela expose this performativity but also use it within their texts, as the main characters in, respectively, *Absalom, Absalom!* and *La familia de Pascual Duarte*, enact a melancholic relationship within the cultures that surround them. In so doing, they respond to mythic codes of Spanishness and Southernness by enacting their own individualistic codes of authenticity and masculinity—ones that appear to contest the dominant structure but only mirror it in a way that ultimately destroys them.

V. K. Ratliff's comparison between European fascism and totalitarian ideologies in the South follows a tradition begun by the Nashville Agrarians, particularly Allen Tate and John Crowe Ransom, in which the "Lost Cause" of the U.S. Civil War became a conflict with transatlantic implications. As Robert Brinkmeyer Jr. describes in *The Fourth Ghost*, Tate's biography of Jefferson Davis conceptualized the war as "a battle between large cultural forces that were remaking both America and Europe" (25). Particularly in *I'll Take My Stand*, the Agrarian attack against "industrialism" stemmed from an idolization of agrarian ideals characterized as European; thus, as Brinkmeyer notes, "Tate rotates the North-South cultural axis characteristically used by southerners to conceptualize their culture (with the North embodying everything that the South was not—urbanism, industrialism, progressivism, etc.) so that the axis points West-East, with the North now as the West, and the South now as the East" (26). In so doing, Tate asserts a Southern exceptionality that is performed—a code rewritten where one was lost in 1864. Indeed, Tate, and a generation of Southerners after him, reimagines that loss as emblematic of a transatlantic battle between "traditional" agrarian purity and the "modern" industrial metropolis. It is a battle, meanwhile, that also defined Spain's Civil War as each side rushed to selectively appropriate various monikers of "tradition" and "modernity" while they claimed a particular image of Spanish authenticity. Conflicting versions of the democratic ideal are not only why Faulkner's V. K. Ratliff calls it a "shibboleth," but they also explain the heavy foreign involvement in the war, particularly from U.S. citizens who saw Spain's struggle as relating to their own—with many of them fighting in the Abraham Lincoln brigades. One of these U.S. citizens was James Yates, the son of former slaves in Mississippi, who went to fight in the Spanish Civil War and, after reading false reports in newspapers that Madrid had fallen to Franco, wrote in his memoir: "Madrid would not fall. Republican Spain would not fall. We would go on to create other Republican states throughout the world! Perhaps even in Mississippi!" (110). The idea that a Republican Spain could be "created" in Mississippi reveals the degree to which "Spain" was an imagined entity that had been split in two—one whose image of democracy fit within that of Europe and an "other" image of exceptional nationhood whose authenticity lay within a "traditional" past. If we look at war as a theater of performed nationhood, then what the Spanish Civil War produced was a situation in which the violent battle over Spanish selfhood ultimately othered Spain from the European and international community, revealing both a fragmented populace and a political regime that had to renegotiate its relationship to a tradition simultaneously, and irrevocably, bound to modernity.

The degree to which Spain had to grapple with a "traditional" nationhood bound up in modernity is apparent in its own "lost" cause: that of the nineteenth-century Carlist Wars fought between the male heir to the Spanish throne, Carlos, and the female heir, Isabel II. Among early twentieth-century writers who most adamantly took up this cause was Ramón del Valle-Inclán, whose three novels comprising the series *La Guerra Carlista* (1908) depicted Carlist soldiers as faithful heroes tasked with fighting for a holy and just cause (Lima 171). While Valle-Inclán was attracted to the Carlist Wars for both ideological and aesthetic reasons (Lima 172), he, not unlike his contemporaries in Spain and Southerners with the Civil War, eventually abandoned the idealism once associated with the nineteenth-century conflict and instead, as Robert Lima notes in *The Dramatic World of Valle-Inclán*, "undertook to hand down a harsh indictment of modern realities when he adopted the point of view of the *Esperpento* to make emphatic the absurdity and grotesqueness of the period" (172). Valle-Inclán's use of irony and grotesque imagery in his adoption of the *esperpento* becomes analogous to the similarly grotesque images and ironic use of the "unreliable" narrator/ main character that characterized Cela's "tremendista" *Pascual Duarte*. Even more, the degree to which grotesque images of death become metaphors for the death of "tradition" within modernity also takes shape across the Atlantic in the development of the Southern "gothic" tradition in which authors like Faulkner and, later, Flannery O'Connor use images of death to wickedly reimagine a decaying agrarian landscape being encroached upon by a "modern," metropolitan South.

While it would seem that civil war and totalitarian authority produced a "winner" between tradition and modernity, in reality the institutions of Francoism and Jim Crow produced a selective blending of the two—a performance of national authenticity that no individual can actually live up to. Thus the autonomous thinking subject becomes suspended between images of Spanishness and Southernness as he or she attempts to cope with the loss of integrated authenticity. This loss is at the center of Faulkner's and Cela's novels as Pascual and Sutpen absorb it into their psyches, thus creating a melancholic relationship with a traumatic history. Following Freud's theory of melancholia, both Pascual Duarte and Thomas Sutpen constantly enact a coded image of Spanishness and Southernness that is linked to an unconscious loss of those very forms in the historical past as they cope with the onset of a modern present. While critics, Walter Benjamin in particular, have argued that the condition of modernity is itself melancholic since it is typified by feelings of loss in its glorification of the new, the particular situations of Spain and the South produce a secondary loss—still tied to the ego—that is compounded by an image of national identity, imagined via the institutions of Francoism and Jim Crow. The result is that the melancholic subjects Pascual and Sutpen unconsciously pave a path toward self-destruction as they can never overcome this perceived ego-loss—because it is really located in a performed code—and instead only seek images of their performed selves in every effort to find a means of achieving personal, and national, authenticity.

The degree to which the Spanish and Southern autonomous thinking subject, in this case Pascual and Sutpen, enacts a pathological relationship to the past speaks to Francoist Spain's and the Jim Crow South's own reliance on ritual as a means of solidifying dominance and authority. This process of establishing control entails the selective blending of tradition and modernity as specifically Jim Crow politics and laws claimed allegiance to a "Lost Cause" of national dominance. For both Spain and the South, a ritualized performance of national authenticity went hand in hand with religious fervor; thus churches became allies of the authoritative state. In the South, as Charles Reagan Wilson explains, churches played a major role in promoting secession from the Union and then maintaining morale during the Civil War even when defeat became a certainty. After the war, the religious sector helped the defeated Southerner accept his or her fate as the culture of the Lost Cause took form. Thus as Wilson notes, "The churches' powerful role in the Civil War, and their expansion and dominance after 1865, suggest that if the Confederacy before dying was baptized in blood, Southern religion was likely symbolically baptized, born again in a fiery sacrament that gave it new spiritual life. The Southern churches thus profited from the Holocaust" (8). Throughout his book Wilson outlines the degree to which the Lost Cause became a religion via performance—that is, coming from a need to rehabilitate through ritual a past perceived as lost. For this reason, Wilson makes clear that the church was not a political organization, instead choosing to offer Southerners the ability to reaffirm a civil identity linked to a shared cultural and historical experience (9). While focused on performativity in his novels, Faulkner does not paint Thomas Sutpen as a religious fanatic by any means; quite the contrary, he is noted for his pragmatism—what Cleanth Brooks calls an "innocence" that can be categorized "par excellence [as] the innocence of modern man" (297). What I propose with Sutpen, meanwhile, is to categorize him as neither "innocent" nor "religious" per se, much like I do not subscribe to an image of Jim Crow as being either traditional or modern. Instead, the religion of the Lost Cause and my ideas on Sutpen's melancholia outline how ritual allows the individual and the state to enact a performative sense of authenticity by carefully combining pieces of a fragmented, and often traumatic, past. Thus monikers of "tradition," "religion," and "politics" no longer become essential forms from the past, but ritualized fragments of that past within modernity.

Meanwhile Spain's Civil War, while comprising a clear set of "winners" and "losers" by its end, also grappled with selectively appropriating its own lost cause of imperial superiority as a means of establishing absolute dominance and authenticity. Despite Franco's links to fascism, that effort involved the direct participation of the Roman Catholic Church, with priests serving as local enforcers of the regime and, in many cases, spies on local citizens thought to be "disloyal." As Michael Richards makes clear, despite some obvious contradictions between church doctrine (like Christian charity) and oppressive totalitarian rule in Spain, Castilian nationalism had always been tied to Catholicism (172). Thus by the end of World War II "church, party and military were enmeshed, not only in a network of common ideas, but in a 'pact of blood' entered into during the war itself" (Richards 172). This "pact of blood" is readily apparent throughout Cela's novel, as Pascual's ties to his family as well as a coded Spanish masculinity mark his life with death and violence. Yet the mode of confession and the separation between Pascual the confessor and Pascual the character actually enact the performativity inherent in Cela's novel, as confession itself, though not to a priest, still recalls the need on the part of the individual to enact a forgotten past. Thus while religion per se is by no means the guiding force of Cela's main character—much like it is not for Faulkner's—its ritualized elements appear throughout both authors' novels as a reflection of Spanish and Southern culture. In Spain and the South themselves, the role of wars with such high civilian casualties speaks to the manner in which religion consoled the loss of a populace, yet the very blood of the Spanish and Southern populace became the very means by which the state essentialized their imagined claims to an exceptional, and authoritative, nationhood. Thus the religious fanaticism that accompanied Francoism and Jim Crow—evidenced by the popularity of Opus Dei in Spain and the tent revival movement in the South—contained an inherent effort to ritualize and enact a mythology of an imperial Spain and a Confederate South. Such are images that haunt the histories of both power structures as leaders sought to resurrect those lost nations, almost like Christ himself, in the eyes of their people.

Part of the allure of religious myth is its ties to essential identity. If we reject the idea of Jim Crow and Francoism as unique expressions of Southern and Spanish claims to exceptionality, the question remains how to locate difference within each culture's experience with modernity. The answer arrives in a careful evaluation of what their performances of "tradition" within "modernity" yield, that is, an identity slippage in which the South and Spain become both "self" and "other" within a U.S. and European cultural model. Yet upon examining the careful renegotiation of nationhood and belonging to the "self" while being "othered" by a national or international community, it only emphasizes that no real winners come out of civil strife and that such "loss" makes both the U.S. and Spanish civil wars into sites of trauma that shaped two modern constructions of nationhood. For this reason, Spain's and the South's two most famous authors, and Nobel Prize winners, used their regions' most bloody wars and dark postwar periods as a means of exploring how the autonomous thinking subject copes with an uncanny sense of place: a familiar one located in a traditional past coupled with an inhospitable and traumatic "double" of that past. The inability of tradition to be reenacted, or performed, in the present—the inability to go back to a pre-civil war world—dominated not just William Faulkner's and Camilo José Cela's aesthetics but also their polemical public personas. Faulkner, for example, never claimed to be more than a farmer from Mississippi; yet as a Hollywood screenwriter and "sole owner and proprietor" of his fictional Yoknapatawpha County, he scandalized his native region by depicting it as the home of murderers and idiots. When it came to the topic of integration during the civil rights movement, Faulkner found himself a controversial middle ground, stating support for gradual de-segregation and suggesting that immediate integration would return the United States to 1860—with him fighting for the South if necessary (Blotner 617).

Not unlike Faulkner, Camilo José Cela remained a controversial figure throughout the Francoist era, once responding to a question about what he planned to do at the end of a colloquium by suggesting, "No sé, quizás me vaya de putas" ["I don't know, perhaps I should go to whores"] (quoted in Gibson, epigraph). Part of Cela's polemical persona was that, despite having fought for the Nationalists and later working as a censor, he never ingrained himself in Francoist historiography. As biographer Ian Gibson notes, Cela's attitude toward his country in the early years of Franco remained ambivalent, feeling the "euphoria" of the initial victory yet later finding Francoist Spain both hypocritical and miserable (108). As I show in this chapter, furthermore, Faulkner and Cela create not just characters, but a novelistic form that explores the ambivalent relationship to Southern and Spanish culture by revealing and enacting the performativity that makes these cultures both "self" and "other." This in-betweenness, moreover, characterizes each one's ability to enact the process of national performativity while not becoming victims of it themselves.

For modern subjects like Sutpen and Pascual, the inability to get back to a mythic past in a modern present manifests itself as melancholy, which emerges via another performance: that of gender. Greg Forter sees performative masculinity as emblematic of modernity when, in his article "Against Melancholia: Contemporary Mourning Theory, Fitzgerald's *The Great Gatsby*, and the Politics of Unfinished Grief," he shows how the modern "belief in the colossal power of desire, the possibility of economic and imaginative self-making," is betrayed during the second stage of capitalist production when the possibility of self-fashioning was inhibited by the homogenization of individual production via the assembly line (144). The result, he shows, is a masculinity that "was to be unambiguously hard, aggressive, physically dominative, potent—and this version of manhood was then projected back into the past, imagined as a primal essence eclipsed by a feminizing modernity that it was now the business of men to combat" (145). In Spain and the South, it is understandable how the modern assertion of a hard masculinity during Francoism and Jim Crow hearkens back to a "traditional" Spanish and Southern ideal. Yet again, the inability of the past to effectively replace the present within such a coded masculinity and national identity—that is, the failure to perform a Spanish or Southern manliness—creates a sense of loss for the autonomous thinking subject as well as an uncanny sense of place as the new man is forced to reconcile a familiar past as it is reproduced in a haunting and still-traumatic present.

The degree to which masculinity becomes a measure of national authenticity means that the loss—and subsequent reimagining—of a "traditional" Spain and the South within modernity begins to weigh upon individual subjectivity as the modern subject tries to define himself in an environment that makes him both self and other. Thus just as Forter sees a pathologically hard masculinity as a melancholic response to the loss of feminine expression in late-stage capitalist production, I see a melancholic performativity in the Spanish and Southern masculine subject as he responds to the loss of "tradition" by replacing it with a very personal, yet still reflective, image of present nationhood. For Freud, the melancholic is a pathological figure that unconsciously comes to detest what is lost, which, having been linked to the ego, becomes linked to the self in a manner that compels the subject to suicide—a destruction of the self as a means of eradicating the hated object-loss. Yet such self-destruction proves multifaceted in a Spain and South that simultaneously embody the role of self and other. Thus particularly in novels like *Absalom, Absalom!* and *Pascual Duarte*, the performance of an authentic nationhood produces a willful, and unconscious, desire to obliterate "other" narratives of authenticity that oppose the masculine, authentically Southern or Spanish self. In the case of both of these novels' main characters, however, that "other" is by no means external to the self, as Thomas Sutpen's children and Pascual Duarte's masculine mother constantly threaten their assertions of an authentic nationhood and masculinity. As Pascual and Sutpen constantly try to perform their image of Spanishness and Southernness, the inability of the past to effectively replace the present persists and haunts them, thus placing them within a cycle of violence in which they constantly try to destroy these opposing narratives of authenticity, but unconsciously end up destroying themselves.

The melancholic performativity in Cela's and Faulkner's novels in which their modern subjects pathologically and unconsciously try to regain a "lost" national authenticity is in fact only one level of performance in these novels. In addition, there is a performativity of novelistic form in which the unconscious acts of the new men are revealed to be melancholic through the commentary of an outside narrator—for Faulkner, Quentin Compson, and in Cela's novel, a Pascual writing his confession years later. This ambivalence of novelistic form—the uniting of both past and present in a single narrative—becomes, in accordance with Forter's reading of *Gatsby*, a means by which we can see "the various costs of embracing social melancholy" by showing, at the level of the text, how "unacknowledged rage is directed at the socially vulnerable" (164). In *Absalom, Absalom!* and *Pascual Duarte*, Faulkner and Cela demonstrate such limits by showing how the "old" South and Spain cannot be effectively reproduced in a modern world. Yet both authors do not achieve this form with characters that have arrived at a state of mourning where loss can be overcome. Instead, Quentin and Pascual the confessor become melancholic as they struggle to take Sutpen and Pascual the figure being narrated as fixed entities in the past and reimagine them for a present audience—much like Sutpen and Pascual the character try to make a "traditional" South and Spain "pass" for a modern one. In both cases, the difference between the "real" and the "performed" is a slippage that is unspeakable and traumatic; yet by centering that slippage around personal and national performativity—all centered around two narratives that are separated by the declaration of civil war—Faulkner and Cela enact that ambivalence for the reader, providing no discernible Southern or Spanish "truths," but only suggesting the limitations of such an enterprise.

Throughout Faulkner studies, attempts to draw connections with the Spanish-speaking world have focused on exploring Faulkner's relationship with Latin America. While he did in fact travel to Latin America during his lifetime, Faulkner also enjoyed success in Spain as early as 1934 when *Sanctuary* was first translated (Bravo, *Faulkner en España* 22). In fact, his popularity abroad matched his fame in the United States, especially following World War II when his works became particularly well known in France and Argentina (Bravo, *Faulkner en España* 30). In addition, Faulkner was, as were many other U.S. writers of his era, engaged by Spain's Civil War. He not only signed a short statement in opposition to fascism and Franco, but he also donated the manuscript and first typescripts of *Absalom, Absalom!* to the League of American Writers as a contribution to the Republican cause. As Joseph Blotner, Faulkner's most noted biographer, describes the gesture, "For a man who would later contemptuously recall being labeled 'a Gothic fascist' by leftist literary warriors, it was quite a contribution" (411). The weight of Faulkner's contribution of *Absalom, Absalom!* to the Republican cause does not stand out because of its financial implications. Instead, the story of Thomas Sutpen's "design" to creatively weld past and present in a personal construction of "Southernness" not only reflects that of a series of characters named Snopes that followed, but creates a functional parallel with a figure like Francisco Franco. Born into a middle-class naval family in Galicia, Franco was denied the possibility of becoming an officer because of the strict social constrictions that reserved these positions for the upper class. As discussed earlier, Franco's success did not just come from climbing the social and military ladder; it occurred as a consequence of a creative merging of past and present, of tradition and modernity. Sutpen's rise involves many of those same constructions, as he too is a member of the lower class and attempts to make claims to respectability by bringing slaves from the Caribbean, kidnapping a French architect to build his plantation, and marrying a respectable woman to bear his children. Franco participated in the same sort of social climbing early in his dictatorship, using and displaying relics reserved for royalty at his parades and positioning himself, in Paul Preston's words, as Spain's "medieval warrior-crusader" (323). Yet despite the intense drive that brought these men to re-create themselves anew within a particular Spanish and Southern honor code, it ultimately destroyed them over the course of a generation as their "designs" consumed them into almost complete impotence. While Sutpen is a fictional character, he, and other characters like him, demonstrates Faulkner's engagement with the performativity inherent in trying to re-create a mythic past—an act that, incidentally, is very different from the U.S. "self-made man" described by Benjamin Franklin that belongs to the present. Thus in many ways *Absalom, Absalom!* articulates the danger that Faulkner saw in performed nationhood—one that so worried him in Spain because he had depicted it in his own Yoknapatawpha County.

For Faulkner, what is dangerous about a figure like Sutpen is that his response to the perceived loss of the past is unconscious; thus the desire to assert a modern subjectivity that is immune to outside determiners like history or ideology becomes haunted by the very thing it appears to shirk. Faulkner explores this problem at length in *Absalom, Absalom!* when Quentin Compson's grandfather describes this unawareness as Sutpen's "trouble" (178). Cleanth Brooks goes even further, discussing Sutpen's "innocence" at length in his seminal essay on this novel in *William Faulkner: The Yoknapatawpha County* by calling it a willful rationalism that, to cite Brooks's quotation of Quentin's grandfather, "'believed that the ingredients of morality were like the ingredients of a pie or cake and once you had measured them and balanced them and mixed them and put them into the oven it was all finished and nothing but pie or cake could come out'" (quoted on 297). This view of modernity returns us to the capitalist myth of progress in which success, like morality, can be measured and cooked into a final, finite product. Yet what Sutpen does not realize is that one of his ingredients—an image of a traditional South—does not exist inasmuch as it is performed. As a result, his perfect plantation, Sutpen's Hundred, lies on a shaky foundation of willfully performed selfhood. When it becomes clear that this plantation world is the replacement for one he lost in the past, the mere threat to his new life makes him a slave to his own melancholic performativity. In other words, faced with what he lost in the past, Sutpen's only recourse is to willfully follow his design, thus destroying that threat, but in the end, destroying himself.

Faulkner highlights the very performativity inherent in Sutpen's enterprise by narrating not through his eyes, but through those of Quentin Compson as he tells the story to his Harvard roommate, Shreve. Like Cela's distinction between Pascual the narrator/confessor and the character described, Quentin's narration of the events at Sutpen's Hundred is, at best, a willful remembrance of the past. He does not know the entire story, and, at key moments, he and Shreve are forced to invent details to give certain aspects meaning. Not only does Faulkner understand the performativity inherent in constructing narrative, he exploits it much as Cela does with confession. In other words, it is in the act of creating narrative that we realize our subjectivity as it exists within the realm of performance. In short, we are because we act. By the novel's end, Quentin realizes this idea as he insists to Shreve that he does not hate the South just as he, at least to Shreve, has spent hours enacting a narrative that suggests otherwise.

From Quentin's and Shreve's perspective, the threat to Sutpen's Hundred appears in Charles Bon, Sutpen's son from a previous marriage with a woman whose parents lied about her black ancestry, causing him to abandon them both. Bon reenters the Sutpen family when Thomas's son, Henry, meets him at college and brings his new friend home. Soon an engagement between Bon and Sutpen's daughter, Judith, is arranged. The plan fails, however, when Sutpen realizes that Bon is his son and tells Henry that Bon is his brother, but notably refrains from telling him that Bon is black. Henry abandons his family as he and Bon travel to New Orleans, and before long, all the Sutpen men, including Bon, find themselves fighting in the U.S. Civil War. It is in the background of the South's crumbling defeat that Sutpen's design is truly dismantled. When Sutpen tells Henry that Bon is a black man, Henry is horrified, and it becomes clear that, in Quentin's and Shreve's minds, the prevailing threat to Sutpen's respectable identity is miscegenation, not incest. Thus they imagine him telling Henry that his father only needed to acknowledge Bon as his son in order to prevent the marriage: "That was all. He would not have needed to ask it, require it, of me. I would have offered it. I would have said, I will never see her again before he could have asked it of me. He did not have to do this, Henry. He didn't need to tell you that I am a nigger to stop me" (285).

As the story unfolds, all Bon seeks from the Sutpen family is paternal recognition—a sense of patriarchal authenticity that comes from discovering one's origin. What Bon does not realize, however, is that he is seeking something that, in Sutpen's world, proves to be nothing more than a construction, again, a mix of ingredients combined together. What Sutpen sees in Bon, furthermore, is not a son, but a "mistake," a blip in his rational, logical plan. He says as much to Quentin's grandfather when he calmly notes, "'You see, I had a design in mind. Whether it was a good or bad design is beside the point; the question is, Where did I make the mistake in it, what did I do or misdo in it, whom or what injure by it to the extent which this [his downfall] would indicate. I had a design'" (212). As Sutpen sees his son as a simple "mistake" and the legitimacy of his design as inconsequential, he makes the same mistake as Bon, who continues believing he will marry Judith until his father recognizes him. He even rides with Henry to Sutpen's Hundred on what is supposed to be the couple's wedding day, but before he can even enter the gates of the plantation, Henry shoots his brother, thus eliminating the threat to his father's design and his brother's belief, like his father's, that sheer strength of will permits the achievement of authentic selfhood.

Such a demonstration of Sutpen's and Bon's will illustrates how "authenticity" is something that can neither be sought nor created, partially because rational modernity, and its subsequent capitalist progress, allows us to believe that selfhood is attainable when, at least within the confines of Faulkner's novel, it is not. Herein exists the trauma of modernity, as Faulkner envisions it within the historical milieu of the pre– and post–Civil War South and as it is remembered and dissected by various twentieth-century characters in the novel, above all Quentin and his Canadian roommate, Shreve. Indeed, there is a persistent link between Sutpen's design and that of the South, which serves as a poignant contrast to his father-in-law's refusal to fight in the Civil War so that he can be "present on that day when the South would realize that it was now paying the price for having erected its economic edifice not on the rock of stern morality but on the shifting rocks of opportunism and moral brigandage" (209). This refusal, coupled with Sutpen's resolve to fight, demonstrates the degree to which Faulkner is aware that coded images of essential identity—particularly religious codes of "stern morality" and "moral brigandage"—are pliable and moldable when the modern subject wills it.

The manner in which authenticity is constantly sought and never found in the novel means that Sutpen's "design" is threatened, thus contested, by various oppositional "narratives," which in themselves represent the intense fears and threat to any sense of a constructed post–Civil War Southern authenticity: that of miscegenation and feminization. Thus both the distinctions of "blackness" and "feminization" become performances of "otherness" that contest the Southern narrative of white male dominance. Such performances, furthermore, demonstrate the degree to which Sutpen performs his "Southern" design for the entire community of Jefferson, and when attempts to make that design "pass" as a model of traditional Southernness fail, "blackness" becomes an opposing, uncanny narrative that appears as a measure of the difference between performed and actual subjectivity (Kreiswirth 130). J. G. Brister makes a similar point in his essay "*Absalom, Absalom!* and the Semiotic Other" when he links "blackness" to Julia Kristeva's idea of the "semiotic" and says, "From this perspective, race in *Absalom, Absalom!* emerges as a dramatization of the dialectic between the symbolic and the semiotic— where the latter ultimately undermines and challenges the hegemony of the former" (39). It is important to note, however, that Bon's blackness is not an issue until it is performed before his father and brother. In other words, Bon is not black until he tries to marry Judith and enact the miscegenation. For this reason, Henry rides with Bon to Jefferson as a friend, knowing that he must kill his brother. Yet he never even conceives of actually doing so until Bon attempts to cross the gates into the plantation property, waiting until the performance of blackness trumps the seemingly innate bond of siblings. In other words, neither Henry nor his father cares that Bon is black, so long as his actions do not force them to recognize his blackness. Thus it becomes an issue of perceived and constructed, not innate, identity.

The idea that Bon's blackness is a threat to Sutpen becomes gendered upon realizing the contradiction that Henry and Judith have a black half-sister, Clytie, who openly lives on the plantation with them and apparently poses no such threat. Yet the feminine is clearly the "other" in this novel as Quentin's father tells him, "'Yes. They lead beautiful lives—women. Lives not only divorced from, but irrevocably excommunicated from, all reality'" (156). The divorce of male and female worlds includes Sutpen as he consistently tries to assert, through performance, his masculinity by putting on bloody spectacles in which he fights his slaves in front of the entire community. Yet much like race, gender becomes another malleable narrative that questions any sense of authentic "Southernness" in Sutpen's world. Indeed, Sutpen's own children question this narrative when they watch his fights: while the male Henry cannot watch the bloody brawls, Judith observes them oddly "unmoved" (30). Following the Civil War and Bon's murder, the dismantling of the South and Sutpen's design suddenly allows for a challenge to the narrative of masculinity—and femininity—that previously dominated the novel. Yet as with Bon, the "otherness" that threatens Sutpen's design is not external; instead, it comes in the form of his own child, Judith.

Judith participates in a performance of gender throughout *Absalom, Absalom!* by, ironically, displaying the same force of will that her father possesses. The novel codes such will as masculine and performative when Sutpen tells Henry that Bon cannot marry his own sister, and the brothers leave, never telling Judith the reason why. Quentin deduces that Henry leaves his sister in ignorance because he knows that his sister will fight back. Indeed, Henry admits that they are "both doubtless aware that when that point was reached she would, and with the same calm, the same refusal to accept or give because of any traditional weakness of sex, recall the armistice and face him as foe, not requiring or even wishing that Bon be present to support her, doubtless even refusing to allow him to intervene if he were, fighting the matter out with Henry like a man first before consenting to revert to the woman, the loved, the bride" (73). Here Judith's masculine role as foe and feminine role as bride can be put on and taken off like a mask in a way that is completely divorced from any "traditional" idea of "sex" and instead linked to the same willful rationalism that her father possesses. Like Bon, and specifically unlike Sutpen, Judith learns that sheer will cannot allow her to make herself the authentically feminine "loved, the bride" when, on her wedding day, she watches Henry murder her fiancé and proceeds to bury his body herself. Following his murder, Judith's story becomes one that seems to merge her father's masculine will and her own feminine compassion. For example, she sees to it that Bon's octoroon mistress visits his grave, raises Bon's son when his mistress dies, and dies herself nursing the boy, whom she insists call her aunt, during a yellow fever epidemic. As Brooks describes her, "She is one of Faulkner's finest characters of endurance—and not merely through numb, bleak Stoicism but also through compassion and love. Judith is doomed by misfortunes not of her making, but she is not warped and twisted by them. Her humanity survives them" (319). Note here that Brooks says "humanity" and not "masculinity" or "femininity." What makes Judith more "human" in this instance is her response to loss, which is where she differs from her father. Not the pathological melancholic who unconsciously needs to destroy the "other," Judith is able, in her nephew, to find a new object of love, thus mourning Bon's loss and arriving at a moment of healing.

The expression of love that Judith possesses and Sutpen ignores causes his demise. When Sutpen returns from the war, he struggles to replace the male heirs he has lost, asking his sister-in-law to marry him but only after she has produced a son. When she refuses, he begins an affair with a fifteen-year-old white girl, Milly, who gives birth to their daughter. Again, in an attempt to perform what has been lost, Sutpen is left with a failed double, a baby girl that, like the "other" son he refused to acknowledge, he abandons. This indefatigable will to enact a "design" is coded via an image of white male Southernness that destroys Sutpen when he is murdered by Milly's grandfather for failing to acknowledge the child. While it appears that Sutpen's Hundred survives, especially when, years later, Henry comes home to die, even the plantation is destroyed by a feminine force when Rosa comes to take Henry away in an ambulance and Clytie burns the house to the ground, killing herself and her half-brother. Thus in Sutpen's failed attempt to create a white male construction of authenticity and progeny, his "design" ultimately, and symbolically, is destroyed by his black daughter.

The manner in which race and gender become "other" narratives that threaten the white male South that Sutpen tries to embody demonstrates the multiplicity of language and narrative structure in the novel. Such varying narratives of the South—its hopes for a white male empire coupled with its fears of miscegenation and feminization—demonstrate how the "South" itself is a construction adopted by Sutpen and performed for the community that he hopes to join. Further, through Sutpen, Faulkner shows how the modern male subject's blind will emerges when he is unable to construct an authentic sense of self. This lack, per Roach's model of performance, produces a need for a surrogate, what Freud sees as transference to a new object-love. Sutpen fails, furthermore, because performance always fails by virtue of its rigidity—the inability to move on—enacted in the refusal to incorporate a diverse narrative. Thus all that remains is fear and intense paranoia of that which has been othered, which not only results in violence but serves to bring all these diverse narratives to the fore.

While the opposing narratives of the South expose the very performance of Southernness, Faulkner embeds another level of performance that exposes the South's exceptionality within a national aesthetic. When Quentin Compson responds to his Canadian roommate's (Shreve) request to "tell about the South," Quentin responds with Sutpen's story. The fact that Shreve is not even from the United States is pertinent to a discussion of performed nationhood since, as Quentin describes Sutpen's performance, he performs the South to a modern, liberal, twentieth-century thinker (Brooks 313). Despite the fact that Quentin hears the story from Rosa Colfield, Sutpen's sister-in-law, and does not witness it firsthand, he does not seem divorced from the narrative. Indeed, as Quentin listens to Rosa, he is suspended both in the past and the present as he describes listening to "two separate Quentins now—the Quentin Compson preparing for Harvard in the South, the deep South dead since 1865 and people with garrulous outraged baffled ghosts, listening, having to listen, to one of the ghosts which had refused to lie still even longer than most had, telling him about old ghost-times; and the Quentin Compson who was still too young to deserve yet to be a ghost but nevertheless having to be one for all that, since he was born and bred in the deep South the same as she was" (4). The idea that Quentin is both haunted by ghosts as a Harvard student yet is irrevocably tied to the past as a ghost himself suggests that the past, or "history," is a construction that is never finished, never laid to rest, and not adequately mourned. In other words, as Quentin describes Sutpen's "design," he and Shreve provide their own interpretations, hypotheses, and commentary, and Shreve flippantly observes, "Jesus, the South is fine, isn't it. It's better than the theatre, isn't it. It's better than Ben Hur, isn't it. No wonder you have to come away now and then, isn't it" (176). As Quentin and Shreve wind their way through the tale, it becomes clear that the "two Quentins" are at odds with one another: one is tied to the past, to Sutpen's performed South, cannot escape it; the other (like Shreve) can see the very performance in front of him—how it is even better than stage performance—which is why he can add his own spin to the narrative.

The manner in which Quentin, unlike Shreve, is tied to Sutpen's story suggests how Quentin's performance of Southernness for his roommate, like Sutpen's for Jefferson, is doomed to fail in its rigidity. Leigh Anne Duck suggests as much in her essay "Haunting Yoknapatawpha: Faulkner and Traumatic Memory" when she says, "*Absalom, Absalom!* suggests that regional memories are neither inherent nor productive: individuals who maintain this traumatic relationship to the past do not participate in a community of shared suffering and gained wisdom, but are each isolated in an encounter with the unique moment that they cannot understand, whether because it proved too destructive in their own lives or because it seems to provide a key to another, more personal trauma" (94). The fact that Quentin the ghost becomes totally isolated from Quentin the student-storyteller suggests that he is just as tied to his constructed image of Southernness as Sutpen is. Thus Quentin's renewed image of the South consumes him in a willful and pathological melancholia that appears in the novel's famous final scene. Shreve, providing a final commentary on the story that seeks a communal, universal theme, deduces that miscegenation will prevail in the world and that, in a thousand years, that which threatened Sutpen's Southern performance so much will become so common that he, a Canadian, will "have sprung from the loins of African kings" (302). Shreve makes this observation despite Quentin's obvious annoyance with the cheeky Canadian, yet Shreve's next question to his roommate—"Why do you hate the South?"—marks a striking contrast with Quentin, who reveals his own melancholy. Quentin says quickly, "I don't hate it" and repeats this phrase in his mind as he lies in "the iron New England dark" (303)—an environment completely removed from his Southern experience. In this final scene, Quentin brings full circle the modern subject's engagement with a rational modernity as he, like Sutpen, thinks that sheer force of will can forge his authenticity: he does not hate the South. The pathological manner in which Quentin repeats these words implies that he suffers from the same melancholia as Sutpen. Therefore, as he "performs" the South for Shreve by "telling" about it, he unknowingly comes to self-identify with the past, causing him to internalize his unconscious hatred of that "other" South with a self-reviling in the present. What Quentin also does not realize is that he does not hate the South because he says so, but because the exceptional South from which he cannot detach himself does not exist inasmuch as it is performed; thus he can never overcome his ambivalent relationship to that uncanny time and place that is both self and other, existing in the past and the present.

The persistent will of Quentin Compson in particular has caused scholars, such as Montserrat Ginès in her *Southern Inheritors of Don Quijote*, to link the innocent man in Faulkner's novels to Cervantes's Don Quijote. Indeed, it was the mad hidalgo's will that caused Ortega to call him a hero in his *Meditaciones del Quijote*, and it is easy to note the functional parallel between the modern subject and the Spanish hidalgo who wills his authenticity into being by giving himself a new name and going on adventures. Faulkner greatly admired Cervantes's character for these traits, as he admitted in an interview, "It's admiration and pity and amusement—that's what I get from him—and the reason is that he is a man trying to do the best he can in this ramshackle universe he's compelled to live in. He has ideals which by the pharisaical standards are nonsensical. His practice of trying to put them into practice is tragic and comic" (Fant and Ashley 94). By linking

Quentin Compson to Camilo José Cela's Pascual Duarte, it seems pertinent to note that *La familia de Pascual Duarte* emerges from the same picaresque tradition that produced *Don Quijote* (Gibson 108). Yet unlike Cervantes's hero, and more like Quentin, Pascual always returns home and is bound to his family in a manner that subsists only through violence.

Much like describing Faulkner and the "South," exploring Camilo José Cela's relationship to "Spain" proves difficult, especially considering that Cela fought for the Nationalists during the Civil War but, in the end, was one of the dictatorship's most ardent critics. Much like Faulkner, Cela's ambivalent relationship with his native country is exemplified most in his first novel and the first published after the Spanish Civil War, *La familia de Pascual Duarte*. While not about Spanish nationhood per se, Cela's novel still reflects the fragmented and divided nation of this period by utilizing many of the themes and styles of both predecessors and contemporaries. In many ways, the novel emerges from the realist tradition characterized by Benito Pérez Galdós's novels and the grim themes of Pío Baroja, whom Cela asked to write a preface but was turned down when Baroja said he did not want to go to jail for doing so (Charlebois 4). Yet Cela's terse prose and realist style, coupled with extreme narrative experimentation, caused critics and scholars to label his work *tremendista* [tremendist], a term that was meant to characterize his violent, often grotesque style, but one that Cela often rejected. Even more, Cela's efforts to erase the presence of author/narrator in the novel become analogous to a subtle absence of explicit ideas of nationhood in the novel. Not only does the lack of said narrator highlight Cela's authorial presence even more, the only slight mention of the Spanish Civil War in the novel actually highlights the novel's "Spanishness"—similar to Quentin Compson's assertion that he "doesn't hate the South." As with Faulkner studies, Cela scholarship has, in large part, centered on "defining" the polemical author and style when, in reality, Cela's work, again like Faulkner's, unequivocally rejects static definition as the Spanish author opts for a multiplicity of narratives that questions his home.

Throughout *La familia de Pascual Duarte*, Cela works very hard to make it appear that he has not written a novel, but instead is narrating the confessions of a real man. Much like Cervantes's *Don Quijote*, we are confronted with a note from a transcriber as well as letters from Pascual's jailers about his death and the writing of his confession. Taken in such a form, we see Cela working within the realist tradition, characterized in Spain by works such as Galdós's *Doña Perfecta* (1876), which employs a similar style coupling letters and narrative. Yet upon reading the confession that dominates this novel, it becomes clear that Cela is reinventing this modern figure upon discovering that Pascual is in jail for a murder he never describes and that the almost-poetic style comes from a peasant born in the remote western region of Extremadura. In addition, as Pascual describes his life, family, and the circumstances that compel him to commit the various acts of violence, we observe a man who at almost every point believed he could determine his fate and, in some ways, still thinks he can by writing his confession. John Kronik makes this point in his essay "Pascual's Parole" when he observes how "it is easy to understand why Pascual should wish to rewrite a life like his which society condemns to eradication" (115). Thus once again, the very act of creating narrative becomes part of creating an authentic selfhood, and Pascual engages in such self-imagination as a way of fighting against the world that already has appeared to determine his fate.

Understanding Pascual Duarte as a modern subject faced with a code of Spanish honor allows for a more complete view of a character that has divided critics between those who see him as a hapless victim and those who see him as an irredeemable criminal. Such a complex view of Pascual becomes evidenced, furthermore, by the multiplicity of narratives in this novel. Aside from a note from a transcriber and a letter from his jailor, there is also a stark divide between Pascual as narrator of his life and the character he describes leading it. As such, Pascual is like Quentin Compson, who explores the past externally but is still irrevocably tied to it. Kronik makes a similar point when exploring the semiotics of Cela's novel: "There exists a text about Pascual, and Pascual exists as a text. His textuality is his parole—in both the current and the etymological sense of the term. Locked in his pen, Pascual takes up his pen and absolves himself of his sentence with recourse to the sentence. Society's campaign of erasure meets the enduring imprint of art" (117). If the modern subject exercises a rational, and indomitable, will to forge authenticity, then Pascual's admission of guilt in reality becomes a similarly willful attempt to define himself, which he does in the very first line of his confession when he says, "Yo, señor, no soy malo, aunque no me faltarían motivos para serlo" ["I, sir, am not a bad man, even though I am not lacking motives to be so"] (25). In this single line from his murderer main-character, Cela inscribes in his novel two levels of performativity: the first is that of Pascual the character whose fated existence makes him melancholically yearn and perform a self-identity unavailable to him. The second is that of the text itself in which, like Faulkner's Quentin Compson, Pascual as narrator wrestles with a past that haunts him by trying to enact it in a present text. Within these two levels of performativity, the enactment of what Kronik calls Pascual's "parole," we see the ambivalence inherent in Pascual's relationship between past and present come to the forefront. The result is not an integrated subjectivity, however, but only profound doubt.

Pascual's assertion that he is not a "bad" man despite his environment takes an ironic tone when one considers the letter preceding his confession to a friend of his murder victim. He says, "Pesaroso estoy ahora de haber equivocado mi camino, pero ya ni pido perdón en esta vida. ¿Para qué? Tal vez sea mejor que hagan conmigo lo que está dispuesto, porque es más que probable que si no lo hicieran volviera a las andadas" ["It weighs on me now having erred in my path, but I don't ask forgiveness in this life. What for? Perhaps it is better that they do with me what they can because it is more likely that if they don't, I will return to my previous ways"] (19). Indeed, as Pascual tells his life story, his intense desire to live a decent life with his wife and children represents the desires of most citizens following the bloody Spanish Civil War, and it was certainly the image of the Spanish nuclear family that the Franco regime wished to project to its own populace and, to some degree, the world. Yet much like Sutpen, who calls his failed performance of Southernness a "mistake," Pascual identifies his "erred path" and almost wills his guilt and his identity, denying even the possibility of redemption or change. By willing this fate on the page, Pascual makes his life into a "parole"—an utterance that is not fated by modernity, but that is his own and under the influence of his own performativity.

The idea of Pascual as a victim of an environment beyond his control versus that of a murderous manipulator is further developed at the textual level when he does not confess to the murder for which he is imprisoned, that of the town's noble, don Jesús González de la Riva, but instead details the premeditated murder of his mother—a crime for which, as far as we know, he is never prosecuted. Again, as a modern subject, Pascual faces coded images of masculinity as he attempts to control his fate. Meanwhile, he also suffers losses that threaten his claims to integrated subjectivity, particularly when it comes to masculinity. For example, after raping and impregnating a local young woman, Lola, he marries her and looks forward to the birth of their child. Yet when a horse throws Lola and causes her to miscarry, Pascual kills the horse in an act of rage. This incident foreshadows a cycle of violence throughout the novel as Pascual tries to be the agent of his own destiny while playing the role of father and protector. However, like Sutpen, the conflict between being a modern, self-determining subject using a national model located in a constructed past creates a slippage, a constant threat of loss that is "other," that Pascual is compelled to destroy through violence. The result is a pathological condition in which Pascual performs a coded Spanish masculinity that he feels is constantly threatened, producing an ambivalent relationship between past and present, between self and other, which Freud sees as being produced from "those experiences that involved the threat of losing the object" ("Uncanny" 256).

The threats to Pascual's attempts at authenticity and happiness come from within his own environment and family. Such threats, furthermore, present "other" narratives of Spanishness that posed threats to any sense of nationalism: both the creature lurking within that represents the ever-present sense of Francoism that was always watching and that of feminization, something that also appeared in Faulkner's vision of the U.S. South. In many ways, both threats are symbolized in *La familia de Pascual Duarte*'s first chapter, which takes place after Lola has miscarried their child. As Pascual sits at the crossroad of his town, he talks to his dog, Chispa. While the dog sits before him and stares, Pascual realizes "que tenía la mirada de los confesores, escrutadora y fría, como dicen que es la de los linces. . . . La perra seguía mirándome fija, como si fuese a culparme de algo de un momento a otro" ["that she had the look of confessors, scrutinizing and cold, like they call that of a lynx. . . . The dog continued staring into me, as if she were accusing me of something from one moment to another"] (33). The description of Chispa's gaze as that of a confessor returns us to the image of religious piety as a pliable code that weighs on individual subjectivity as a performed entity—hence the reason it becomes manifested in Chispa via Pascual's own paranoia. Meanwhile, Michel Foucault's discussion of confession in *The History of Sexuality* describes it as such an omnipresent aspect of daily life that confession subjects us to its weighty power while simultaneously making us realize that we are autonomous thinking subjects in the ability to construct a self-narrative. This early moment in the novel indeed is the moment where Pascual is divided into two subjects: one that is fated by the confession, but one that realizes his own subjectivity. Here we see both these figures as Pascual describes feeling the weight of the dog's gaze, cannot tolerate it, and shoots her. That is, we see Pascual the subject feel the weight of the confessor, and he tries to obliterate that threat with violence, a cycle repeated throughout the novel. Yet we also see Pascual as the confessor, relaying this story at the very beginning of his exploration of self. Thus in this one act the two levels of performativity emerge in Cela's novel: the one in which Pascual the character enacts a hard and violent masculinity when faced with the threat of losing that very thing, the other as Pascual narrates that brutal violence in an apparently seamless narrative, with many details omitted, as he paints the picture of himself as a man who is not "bad" growing up and living in rural Spain.

The fact that Chispa the dog is female (and that the horse that caused his wife to miscarry is a mare) is not without symbolism in Cela's novel since the prevailing threat to Pascual's sense of self emerges in the ever-present threat to his masculinity. In his article "Pascual Duarte y la susceptibilidad viril," Carlos Jerez-Farrán explores the code of Spanish masculinity according to Cela and determines that "la crueldad de Pascual, lejos de ser fortuita o resultante de un caso psicópata o sádico, es producto de unos determinantes socioeconómicos y psicológicos que fuerzan al protagonista a proceder de un modo física y sexualmente agresivo" ["Pascual's cruelty, far from being fortuitous or the result of a sadistic or psychopathic case, is a product of some socio-economic and psychological determinants that force the protagonist to proceed in a physical and sexually aggressive manner"] (48). While, again, I do not see Pascual as the psychological victim of his environment, I do see him as willfully trying to assert authenticity in a world that has conditioned his masculinity. Thus when he returns after a long absence from his family to find his wife pregnant by another man, el Estirao, he feels the need to defend both his, and his wife's, honor. Pascual goes looking for the man, who was also his sister's lover, despite the fact that he promises Lola he will not kill him. The man that Pascual sees as having "killed" his wife is unrepentant and mocks his adversary in public, saying that he does not know how to kill Pascual "porque aún no nació el hombre" ["because the man hasn't even been born"] (149). When Pascual informs el Estirao of his promise to Lola not to kill him, Estirao responds, "¿Entonces, me querría?" ["She loved me, then?"] (149). In both his desire to avenge his wife's and sister's honor while not breaking his promise to Lola, Pascual plays the role of chivalric savoir and moral victor. Yet once again the inability for the past to appear in the present produces a difference that, for Pascual, usually results in violence. Estirao's taunting proves too much for Pascual, causing him to murder his wife's and sister's lover—an act that puts him in jail for three years and allegedly kills his wife.

Throughout the novel, Pascual's masculinity appears as performance, and the failure of that performance is highlighted by the "other" narrative of masculinity in the novel: that of his mentally disabled brother, Mario. Much as Charles Bon presents a threat to his father's masculine and biologically pure design in *Absalom, Absalom!*, Mario haunts Cela's main character by serving as a counterpoint—an unmasculine, biologically inferior narrative to which Pascual can repeatedly, and traumatically, be compared. Pascual tries to hide this comparison early in the novel when he describes his mother's boyfriend, don Rafael, beating Mario. Despite insinuating that he was too young to defend his brother, as Lucile Charlebois notes in her book *Understanding Camilo José Cela*, "the astute reader is reminded that Pascual was twenty-four years old when the beating occurred" (13). The idea of Mario as an "other" narrative of masculinity that questions the Spanish code of manhood emerges in Cela's continuously grotesque images of him, which reach a pinnacle when Mario dies drowning in a vat of olive oil. Even after his brother's death, the ghost of his brother's unmanliness haunts Pascual as early as Mario's funeral when he meets Lola. In fact, Lola's assertion to Pascual, "¡Eres como tu hermano!" ["You are like your brother!"] (68), causes him to rape her, thus reaffirming his manhood. After, he asks her if that was what she wanted, and when she responds affirmatively, she also tells him, "¡No eres como tu hermano . . . ! ¡Eres un hombre . . . !" ["You are not like your brother . . . ! You are a man . . . !"] (68). Thus just as Charles Bon provides an "other" narrative that questions Southern white masculinity, Mario presents a similar tale that challenges Pascual's performance of virile Spanish masculinity, one that he is compared to more than once in the novel.

Such threats to Pascual's masculinity also come from the women in his life. For example, his mother, wife, and sister all blame his weak blood for the death of his eleven-month-old son, Pascualillo. What proves ironic about the representation of gender in this novel is the fact that no one, including Pascual, seems to effectively adhere to gender roles. In fact, the women appear as cold, masculine figures. His mother, for example, drinks and engages in numerous affairs with men while his sister, Rosario, leaves home at fourteen to become a prostitute. It would appear that, just as Pascual is fated to fail as a "man," his wife, mother, and sister all represent images of failed Spanish womanhood. Such "failure" again comes from the slippage between trying to take an image of womanhood from the past—that of the untouchable Virgin Mary figure that exists as early as the creatively imagined Dulcinea figure in *Don Quijote*—and make it "pass" for a figure in the present. Throughout *Pascual Duarte*, the women become figures who respond to that slippage not with an overt femininity, but instead, like the modern subject, with a hard masculinity as they respond to a patriarchal world by adopting the very coded identity that attempts to subdue them. The one exception to this rule is Pascual's sister, Rosario, who is a failed image of Spanish womanhood in that she is unable to have children supposedly as a result of the many venereal diseases she contracted as a prostitute. Rosario stands out in the novel as the only character who responds to loss in non-violent, nonpathological ways—for example, when Pascual returns home to find his wife has died, Rosario is the one who helps him find a new wife. The exact opposite of the perfect image of Spanish womanhood, Cela uses this childless prostitute to show a character driven by love, not fear; thus she is never fated by the frustrated performance of gender that constantly threatens Pascual.

Pascual's relationship with Rosario stands as a contrast to that with his mother—a figure that threatens Pascual's masculinity by literally being more manly than he is. Given the cycle of violence that exists in the novel, Pascual's premeditated matricide, and in particular his description of it, seems to be a foregone conclusion. While her death becomes an assertion of his masculine self, the initial fight between Pascual and his mother finds her matching him blow for blow until he manages to strangle her while his new wife watches in the doorway. When she dies, he describes the feeling of affirmation, saying, "La solté y salí huyendo. Choqué con mi mujer a la salida; se le apagó el candil. Cogí el campo y corrí, corrí sin descanso, durante horas enteras. El campo estaba fresco y una sensación como de alivio me corrió las venas. Podía respirar" ["I let her go and fled. I collided with my wife on the way out; she dropped her candleholder. I seized the countryside and ran, ran without rest, for endless hours. The countryside was fresh and a sensation of life ran through my veins. I could breath"] (179). As Pascual runs through the countryside, the image of nature returns us to Forter's idea that the affirmation of masculinity involves the perception of a strong manhood that is primal. In other words, in killing his mother, Pascual has returned to a more "natural" state imagined in the past. Thus Pascual naively believes he has eliminated the eternal threat to his masculinity by eliminating this feminine threat that seems tougher than he is. Yet in reality, Pascual is a melancholic who responds to the mere threat of "lost" masculinity by, unlike Rosario and within Freud's description, losing his capacity to love and seeing his mother as representative of his lost liberty and masculinity. In other words, he grows to hate in her what he sees as missing in himself; thus Pascual's killing of his mother becomes a mode of self-hatred, and the ellipsis at the end of the novel suggests that there is far more to this story—that Pascual's cycle of violence will not end. In fact, the careful reader reminds himself or herself that he ends up in jail for another murder and dies there just before the beginning of the Civil War.

What ultimately marks Pascual as a character is that he is embedded in a narrative that he controls only in retrospect, which is why he feels the need to rewrite his story as a confession. Yet what Cela shows in Pascual's environment is what Eloy E. Merino sees as an allegory for Falangist Spain: "Es posible interpretar esa brutalidad de Pascual no como aquella parte de la balanza que sirve de contrapartida necesaria para su inevitable e imprescindible condena y redención (Schaeffer), sino como la elaboración poético-estética del ideal masculino, macho, de la Falange, en un medio tan tradicionalmente inclemente como el rural español" ["It is possible to interpret Pascual's brutality not as part of a balance that serves as the necessary counterpart for an inevitable and unavoidable condemnation and redemption (Schaeffer), but as the poetic-aesthetic elaboration and masculine, macho ideal of the Falange, in an environment so traditionally inclined as that of the rural Spaniard"] (4). Seeing Cela's novel in such a light returns us to figures like Thomas Sutpen and how he tries to will an imagined authenticity into actuality by asserting a masculine ideal that has nationalist implications. While *Pascual Duarte* does not specifically address his "Spanishness," his brand of masculinity is coded by a national ideal. The degree to which this ideal is located in the past, and its enactment in the present is an unconscious re-remembering of the past, speaks to the degree to which such national performativity becomes an uncanny form that we are blind to, thus producing Pascual's and Sutpen's willful rationalism within modernity—one that ironically can be compared to a similarly performative religious discourse in that period. The moment in which we see ideas of "Spanishness" or "Southernness" unfold in Pascual's and Quentin's performative narratives occurs in the unspeakable difference between the past and their reconstructed history in the present. In that difference, furthermore, one readily observes the ambivalent relationship between tradition and modernity—an ambivalence reflected in the "macho ideal" of the Falange that attempted to reconstruct Spanish glory (and repopulate the country) in a modern environment. Thus in Sutpen's intense desire to have a son, Pascual's murders of emasculating adversaries, and, in a later context, Franco's posturing as Spain's "el Cid" reincarnated, we readily observe the struggle to determine a masculine authenticity that is consistently threatened from within, by one's own community or family.

The fact that the threat of a feminized or inauthentic nationhood comes from within—in Sutpen's and Pascual's cases, from their families—suggests that these "other" narratives of nationhood are by no means external verities. For this reason, furthermore, the legacy and consequences—particularly the appropriation of a rhetoric of "loss" among political and religious figures—prove vital within a discussion of novelists like Faulkner and Cela and how such internal fragmentation comes to typify the Spanish and Southern experience with modernity. In other words, there is a shift from the nineteenth-century period when Spanish and Southern exceptionality emerged as a construction configured by thinkers and writers outside of these areas—usually by French and Northern travelers, respectively—who saw these geographic landscapes as exotic and primal versions of Europe and America. In fact, such predeterminations wane in the face of a modernity that seemed to provide the individual with the opportunity for self-determination by freeing him or her from the heady weight of the past and external judgment. As a result, the modern subject's wrestling with a national selfhood that stands as a European and U.S. "other" becomes internalized by the ego in a manner that makes that "otherness" a measure of the self—evidenced by Quentin Compson and Pascual the narrator who self-identify with the characters that belong to the past in a manner that literally divides their subjectivity into ghost and narrator. Indeed, that fragmentation, the conflict between a new self and a haunting other, is very much embodied by Spain's and the South's experiences with ideas of "loss" following their civil wars. Thus while it becomes easy to view Jim Crow and Francoism as two sides of a war that, respectively, "lost" and "won," in reality they embody the sum of that entire conflict as the fear of fragmentation haunts and, in many ways, consumes their assertions of authentic nationhood. In other words, Francoist and Jim Crow ideologies relied heavily not just on a monolithic understanding of a national self that is pure or masculine but also on an intense fear of the "other" that comes from within. That fear, furthermore, not only drives Sutpen's and Pascual's cycles of violence but also typified a Francoist and Jim Crow oppression that focused not as much on French and Northern "interlopers" but on Spanish and Southern "traitors."[1]

The simultaneous presence of the assertion of self versus the fear of the creature lurking within means that, if we discuss performative nationalism during Jim Crow and Francoism, *everyone* feels compelled to "pass" for an authentic Spaniard and Southerner, even those who fit the mold. Such a need to perform, furthermore, emerges as national exceptionality becomes configured from within, which also explains why both Faulkner's and Cela's novels center heavily around the spaces their characters occupy, coding them as specifically Spanish or Southern. María Elena Bravo, in her comparison between *La familia de Pascual Duarte* and Faulkner's novel *Sanctuary*, points to a metonymic relationship between both authors' characters and their environments ("Los parientes faulknerianos" 43). Kronik, furthermore, suggests that this relationship is a modern one when he links Pascual

Duarte "to the modern tradition of Kafka, whose fictional spaces threaten, transform, and stifle the individual. Whether the withdrawal is voluntary, as it is in Proust and in most of the anguished successors to Dostoyevsky's underground man, or imposed, as in Pascual's case, the result is a painful social and personal alienation" (114). Similar to the manner in which Pascual's cell appears to protect him from the deterministic fate of the home he describes, Quentin Compson's cold Harvard dorm room serves as a counterpoint for the stifling South that haunts him. In other words, by leaving the Spanish and Southern spaces that define these characters, they attempt to break free from this metonymic relationship: Pascual and Quentin are not fated to be exceptionally Spanish or Southern by virtue of a spatial existence, and it is only outside of these spaces that they can tell their stories.

The degree to which Spanish and Southern exceptionality are imagined as internal forms occurs as a result of the melancholy that plagues many of Faulkner's and Cela's characters. In effect, by losing an "exceptional" Spanish and Southern tradition, particularly through civil strife, there is an ego-identification with that lost exceptionality that reconfigures it as an internal form—not judgment from "outsiders." In fact, such a configuration of Spanish and Southern exceptionality actually seeks freedom from external verities, which, in effect, makes it a modern attempt at a national ideal. Specifically, Pascual's and Quentin's narratives are modern attempts to shirk an "exceptional" past by reimagining it for themselves in the present. Yet as McGowan argues in *Postmodernism and Its Critics*, these modern attempts at expression seem to proclaim "a heady freedom from traditions, from social environment, from reality itself. Yet throughout its dizzying experiments, modernism remains haunted by that scarcely repressed fear that the negative liberty it annexes to itself carries with it an inescapable impotence" (8). This fear of "inescapable impotence"—a reformulation that seems completely arbitrary—causes Pascual to claim that he is not a "bad" man, despite the fact that he should be, and compels Quentin to declare that he does not hate the South, even though his own performance of Southernness suggests otherwise.

As we observe the metonymic relationship between the modern subject and his or her environment, there emerges a similar relationship between exceptionality and place, even as figures like Sutpen and Pascual attempt to shirk that link to the past. The reason exceptionality lingers, furthermore, is that Pascual's and Quentin's attempts to reconfigure national authenticity is uncanny at its core—it contains a traumatic past that has not been laid to rest and whose reemergence they are not aware of. Thus contained in their narratives of place are expressions of selfhood that are simultaneously othered; thus the hatred for "other" narratives of national authenticity and exceptionality becomes a blind self-hatred that results, specifically, in Pascual's and Sutpen's isolation and destruction. Yet by enacting that phenomenon in their own texts—literally taking the past and reconstructing it in a present narrative—Faulkner and Cela expose the politics of exceptionality by exposing how a melancholic relationship to the past yields a performance of nationhood that converts collective memory into an uncanny "other." The sum of these novelists' achievement, furthermore, comes as they break down the metonymic relationship between Spain and the South and "different" by showing how exceptionality has nothing to do with a cohesive national subjectivity. Instead, in their novels' form, there is actually a blurring of subjectivity and a plurality of narrative that does not destroy "other" claims to authenticity, but exposes them. In addition, in seeing Faulkner and Cela as polemical public figures who chose never to leave the homes in which they wrote, I am not arguing that these authors sought to reject a coherent, or even a traditional, idea of "Spain" and the "South." Instead, they show the costs of pathologically trying to reproduce that tradition in a vacuum, refusing to look to the outside world, and being incapable of mapping national boundaries and conceptualizing time in a way that allows the individual to effectively mourn the trauma of civil conflict and forge subjectivity via a new idea of nationhood.

Chapter 3

FLEEING EXCEPTIONALITY IN A LITTLE RED MG

Driving through National Melancholia

J udith Butler's claim that gender is a performed identity constituted by "a stylized repetition of acts" makes a vital connection between ritual- ized act and the methods we use to define individuals. Given Butler's claim, one easily observes the performed aspect of melancholia when the individual's dejection from the world becomes a ritualized response to in- tangible loss. For the modern subject in the early twentieth century, leading into Francoism and Jim Crow, this loss stemmed from the various questions of what constituted Spain and the South—questions begun by Unamuno, Ortega, Ransom, and Tate that echoed throughout the century. While chap- ter 2 showed how the male melancholic's ego-identification with a Spanish or Southern "self" compels him to destroy any "other" claims to nationality, this chapter explains how that same loss is manifested in the individual, creating a self-reviling and compulsion toward suicide that recasts the na- tional question of "What is Spain/the South?" in existential terms. Within this model, the modern subject's quest for a new, and personal, idea of sub- jectivity produces a deconstructed nationality that rejects nationhood as a coded, communal form. Thus it becomes a concept that is not dominated by concrete binaries of self and other—Southern and Northern, Spanish and French or German—but a myriad of identities that the subject must accept before he or she can let go of the object-loss. That is, he or she can let go of a performance of nationhood imagined in the past in order to reach a state of mourning.

The means by which melancholia takes national crisis to existential lev- els is a measure of the modern subject's detachment from the world around him or her or, more specifically, his or her detachment from competing ver- sions of Spain and the South; thus the modern subject embodies the image of the autonomous thinking subject typified by modernity. This figure is thrown into existential crisis when the eternal "truths" of coded nationhood no longer hold, prompting a melancholia that causes him or her to violently cling to that truth (see Sutpen or Pascual) or to detach himself or herself from it as a means of observing its origins. Particularly, the new men in Pío Baroja's and Walker Percy's novels, *El árbol de la ciencia* [*The Tree of Knowledge*] (1902) and *The Moviegoer* (1961), respectively, find themselves suspended between the same dichotomy of a "traditional" and "modern" Spain and South seen throughout this study—two nations that are both "self" and "other" as they selectively reject and accept U.S. and European efforts to modernize and industrialize while clinging to a "tradition" of stoicism that stems from military defeat. By remaining suspended between these two images, the modern subject engages national exceptionality as an uncanny form. In other words, coping with both "self" and "other," the melancholic responds to Spanish and Southern exceptionality by being both attracted to its familiarity—longing for the return of the object-loss—and horrified by what is unfamiliar, that is, the various claims to authenticity designed to alienate and oppress. Faced with the horror of the uncanny object-loss, the modern subject detaches himself or herself so much from the world that he or she can begin to understand that loss and can potentially move to a place of mourning where it can be let go. Within mourning exists the possibility of freedom from the performance of national exceptionality by exposing the performative inherent in seeking an image of nationhood that was not just lost, but that was an image to begin with.

While dejection from the outside world allows the autonomous subject to engage, and examine, national exceptionality, it is by no means the purpose of this chapter—or this book—to assert that melancholia is a productive, or uniform, process. Freud tells us, after all, that the result of melancholia is suicide. Yet by linking the melancholia of the individual to that of nation, Spanish and Southern authors across the twentieth century have been able to explore the ambivalent relationship between Spain and Europe, the South and the United States, and expose how one's claims to exceptionality are, in large part, reliant upon and inform the other's. Only through the assertion of a "modern" North, for example, can one assert to be from a "traditional" South. Yet in Baroja's and Percy's novels, Andrés Hurtado and Binx Bolling are determined to remain suspended between these two distinctions. This very liminality is what dominates *El árbol* and *The Moviegoer* as one claim to truth or exceptionality never becomes as important as the search for those ideas. While detached from the world around them, Andrés and Binx still reach a point where they begin to identify with the object-loss as they see themselves embodied in a defeated Spain and South. In turn, they then enact the very gendered and nationalized roles they want to escape. Andrés and Binx do become aware of this performance, and, in the end, their decision to remain suspended between competing versions of the South and Spain (which, for Andrés, means suicide) means they never stop searching for a renewed sense of self or nation, a new object-love.

Part of the detachment that Andrés and Binx experience becomes analogous to that of their creators who, despite the large span of time that separates them, hold a unique place in Spanish and Southern letters for their status as outsiders of sorts: Percy as a Catholic in the evangelical South of the 1960s and Baroja as a Basque whose anarchist ideas never firmly planted him on either side of Spain's civil conflicts. Meanwhile, given both authors' training as medical doctors who later left the profession (Percy because of health, Baroja because of boredom) in order to write, they also similarly adopt a clinical point of view that they pass on to their characters; thus Andrés and Binx are allowed to frequent the world and observe it without really participating in it. In addition, Binx and Andrés face a brand of Southern and Spanish stoicism—embodied by their respective aunt Emily and uncle Iturrioz—that compels them to seek an alternative even as they know they cannot escape the familial and national pasts that constrain them. Thus Percy, despite his contradictory role as a Southern Catholic novelist, saw no disjointed state between his regional affinity and his religion, as both informed his decision to be what scholars and the author himself have termed a "wayfarer"—an autonomous thinking subject that is always searching for truth but never apt to find it. Such a quest also defines Baroja's writings. A search even titles a trilogy of novels written early in his career. Like Percy's Catholicism, Baroja's anarchism allowed his search to exist on the fringe of a Spain driven toward static definitions, much like his existential main character. The detachment that Baroja's and Percy's main characters have from the world around them is mirrored in these novels' chronological distance from the periods dominated by Francoism and Jim Crow. Baroja published *El árbol* in 1902, decades before the Civil War, and Percy wrote *The Moviegoer* at the height of the civil rights movement and only a few years before the Civil Rights Act of 1964 was passed. Yet this detachment from the specific experiences of Spanishness and Southernness again reflects these authors' own detachment from Spanish and Southern tradition. A Catholic who chose a self-imposed exile in rural Louisiana toward the end of his life, Percy did not identify himself exclusively (at times at all) as a Southern writer, choosing instead to locate his work among European and Russian writers like Camus and Dostoyevsky. Meanwhile, while Baroja was Basque, he categorically rejected Basque nationalism and denied any national underpinning throughout his career, making various comments against any claim to specific identity.

While both Baroja and Percy seem to exist in different times, regions, and thus planes of existence, the existential character's search defines both of their aesthetics. Meanwhile, the degree to which this "search" defines the new man becomes more complicated when we consider the degree to which both *El árbol* and *The Moviegoer* do have autobiographical elements, that is, portions of a narrative that should provide a level of certainty. Yet what Baroja and Percy do with their personal histories is exploit the performance inherent in exposing an "assured" history as a contrast to the national doubt their characters experience. This contrast does not produce a seamless narrative of self-reflection, but a collection of fragmented images that show the individual grappling with the various, and at time contrasting, implications of a perceived nationhood. Thus novelistic form becomes an allegory for the manner by which the individual imagines national identity. These novels are by no means "autobiographical" inasmuch as the fragmented use of autobiography becomes a means of exploiting the performed nature of how we creatively relay narratives perceived as fact. In this respect, these novels contain characters who respond to the loss of nationhood by fleeing it. At the level of form, these authors engage that performance not by clinging to a lost sense of selfhood, but by abandoning it altogether, breaking their own stories into fragments, and repositioning the pieces as a means of exposing how coded identity, in all forms, is enacted through nationalized, and gendered, ritual.

While half a century separates these authors' major novels, both *El árbol* and *The Moviegoer* provide very similar portrayals of what Christopher Soufas calls the Spanish and Southern "new man": a figure plunged into existential doubt to such a degree that he becomes suspended between a national tradition that haunts him and a modern world defined by scientific sterility and bourgeois social-climbing (*Subject* 14). Living between these two worlds, this figure struggles to decipher the roles people play and how to know the world while being in it. Even more, both main characters encounter a stoic sense of place in which to live in a particular Spain and South is to accept the limitations of its performativity—as both Aunt Emily and Uncle Iturrioz have done and encourage their respective nephews to do. Percy and Baroja confront this struggle through their emotionally fragile protagonists who face the world from the dual perspectives of observant medical doctor and contemplative philosopher. Like Faulkner's and Cela's new men, Percy's Binx Bolling and Baroja's Andrés Hurtado are haunted by the "traditional" and stoic South and Spain they have known their whole lives, yet are also dissatisfied by the scientific relativism they see in the "modern" medical profession. Struggling between a modern and traditional nation, Binx's and Andrés's only resolve is to remain there, to flee exceptionality if only to explore these opposing senses of nationhood in greater detail. Yet still melancholic, Binx's and Andrés's "loss" of certainty means they either have to find a new object-love or eventually succumb to suicide. While these characters choose very different ends—with Binx deciding to marry his stepcousin Kate and Andrés killing himself—both characters still embody the autonomous thinking subject's ever-present search for integrated selfhood by knowing the world around them. What separates Binx and Andrés from characters like Sutpen and Pascual, furthermore, is this very quest for knowledge. While we could argue, given the novels' different endings, whether one or both of them fail in the search, I instead argue that the search itself proves fruitful to examining Spanish and Southern exceptionality in these novels. In other words, what becomes important in *El árbol de la ciencia* and *The Moviegoer* is not a singular image of sought-out nationhood. In fact, Binx never really defines what it is he is looking for, vaguely and ironically describing the search for "it." Instead, what stands out is how these characters negotiate the roles of active participant in and passive observer of the world around them, exploring not the image of an "exceptional" Spain or South itself, but, more important, how that image is imagined and enacted for an audience.

While time seems to separate these writers, one thing that unites their work is an engagement with stoicism and its link to geographic exceptionality. In both cases, both writers not only saw a link to stoic philosophy and Spanish and Southern exceptionality, they personify it in their novels through characters who philosophically challenge their protagonists. In the case of Spain, stoic philosophy had dominated early twentieth-century thought as writers like Ortega y Gasset promote individual will and freedom—coupled with an ability to mold one's environment based on said will—as the hallmark of Spanish exceptionality and the qualities most admired in its national hero, Don Quijote. Ortega's focus on Spanish stoicism as well as its link to the Córdoba-born Roman philosopher Seneca influenced generations of Spanish philosophers who identified a particular *estoicismo español* because of an inherent *senequismo* in the Spanish nation.

In particular, Ortega's protégé, María Zambrano, chose to write most about Seneca during the rise and fall of the First and Second Spanish Republics, publishing these works following her exile after the Spanish Civil War (Murcia Serrano 271). Zambrano, like Baroja and Ortega before her, intimately links the questions of stoic philosophy to the "problem of Spain" at the beginning of the twentieth century. Yet despite efforts to locate Spain within a philosophy, the "problem" of Spain and the questions prompted by Senequismo are ones that have no answer within Baroja's novel; thus Andrés must wander through his life and the Spanish landscape in search of answers and an exceptional nationhood that never arrive.

Although Walker Percy seems to be a generation and an ocean away, he too addresses a change in Southern exceptionality in his essay "Stoicism in the South" when he writes how the Southern aristocrat is no longer the defender of African American causes as he or she once was, noticing how the new public ally of African Americans is now the poor white political candidate—a figure once their enemy. Almost adopting an Agrarian and quixotic perspective, Percy champions Southern stoicism as an alternative to what Faulkner described as Snopesism, that is, a move toward bourgeois consumerism versus "the stern inner summons to man's full estate, to duty, to honor, to generosity toward his fellow men and above all to his inferiors" (85). While Percy locates stoicism in the South, he again attempts to shirk claims to Southernness when he declares: "It is not just Faulkner who bears witness to the coming of the mass man, to the alienation and the vulgarization of the urban consumer. Ortega y Gasset and Marcel are neither Southern nor stoic" (86). Once again, we observe Percy as a writer in between spaces, linking his ideas to Spanish and French philosophy as a means of understanding the South—the hallmark of a Catholic novelist in the evangelical South who linked himself to Camus as easily as he did to Faulkner. Yet again, what prevails is the loss of a national philosophical ideal that Percy's Binx, like Baroja's Andrés, feels the need to reject and recoup simultaneously. The inability to do either is the source of his melancholia, what Binx calls the "malaise."

Inherent in the lost national ideal that haunts Baroja's and Percy's main characters are also coded gender roles that they reject but, at times, seem to embody. For example, Andrés and Binx often find themselves disgusted by traditional modes of Spanish and Southern masculinity—represented by the macho suitor or the Southern gentleman. Yet simultaneously, these men seem to yearn for the certainty that role provides, causing them to self-identify with the masculine ideal and seek relationships with women that lead nowhere and, in Andrés's case, to consider himself and be seen by others as a violent man. Yet because that self-identification emerges from the melancholic's ego-identification with the object-loss, neither can ever live up to his imagined masculinity. The result is not only a self-hatred, but a simultaneous need for a new object-love. For Binx and Andrés, this new object-love is one that represents the constant reconsideration of nationalized gender roles as they choose neither a Southern belle nor a virtuous Spanish Dulcinea, but almost-masculine, similarly cerebral women reminiscent of the female characters in Faulkner's and Cela's novels. These women not only cause the modern subject to reconsider his own masculinity by being more manly than he is, they become objects of intersubjectivity—women who engage in the same search for "truth" as their male counterparts. Again, while this search never leads to certainty or to a view of gender or nation that is not a performative or a ritualized act, the search for these truths means that no one idea of self or nation reigns supreme, thus casting exceptionality as an eternal form into doubt.

Pío Baroja was, personally and aesthetically, suspended between two conflicting worlds. Often identified as one of the youngest members of so-called Generation of '98, Baroja's work transcends the arbitrary boundaries of this generational grouping as he became a prominent literary figure in the early years of the Franco regime—only leaving Spain during a four-year self-imposed exile during the Civil War. While there have been numerous critical efforts to firmly root Baroja within a generation, philosophical underpinning, or nationalist leaning, my study of Baroja's work explores his navigation around and between these distinctions through a character suspended between the draw of "Spanish" tradition and "European" modernity. By remaining between these two worlds, Andrés returns us to the image of the autonomous thinking subject as a quixotic figure. Like the Quijote who escapes his bourgeois everydayness by clinging to a performed ideal of a Spanish "Gilded Age," Baroja takes Don Quijote's quest as a performative and creates a character that is similarly torn between two Spains; yet while the Quijote clings to his performance of Spain's Golden Age (again like Thomas Sutpen and Pascual Duarte), Andrés's melancholia progresses to a point where the loss of a "traditional" nation-ideal becomes absorbed into his psyche—which is why the young medical student remains constantly unsatisfied with his profession and his philosophical ideals, jumping from Kant to Schopenhauer in his readings and worldview. Thus Andrés's flight from exceptionality, both Spanish and European, is how he can expose both ideas of nationality as performatives, that is, as fragments of ritualized culture that we use to code people and spaces.

Throughout *El árbol de la ciencia*, Baroja's character remains suspended between two distinct environments and is openly, and sometimes violently, reactive to both: the Spanish landscape, plagued by a romanticism that Andrés criticizes and a sterile medical profession that he links to a "modern" Europe as his classmates constantly try to convince him to take his education and move to France or Germany. Much like Baroja in this period, Andrés expresses disdain for Spain, saying, "España entera, y Madrid sobre todo vivía en un ambiente de optimismo absurdo. Todo lo español era lo mejor" ["All of Spain, and Madrid above all, was living in a world of absurd optimism. Everything Spanish was the best"] (39). Yet Andrés is just as skeptical of scientific reason and its ability to provide certainty, particularly as his medical study becomes an exercise in antiquated practices with professors who are, pointedly, performers of dead science instead of teachers of ideas. As Andrés begins his medical work he notes, "A los pocos días de frecuentar el hospital, Andrés se inclinaba a creer que el pesimismo de Schopenhauer era una verdad casi matemática. El mundo le parecía una mezcla de manicomio y de hospital; ser inteligente constituía una desgracia, y sólo la felicidad podía venir de la inconsciencia y de la locura" ["A few days after frequenting the hospital, Andrés was inclined to believe that Schopenhauer's pessimism was an almost mathematical truth. The world seemed to him a mix of a psych ward and a hospital; to be intelligent constituted a disgrace, and happiness could only come from unconsciousness and insanity"] (78). Confronted with the options of blind romanticism or insanity, Andrés chooses neither, taking refuge in philosophical study that gives him no concrete truths by which to navigate his conflicting sense of self and nation.

Andrés's constant uncertainty produces a situation where he opts between active participation in the world—which he demonstrates by traveling to the country as a doctor—and passive observation, becoming a reclusive medical translator by the novel's end. His quest for subjective truth, and the dual role of participant and observer it gives him, thus becomes imagined as a constant search that attempts to extract him from coded "Spanishness" as a means of observing it. Yet Andrés is constantly tempted by assertions of truth, represented best in *El árbol* by his uncle Iturrioz. In her book on Baroja's body of work, Mary Lee Bretz best describes this character: "Caso clásico del intelectual encasillado, del diletante de la filosofía,

Iturrioz pasa del voluntarismo al estoicismo sin la menor dificultad" ["Classic case of the hermit intellectual, of the philosophical dilettante, Iturrioz passes from voluntarism to stoicism with minor difficulty"] (*La evolución novelística* 386). The major difference between Iturrioz and his nephew, furthermore, appears in their views on a person's individual will: Iturrioz is a stoic who believes that the "Semitic," or Judeo-Christian, approach will prevail as humans seek freedom by bending their environment to an imaginative will. Andrés, in contrast, posits himself as an anti-Semitic who rejects religious positivism and seeks scientific understanding of the world in order to exercise his will within the parameters of knowledge and personal experience. This divide between Andrés and his uncle, furthermore, appears during their discussion of the tree of life and the tree of knowledge in the Bible's book of Genesis. As Iturrioz recounts the story to his nephew, he notes how the desire for knowledge, symbolized by Adam and Eve eating the fruit of the tree, has the ability to compromise life itself, as it did for the Edenic couple (167). Iturrioz rejects the idea of man as "un puro intelecto, ni una maquina de desear" ["a pure intellect or a machine of desire"]—an idea he associates with German intellectualism (171, 175). Thus within Andrés and Iturrioz's conversation, one observes the young man's rejection of his uncle's Spanish stoicism—which sees math and logic not as a truth, but as a performative, calling it a "baile de máscaras" ["dance of masks"] that only disorients truth (172). For Iturrioz, when one claims truth on the basis of science, one is really *doing* something else, and he asks what scientific knowledge "esconde debajo de su capa gris" ["hides under its gray cape"] (172). Drawing this observation back into a question of real-time events occurring in Spain at the time, most notably the question of monarchy versus republic, Iturrioz sees his debate with his nephew as having national implications that exist outside his nephew's limited worldview. Yet Andrés still chooses the tree of knowledge, which he sees as void of fanaticism and prejudice, even as he recognizes at the end of this chapter that the famous apple from the tree of knowledge carries with it the possibility of death, just as it did for Adam and Eve.

The comment that sparks this philosophical debate on the tree of life versus the tree of knowledge is Andrés's observation of Don Quijote—a prototype of sorts for the brand of stoic willfulness that Iturrioz represents. Andrés's comment about Don Quijote proves ironic, however, since it mixes his usual skepticism with a hint of admiration: "Don Quijote, a quien Cervantes quiso dar una sentido negativo, es un símbolo de la afirmación de la vida. Don Quijote vive más que todas las personas cuerdas que le rodean, vive más y con más intensidad que los otros. . . . El instinto vital necesita la ficción para afirmarse. La ciencia entonces, el instinto de crítica, el instinto de averiguación, debe encontrar una verdad: la cantidad de mentira que es necesaria para la vida" ["Don Quijote, whom Cervantes wanted to give a negative sense, is a symbol of the affirmation of life. Don Quijote lives more than all of the sane people that surround him, he lives with more intensity than the others. . . . The vital instinct needs fiction to affirm itself. Science, then, the critical instinct, the inquisitive instinct, should find a truth: the amount of lies that is necessary for life"] (167). Here Andrés's admiration is similar to Unamuno's and Ortega's praise for Don Quijote's will. In addition, what Andrés seems to experience is the melancholic's ego-identification with the object-loss. While Andrés shows disdain for blind Spanish romanticism throughout the novel, he identifies with the "affirmation" of life that the mad hidalgo represents and that is lacking in the Spanish imperial enterprise but also in the sterile scientific world of medicine. Andrés recognizes the need for "fiction" in the search for truth and even feels that science should embrace that paradigm. Yet what also stands out here in Andrés's admiration for Don Quijote is the Spanish landscape itself. We are reminded that Andrés has not chosen Robinson Crusoe as his idol, but Spain's national hero, and Baroja's young protagonist never leaves his home country despite his friends' suggestions to do so. Andrés's identification with Don Quijote reaches its culmination as he mirrors his quest, retreating to the hidalgo's home region—a fictional town in La Mancha called Alcolea del Campo where he is given a job as a doctor.

While Andrés's retreat to Don Quijote's native region seems like the exact opposite of a rejection of Spanish exceptionality, as a member of the Madrid bourgeoisie, his voyage to the country is an effort to flee the modern implications of coded nationhood. Yet again, there is a performed quality to Andrés's escape in the sense that he *has* chosen to stay in Spain and seek an existence that is completely opposite to his own. And, upon arrival, Andrés encounters all of the challenges that a boy from Madrid who goes to the country might expect to face: religious fervor, hearty resistance to modern medicine, a lack of modern conveniences, and, above all, bathing in a place where water is a huge luxury (193). During Andrés's time in this town, we can observe how the city has feminized Baroja's main character since, as he has to eat strong meat and bathe rarely, he is constantly "excitado" (193)—a word translated as "agitated," but that carries the connotation of sexual excitement. Returning to the idea of the countryside as the ideal place to assert and return to a primal masculinity, it would appear as if

Andrés thwarts such an idea and that Baroja's image of the search for existential selfhood has little to do with masculinity. Yet critics note a masculine tone to Baroja's work, and a close examination of Andrés's final days in Alcolea del Campo and return to Madrid reveal a gendered quality to Andrés's rejection of his Madrid life. Andrés spends that final night with Dorotea, a local woman who is married to a stereotypical rough countryman and who shares a name with one of *Don Quijote*'s most compelling female characters. Andrés's admiration for this woman lasts for most of his stay in town, yet he only professes his love on his last night when they are alone and he initiates physical love. It is then that Andrés transforms himself from the seemingly feminized intellectual to a masculine lover, thus choosing to engage a national ideal that he seems to reject:

> Andrés se tuvo que apoyar en el hierro de la cama, pálido y tembloroso.
> —¿Se pone usted malo? –murmió Dorotea con voz ronca.
> —No; no es nada.
> Ella estaba también turbada, palpitante. Andrés apagó la luz y se acercó a ella.
> Dorotea no resistió. Andrés estaba en aquel momento en plena inconsciencia.
> [Andrés had to support himself on the headboard of the bed, pale and trembling.
> "Is something wrong?" Dorotea murmured.
> "No, it's nothing."
> She was also nervous, her heart beating. Andrés turned off the light and approached her.
> Dorotea didn't resist. Andrés was in that moment in full oblivion.]
> (231)

For the young man from Madrid who sees full consciousness of the world around him as the only hope of seeking "truth," his arrival at oblivion suggests an ego-identification with a rural Spanish masculinity that he achieves by making a married woman (aptly named after Cervantes's wronged woman) into a conquest. Dorotea's lack of "resistance" only further completes the image of Andrés taking her in his arms as only a masculine hero can. Yet always the melancholic, Andrés's identification with a "lost" Spanish masculinity causes him to hate that image of himself. Not realizing that he is performing an image, Andrés reverts to hating himself as he rejects country life and returns to Madrid more depressed than ever. Baroja paints Andrés's loss of Dorotea, and the coordinating masculinity, under the guise of Spain's national loss at the turn of the twentieth century. *El árbol*'s final section begins with Spain's declaration of war on the United States. Andrés, the constant recluse, does not care about the war; it only crosses his mind when he remembers Dorotea's maid singing a patriotic song about Cuba as the "flower of Spain" (235). Baroja's textual coupling of Andres's loss with Spain's imminent imperial failure becomes the way in which he exposes Andrés's assertion of rural Spanish masculinity as a performative. In other words, much like a Spain that is blindly assured of its own victory, Baroja paints a main character clinging to an image of a relationship he cannot realize (for several reasons, among them, Dorotea is married). In so doing, Baroja subtly links the image of strong, masculine lover and Spanish imperial victor, demonstrating how both are performances that rely on pathological blindness.

Baroja does not let his character completely plunge into depression, instead creating a woman that represents a new object-love for Andrés—one that also presents a very different version of Spanish femininity. The character of Lulú, briefly introduced as an odd young woman early in the novel, is a masculinized female character, reminiscent of Pascual Duarte's mother or Judith Sutpen. Lulú herself provides what Andrés calls at one point a "caso de estudio" ["case study"] (270) in the sense that she differs greatly from both Dorotea and her own sister, Niní, who maniacally hunts a husband. Andrés recognizes Lulú's difference early on when he describes his future wife as "una mujer inteligente, cerebral, como la mayoría de las muchachas que viven trabajando en las grandes ciudades, con una aspiración mayor por ver, por enterarse, por distinguirse, que por sentir placeres sensuales" ["an intelligent woman, cerebral, like the majority of the girls who live working in the big cities, with a larger aspiration to see, to involve herself, to distinguish herself, to feel sensual pleasures"] (106). Despite his intense admiration for Lulú, Andrés also admits here that he would never think of courting her. This opinion changes following his return from the country and his experience with "oblivious" love. Upon Andrés's arrival in Madrid, he finds that Lulú has only further thwarted society's gendered expectations by opening a store with her brother-in-law's money to support herself. Lulú even takes a masculine role in her and Andrés's relationship by being the first to profess her love. As Andrés realizes his own feelings for Lulú, he seeks less an absolute "truth" and instead a knowledge that comes from an intersubjectivity with Lulú. In addition to describing how they "se entendían muy bien" ["understood each other very well"] (285), the novel shows two figures engaged not in the ritualized act of suitor and maid, but two people engaged in the same search and need for self-definition who find it by seeking a kind of intersubjective truth about each other.

In comparison to his relationship with Dorotea, Andrés and Lulú's relationship presents a different idea of gender roles in the novel as their domestic arrangement and life together entail a complete reversal of the gender roles Spanish society had for husbands and wives. Virginia Trueba Mira, in her article "Lulú: El extraño personaje de El árbol de la ciencia de Pío Baroja," explores the "nationalist" implications of Lulú as a character and surmises, "Lulú es conciencia lúcida de una España decadente en la que los hombres y las mujeres viven todavía inmersos en la corriente de una conservadurismo ignorante, injusto e inmoral que les arrastra sin que nadie le oponga resistencia" ["Lulú is a lucid consciousness of a decadent Spain in which women and men were still living within a current of ignorant conservatism, injustice and immorality that surrounded them without anyone putting up resistance"] (186). Evidence for such a portrayal of Lulú is the domestic space she shares with Andrés. In traditional Spanish homes of the period, male and female spaces were kept separate to such a degree that rooms often seemed like pigeon holes. Yet Andrés chooses a home with one room that serves as a common space for all activities. In addition, Lulú keeps her store while Andrés happily stays home, receiving few visitors while he translates medical articles. Andrés and Lulú live in blissful and quiet isolation from society, that is, until Lulú confesses that she wants a child. Despite Andrés's protests, Lulú becomes pregnant and, as Andrés sees it, "La naturaleza recobraba sus derechos" ["Nature was recovering its rights"] (287). She becomes both jealous and sensitive, and Andrés worries about the state of his medically frail wife and their marriage—fears that are realized when Lulú dies in childbirth. Andrés responds to his wife's death by refuting nature's will, and asserting his own, when he kills himself—an act that is summed up in the doctor's comment and the novel's final line: "Pero en él había algo de precursor" ["There was always something of a precursor about him"] (292). Unable to control the world around him, Andrés appears doomed to fulfill the existential desire to control his fate—even if it means self-annihilation.

The idea of Andrés as a "precursor" has produced a series of controversial readings of the novel's final scene—with some seeing him as a hero and others a victim of nature. Yet I argue that Andrés, as a modern figure, stands out as a victim not of nature, but of the negative liberty that appears when the search for selfhood within modernity fails (McGowan 8). Given such an image of modernity, Lulú herself is also what Mira calls a "precursora" ["feminine precursor"] in the sense that she also thwarts traditional gender expectations, yet fails and is left with an almost maniacal love, what Andrés calls "un amor animal" ["animal love"], and dies fulfilling a feminine role. Yet what stands out for both of these characters is their ever-present will, a constant search that, for critics like Bretz, not only explains the suicide but also finds a solution to the constant struggle between Andrés as a man both of action and contemplation. She says, "Evidentemente, no es precursor del hombre voluntarioso ni tampoco del intelectual abstencionista, pues como hemos visto, tanto el ensayo contemplativo como el de la acción termine en el fracaso. A este respecto, parece más acertada la teoría de José Alberich de que Baroja no cree en la filosofía aunque sí en la búsqueda. Así Andrés se adelanta al hombre posterior más por esa actitud de indagador perseverante que por las ideas expresadas" ["Evidently, he is not a precursor to the voluntaristic man nor of the intellectual abstentionist since, as we have seen, the contemplative project fails as much as the one that inspires action. In this respect, Andrés appears closer to José Alberich's theory that Baroja does not believe in philosophy as much as he does believe in the search for it. Here is how Andrés gets closer to this precursor through the pervasive attitude of the investigator than for already expressed ideas"] (*La evolución novelística* 389).

Ultimately, what Andrés searches for is not something he is unable to find, but something that he cannot achieve through his own knowledge— hence the desperation he feels when Lulú's doctor says maybe she would have lived had nature taken its course and medicine not intervened (291). Thus he exercises the only will he has and uses his medical knowledge to do so, as Bretz points out in *Encounters Across Borders: The Changing Visions of Spanish Modernism, 1890–1930*. In such an act, Andrés has not chosen scientific truth per se, but has used science to exercise his own will—thus he remains suspended between two modes of being, between the tree of life and knowledge, by fusing these modes on his own terms, free from the coded norms of gender, class, and nation.

Andrés's suicide, in many ways, fulfills the image of Freud's melancholic whose inability to find a new object-love produces a pathological self-reviling so strong that the only logical step is suicide. Yet Baroja's novel is far more ambiguous than Andrés's end suggests. As his suicide becomes a continuation of the "search" for philosophy rather than its conclusion, Andrés's melancholia becomes an exploration of the "loss" that prompted the assertion of Spanish exceptionality at the turn of the twentieth century. While Andrés rejects any idea of a coded Spanish self, his rejection, at the beginn ng of the novel, simply becomes another performative that leads his ego to identify with this "lost" Spain, which occurs in his relationship with Dorotea. Andrés, as a modern subject, is not unlike Pascual and Quentin Compson in that he finds himself suspended between the present need to cope with the loss of a masculine, imperial sense of self in the past. While this loss, in many ways, defines a series of responses to "modernity" in the early twentieth century, Spain and the South stand out for two reasons: the experience of military defeat that, instead of implicating them in a U.S. and European modernity, placed them at an ironic distance from the cultural milieus in which both Spain and the South did in fact participate. Even more, Baroja re-creates this ironic distance between two exceptional claims to authentic, and exceptional, nationhood in *El árbol* by re-creating that relationship between Andrés and what Bretz calls his "contradictory characters" (*Encounters Across Borders* 392). While Bretz asserts that this distancing is meant to leave the reader feeling disjointed, as if no rational solution to Andrés's existential problem is attainable (*Encounters Across Borders* 392), I argue that Andrés's suspension between a European and a Spanish sense of self, with these "contradictory characters" that represent both sides, is an effort to examine the competing claims to exceptionality not as a logical relationship of oppositions, but an ironic one in which both sides make the same claims to an authentic and exceptional sense of self. After all, Andrés is just as skeptical of his friends' finding "freedom" in France and Germany as he is of his uncle's Spanish stoicism. The constant melancholic, Andrés soon realizes that these two sides are one and the same—even his precious Lulú succumbs to the prescribed role of motherhood and dies for it—thus Andrés's only recourse to not fully understanding the world is to remove himself from it.

The disjointed feeling that results from the ironic distance between protagonist and the characters that challenge his sense of self seems ironic when we consider the strong autobiographical aspect of this novel. Yet in many ways, the struggle between two claims to exceptionality that Andrés experiences reflects that of his creator who chose, like many Basques of his generation (including Miguel de Unamuno), to reject Basque nationalism and make a series of controversial comments on various other European nations that ranged from praising Germany and France to expressing sometimes anarchist ideas (Patt 58). Indeed, Baroja reproduces his ambivalence about claims to national exceptionality not just in *El árbol*'s main character but also in the novel's form as he creates a disjointed narrative that reproduces the frustration Andrés feels, never giving the reader the satisfaction of relying exclusively on any philosophical or national ideal. Within this context, Baroja's own use of autobiographical details becomes ironic in that, while it tempts the reader into finding some eternal "truth" in the novel's narrative, its disjointed form actually denies us that possibility.

Part of the reason that Andrés never finds a new object-love is that he remains suspended between Spanish "tradition" in the past and European "modernity" in the present—a plight that many modern Southern subjects of the same era experience. The U.S. South found itself in very much the same situation as Spain at the beginning of the twentieth century as its nineteenth-century loss caused it to be suspended between its Confederate past, dominated by an agrarian way of life, and an increasingly industrial present, embodied by U.S. modernity. The response to this loss is varied and contradictory for the Southern male and involves the performance of a national self—one that either clings to conceptions of a "traditional" South or runs from the weight of national exceptionality. Again, we encounter a Southern man who remains suspended between the two. Quentin Compson in Faulkner's *The Sound and the Fury* (1929)[1] embodies such a character, and, like Andrés, the weight of Southern exceptionality at times causes him to cling to a Southern past and later escape it by retreating to Harvard. Quentin's problem, therefore, is that he cannot "know" himself or his place within a national ideal; thus he hears his watch ticking and remembers his father's words: "I give you the mausoleum of all hope and desire; . . . I give it to you not that you may remember time, but that you might forget it now and then for a moment and not spend all your breath trying to conquer it. Because no battle is ever won he said. They are not even fought. The field only reveals to man his own folly and despair, and victory is an illusion of philosophy and fools" (76). Upon the realization that he can neither live in illusion nor battle time, Quentin, like Andrés, exercises the only will he thinks he has by breaking the watch and committing suicide. Thus again, suspended between the borders of past and present, consciousness and unconsciousness, both Baroja's and Faulkner's new men continue their search for integrated selfhood in the only way they see possible: by leaving the "exceptional" worlds they can never fully know.

Walker Percy was well acquainted with the need for escape and the compulsion toward suicide, both in his literary production and in his life, given that his grandfather and father both committed suicide when Percy was a child. A medical doctor turned writer, Percy admitted influences as varied as Kierkegaard to Faulkner. As he described the creation of *The Moviegoer*: "I would like to think of starting where Faulkner left off, of starting with the Quentin Compson who didn't commit suicide. . . . In a way, Binx Bolling is Quentin Compson who didn't commit suicide" (quoted in Allen 19). While Binx does not choose the same end as Andrés and Quentin Compson, Percy's novel by no means depicts Binx's decision as a realization of "truth" or a will to live. In fact, comparing Baroja's and Percy's novels, as well as their biographies, produces a series of striking similarities: Binx Bolling is a dissatisfied upper-class gentleman living in New Orleans who undertakes what he calls a "search" in which his experience in medicine compels him to try and know his world while he wallows in the contemplation of a self-proclaimed "moviegoer." While the act of "moviegoing" seems (on the surface) to be an accessory idea in Percy's novel, in reality film spectatorship theory provides a unique insight into Binx Bolling. Suspended between past and present, isolation and intersubjectivity, Binx is indeed the prototypical moviegoer utterly isolated in the dark theater but who seeks communion with what he encounters on screen. Hence, Binx says, "The movies are onto the search, but they screw it up" (13). In Binx's mind, they screw it up because the endings are too happy, too content with "everydayness."

Throughout his search, Binx encounters a series of characters that oppose him by either drawing him toward the modern "progressive" ambition of becoming a doctor or the "traditional" role of Southern gentleman. Binx remains willfully suspended between both worlds, however, and finds a like-minded figure in his stepcousin Kate. Suddenly, Binx's search becomes bound up not in voluntary isolation but, like Andrés's relationship with Lulú, in the desire for intersubjectivity, that is, communion with a fellow moviegoer. Yet again, Percy's novel never gives the reader complete satisfaction that Kate and Binx are going to overcome their depression or make it as a couple. While Percy's novel, like Baroja's, contains elements from the author's life, autobiography is by no means the way to find a concrete reading of this novel. Instead, it represents an ironic use of form in which the author's own life is a series of fragmented images that do not bring us closer to his main character, but always keeps him at a distance as his thoughts and actions are nothing more than extensions of Binx's constant wandering.

While the 1960s South that Percy describes in *The Moviegoer* seems a far cry from Spain at the turn of the twentieth century, what emerges in these two novels are nations at a crossroads: teetering between the desire to cling to a "traditional" idea of nationhood and a similar desire to give in to the promise of a modern national ideal. The South in Percy's novel is one that has labored under the weight of Jim Crow for decades at this point even as it participates in the post–World War II economic prosperity that the entire United States experienced during this period. As one of Percy's other characters describes in a later novel, *The Last Gentleman* (1966), "The South he came home to was different from the South he had left. It was happy, victorious, Christian, rich, patriotic, and Republican" (185). As a member of New Orleans's upper class, Binx is very much aware of his responsibility to his family's traditions, particularly the Southern tradition of military service (Binx's father fought and died in World War II, and Binx himself is a Korean War vet). Simultaneously, Binx admires science enough that his aunt thinks he should attend medical school but, like Baroja's Andrés, questions the ability of scientific research to reveal truth. Throughout Percy's novel, Binx remains suspended between these two Souths that make claims to the same brand of exceptionality—that is, false claims to authenticity that Binx exposes via his skepticism in both.

While Binx seems to be above the two images of the South, his escapism from those forms proves to be a performative that he vaguely calls the "search." In other words, by engaging in the "search," Binx understands the concept that to say something is to do something else, hence the reason his search becomes an intangible concept throughout the novel. As Binx puts it, "The search is what anyone would undertake if he were not sunk in the everydayness of his own life. . . . To become aware of the possibility of the search is to be onto something. Not to be onto something is to be in despair" (13). The "something" that Binx may be "onto" never becomes clear in the novel as the process of the "search," that is, the ritualized act of seeking knowledge, becomes more fruitful than any absolute "truth" the search can reveal. Again, while Binx's quest seems to remove him from the weight of tradition, which he also attempts to shirk by working as a stockbroker in the New Orleans suburb of Gentilly, in reality his search makes him into a Southern Quijote who wanders in a quest for meaning in the fragmented cosmos around him.

For Binx, such a journey is bearable only through one mode of transport: his little red MG, which he describes as being "immune to the malaise" (122). Part of the reason it is "immune" is the fact that it allows Binx to be "in" the world without being "of" it. He describes the car this way as he speeds across the highway with one of his many girlfriends: "The malaise was gone! We set out in the world, out in the thick summer air between sky and earth. The noise was deafening, the wind was like a hurricane; straight ahead the grains of the concrete rushed at us like mountains" (122). Binx's world is divided between the MG and the movies—both mediums that allow him to remain suspended between past and present and competing versions of Southernness. Yet Binx's search becomes a performance that rejects all claims to Southern exceptionality and temporal distinctions as he wanders through life, watching movies and dating his secretaries, with whom he has no intention of pursuing a serious relationship. Binx's detachment from the world is typical of the melancholic, and his dalliances with secretaries and moviegoing become a pathological need to escape both the "traditional" South that haunts him and the "new" South that tempts him.

As Binx engages in his search, he encounters characters that contest his desire to remain above the claims to Southern exceptionality. Yet like Uncle Iturrioz in *El árbol de la ciencia*, these characters are not caricatures of Southernness but figures that truly challenge Percy's protagonist. In *The Moviegoer*, Binx's Aunt Emily is the novel's Uncle Iturrioz, and she also believes in a stoic nationhood in which one accepts his or her environment and molds to it. As John F. Desmond has noted in his book *Walker Percy's Search for Community*, most critics see Emily as the voice of Southern stoicism in the novel (much like Bretz sees Iturrioz as a hopeless stoic) (46). Emily describes her efforts to pass this philosophy on to Binx when she says, "I gave you all I had. More than anything I wanted to pass on to you the one heritage of the men of our family, a certain quality of spirit, a gaiety, a sense of duty, a nobility worn lightly, a sweetness, a gentleness with women—the only good things the South ever had and the only things that really matter in this life" (224). Though Aunt Emily appears as the voice of blind Southern stoicism, in reality she is a far more complex figure: she once worked in inner-city Chicago and served as a Red Cross volunteer during the Spanish Civil War (26). Emily's idea of Southern "gentility" as the "only good things" the region ever had is a bleak image of nationality. Like Iturrioz, Emily sees Binx's search as evidence that he believes in nothing, that she has failed him somehow (226). Binx assures her that she has not, but, like Andrés, he simply cannot bring himself to subscribe to the social distinctions that Emily admits believing in. Instead, he must "know" his world, even if that effort only produces frustration.

While Binx's search attempts to remain detached from the exceptionality he is escaping, it often leads him down a path where he is haunted by that past, specifically its gendered connotations. Binx himself is no stranger to playing the role of disinterested playboy by having affairs with his secretaries. Yet again, like Andrés before him, Binx makes a trip to the countryside, where he confronts coded masculinity and becomes aware of his own ego-identification with this lost masculinity. This scene occurs when Binx travels to the countryside with his secretary/girlfriend, Sharon, to explore selling his father's duck camp, which was purchased as a result of his father's reading of Robert Browning's poetry and seeing "himself in need of a world of men" (91). As Allen notes about the scene, the camp "is so unrelentingly masculine as to become parodic, with its wild-West name and its insisted-upon absence of beds" (31). When Binx arrives at the camp, however, what he finds is not a masculine oasis in the marsh, but, like Binx himself, a parody of masculinity sandwiched by modern conformity: "A far cry from a duck club now, my patrimony is hemmed in on one side by a housing development and on the other by a police pistol range" (90). Binx's return to the country, furthermore, is by no means a journey to reclaim a primal masculinity, but, like Andrés's affair with Dorotea, is a jaunt into an oblivious world with one of many girlfriends and a rugged masculine world that has become dominated by domesticity on one side and the presence of a carefully mediated masculinity on the other. Binx returns to New Orleans not engaged with the "search" but clinging to a coded idea of masculinity as he refers to himself as "the old Gable, asweat with no thought for her and sick to death with desire" (96). Invoking the South's famous depiction of a Southern rogue gentleman—Clark Gable as Rhett Butler—Binx has identified with what he claims to escape, showing that the "search" is not only a performative, but one that can, unknowingly, conjure up images of a haunted past.

Binx's trip to the countryside and various affairs with his secretaries expose his half-hearted attempt to assert his masculinity; yet like Andrés's night with Dorotea, such assertions pertain to the realm of the "old Gable," disengaged with the search. Instead, what Binx seeks is active engagement with a like-minded person, which he seems to find in his stepcousin Kate. Much like Baroja's Lulú, Kate represents a unique image of Southern womanhood given that, following a car accident that kills her fiancé but leaves her unharmed, she becomes intimately aware of both her sense of self and her mortality. As she becomes far more depressed than Binx, Kate becomes aware of both the positive and negative aspects of the search for an integrated self when she admits discovering one day in therapy "that a person does not have to *be* this or *be* that or be anything, not even oneself. One is free" (114). Later, Kate reveals to Binx that her will to "*be*" only exists as a counterpoint to its opposition: suicide. She tells Binx, "Suicide is the only thing that keeps me alive. Whenever everything else fails, all I have to do is consider suicide and in two seconds I'm as cheerful as a nitwit. But if I could *not* kill myself—ah then, I would" (195). In several ways, Kate demonstrates the willfulness of the modern (male) subject by asserting that not killing herself is simply an exercise of will, hence the reason she admits that she would commit suicide if she were forbidden from doing it. Yet as we have seen before, such willfulness only produces a negative liberty, hence the reason Kate finds no real solace in her self-knowledge and only becomes more fragile as the novel wears on.

Binx's relationship with Kate becomes a union of two like minds, and similar to Andrés and Lulú, they must remove themselves from the outside world, in this case by taking a socially illicit trip to Chicago—a city that, in Binx's mind, is not "Southern" because it is not haunted by its past (202). Yet as with Baroja's young couple, Binx and Kate's isolation is infiltrated by traditional societal expectations. Binx admittedly tries to embody the stereotypical masculine hero who makes love to his heroine in the Southern novel, "with [Kate] dispatched into as sweet a sleep as ever Scarlett enjoyed the morning after Rhett's return" (200). Yet Binx admits, "Flesh poor flesh failed us," and, like Lulú's desire for a child and Kate's need to be cared for, any attempt at a "traditional" relationship will always fail these unconventional characters. While Kate does not "die" like Lulú, she suffers an emotional collapse that gives real-world consequences to the loss felt by these melancholic characters. Critics have attacked Percy for making Kate into a stereotypically hysterical woman in the same way that Baroja's work has been accused of misogyny. Yet while Percy at times offered a mea culpa, saying "I plead ignorance, I don't know enough about women" (Lawson and Kramer 212), in reality Kate and Lulú represent a counterpoint to the "modern" male characters in that the ability to engage in the search is not available to them as women since society denies them the mobility that Binx and Andrés have because of their gender. As a result, both women seem masculine in their willful desire just to be "in" the world while Binx and Andrés simply struggle to "know" it. By adopting diverse gender roles, both women are not just harbingers for female sentimentality or weakness, but instead represent the possibility for the melancholic to engage the world, instead of persisting in a pathological detachment from it. Though their quests fail, both Baroja and Percy make these women no less human and the possibility for a new object-love no less real. Much like Aunt Emily and Uncle Iturrioz, furthermore, these women are far more complex than most readings of them allow, hence the reason they possess both the modern subject's will and the "feminine" desire for human engagement.

What also stands out about the women in these novels is that they are the very human means by which Andrés and Binx exercise their final act of will and realize their roles as both passive observers and active participants in their worlds. In other words, in realizing Lulú's negative liberty, Andrés realizes his own, using his knowledge as a doctor to exercise his will and kill himself. Similarly, Binx is not so unlike Andrés since it is the same type of will that causes him not to kill himself and instead marry Kate. In addition, Binx becomes both a man of action and a passive observer since he also decides to go to medical school in an effort to do research. In the novel's closing scene, it appears as if Binx and Kate have achieved intersubjectivity as the still-fragile Kate describes how she will take the streetcar home with cape jasmine in her lap. When she asks Binx, "And you'll be thinking of me just that way?" (241), he replies that he will, and as they repeat each other's sentences while saying good-bye, Percy provides his character with a sense of integrated selfhood in a way Baroja has not. Yet this final scene has proven just as controversial as the idea of Andrés as a precursor. Critics like Martyn Bone, in his book *The Postsouthern Sense of Place in Contemporary Fiction*, see Binx's decision at the end of the novel as a key example of negative liberty, saying, "Finally, however,—and despite exposing Emily's aristocratic southern stoicism as an anachronistic, rhetorical construct— *The Moviegoer* envisions no escape from the 'spirit' of postsouthern capitalist space other than returning Binx to his aunt's upper-class enclave" (74). Meanwhile, others, like William Rodney Allen, see it as an affirmation of humanity and of Binx's ability to become "the protective father" he never had (43). Yet Percy's inconclusive ending seems something closer to what Bretz identifies in Baroja: a character who is less concerned with realizing selfhood than he is in seeking it. Herein lies the quixotic tendency in both novels, which Desmond sees within the inconclusiveness of *The Moviegoer's* final scene: "Binx and Kate are still subject to the terrors of alienation, to the possibility of despair, and to the challenge of 'everydayness,' but their bond of love, their *solitude à deux* amid the ruins, strengthens them as they go forth as wayfarers, still searching" (80). Binx's search, therefore, has not ended; instead, as with Andrés's search for knowledge, it changes as it becomes not a pathological search for the object-loss, but a search for a new object-love.

In trying to wrestle meaning from Binx's search, it is almost too easy to find solace in Percy's autobiography, particularly the author's own struggle with mental illness. Like Binx, Percy had medical ambitions before taking up his own search as a philosophical observer, but his medical career ended when he contracted tuberculosis during his residency. In addition, Binx is scarred by his father's death, much like Percy himself was. Yet again, autobiography in *The Moviegoer* seems less a sentimental journey into the self, but instead an empirical "search" not unlike Percy's—hence the reason that Percy's prose often appears so clinical and why critics like Edward J. Dupuy have identified the same ironic distancing from his characters that Bretz describes in Baroja. Dupuy asserts that this distancing functions as a method of duplicating the distance between the signifier and signified, which is the reason Binx can accept Emily's stoicism without submitting to it. Again, what emerges in this ironic distancing is a focus on the liminal space of identity; thus autobiography in Percy's novel becomes not a retreat into the past but a willful act of self-examination through narrative. Narrative, therefore, becomes another means of self-knowledge, as Dupuy notes when he describes the theoretical implications of the literary use of autobiography in Percy. He says, "Both autobiography and Percy's novels, then, struggle with the question of time, whose end remains unknown, but which nevertheless seems to demand redemption. That is to say, both Percy's writing and autobiography share a goal of calling the writer (and the reader) back to an awareness of time, of the self's placement in time, through the process of self-naming" (9). In making himself aware of time, furthermore, Percy does begin where Faulkner left off—with a Quentin Compson who knows he cannot "conquer" time, thus choosing to exercise his will and create a personal sense of it.

Binx's and Andrés's search for selfhood ultimately proves integral to those of their authors; yet the existentialist implications of these novels also allow for an exploration of the "exceptional" Spain and South they describe. Because of the focus on their main characters, Baroja and Percy appear to shy away from an exploration of region. Yet in reality there is a subtle commentary on region that exposes the simultaneously capitalized urban spaces of Madrid and New Orleans coupled with a "traditional" image of Southern and Spanish culture. Soufas identifies this dichotomy in *El árbol* when he observes, "[The novel] strongly critiques a spiritual malaise in Spain, one of the consequences of the ignominious defeat in war with the United States. It despairs of a political solution to Spanish social problems, while it seems to be obsessed with a desperate search for the means to regenerate national values and virtues" (*Subject in Question* 87). Similarly, in embracing a suburban life in Gentilly, Martyn Bone sees Binx as a figure that denies the traditional Southern space of uptown New Orleans and instead opts for an existence Bone calls "post-southern" (64). Yet in describing the empirical experience of their characters, Baroja and Percy do not write about "exceptional" Spain and the South but instead create a formal means of "knowing" these spaces by observing two characters who are, in many ways, suspended between these spaces as they are haunted by the past and tempted by the present claims to truth. Dissatisfied with such willful delusion, Andrés and Binx are plagued by existential—and national—doubt. While the only means to avoid the malaise is to engage in a truly endless search, this ritual of the melancholic becomes a performative act—an escape from nation that is actually an engagement with it. Yet that performative allows Andrés and Binx to understand the performances of essential nationhood that surround them without falling victim to them. Andrés and Binx find little solace in neither the modern nor the traditional Spain and South they occupy, but their search is not for a point of arrival but for one of departure to a place where "truth" is a personally realized form, not a nationally mandated one.

The ambiguous endings of Baroja's and Percy's novels beg the question of whether Andrés and Binx have overcome their melancholia, that is, reached a state of mourning. While Andrés's suicide seems to suggest that his melancholia is inherent to his subjectivity, critics like Greg Forter caution against a tendency in contemporary mourning theory to embrace melancholia with the idea that mourning, or the process of letting go of the object-loss, compels forgetting (138). Forter contests that idea by instead suggesting that the process of letting go allows one to build "psychic memorials" that remove memory from the individual ego and instead make it available to the collective. Thus despite the fact that Andrés kills himself and Binx settles in to upper-class domestic bliss, their final moments in the novel suggest moments of letting go, of building "psychic memorials" to what they have lost. At that moment, Freud says the ego is "free" and "uninhibited," thus mobile and open to the new search that is before these new men.

In Baroja's novel, this moment comes when Andrés's two sources of certainty—nature and science, or the tree of life and the tree of knowledge—seem ambiguous and confusing as Lulú's doctor suggests that maybe medicine should not have intervened, that maybe Lulú would have lived if nature had used its own "recursos" ["resources"] (291). Here we are reminded that Freud describes melancholia as an act in which the ego absorbs the object-loss, producing a self-hatred and self-reviling. Yet that is not how Baroja describes the moment before Andrés's death, instead noting how "al oír lo que decían, sintió que le traspasaba el alma" ["upon hearing what they were saying, he felt that his soul was leaving him"] (291). Throughout the novel, Andrés has wandered between roles as an active participant and passive observer of his environment, a feminized city boy and a passionate lover. When Lulú dies—and her death seems to make no sense to the doctor—Andrés's only recourse is to let all those preconceptions go in a single act of personal will. While this moment seems as if it is another moment of escapism on Andrés's part, his death does not suggest such an erasure. Instead, there is an effort to learn something from him, to remember, as Iturrioz bemoans that his nephew was an epicurean and an aristocrat, even if he didn't believe it. The other doctor's reply, "Pero había en él algo de precursor" ["But, there was something of a precursor in him"] (292), suggests that Andrés represents something more, an indication of something in the future—an idea echoed in the novel's vision of a character that is always changing and, more important, moving on to the next place or idea.

While Percy's main character does not commit suicide at the end of *The Moviegoer*, his decision to marry Kate seems like a retreat into bourgeois propriety. Yet the novel's final scene suggests otherwise as Binx experiences a moment of letting go as his stepbrother, Lonnie, whom Binx calls a "moviegoer" like himself, is on the verge of death. The final scene has Binx ready to face his stepbrother's death while Kate leaves to run an errand for him. As she boards the streetcar with cape jasmine in her lap, she confirms her plan with Binx and asks, "And you'll be thinking of me just that way?" (242). Binx says he will, and the novel closes with Binx watching "her walk toward St. Charles, cape jasmine held against her cheek, until my brothers and sisters call out behind me" (242). Here Binx no longer clings to the image of himself as a moviegoer, as the two people who most represented that mode of being to him—Lonnie and Kate—leave him. Instead, what dominates this scene is the act of memory, as Binx has been honest with his young brothers and sisters about Lonnie's death and vows to remember Kate after she has left him. Thus while it seems as if Binx is no longer engaged in the "search" for "it," in reality "it" simply becomes a word whose vagueness represents the diverse depictions of individual subjectivity in this novel. At times Binx is Southern gentleman, a Gentilly businessman, a moviegoer, and a philosopher. The novel's very open ending—coupled with Binx's ability to let go and remember—suggests that his search has not ended, but only increased in scope.

Integral to the process of moving from melancholia to a place of mourning is the realization that the object-loss—in this case national identity—is performed. For Baroja's and Percy's modern subjects, this process occurs as they develop an ambivalent relationship with national exceptionality, at times yearning for the lost "traditional"—and stoic—Spain and South and at other times hating those places. The resulting ambivalence means that no reigning definition of Spain or South exists in these novels, only competing versions of national identity that echo the early twentieth-century questions of whether to modernize or preserve tradition. While the new men experience the ego-identification with the object-loss typical of melancholia, their simultaneous detachment from the world is a pathos that reduces the world around them to a series of signs whose meanings are indecipherable. It is only at this moment that national exceptionality can truly be understood—at the moment when it has been taken into the ego and simultaneously let go, when loss is enacted for the conscious self. In this manner, mourning springs from melancholia via performance as loss moves from an unconscious experience to a ritualized act, meaning that we no longer have to suffer with individual guilt and instead can learn to cope as a collective—just as Iturrioz does with the doctors and Binx does with his brothers and sisters.

Part of the work that involves moving from melancholia to mourning is a process by which the other, the modern subject as outsider, is made into the self, the free and mobile citizen. What Baroja and Percy have done with their novels is reverse a social order in which one relies on their other in order to stabilize their identities, that is, "I know I am Southern because I am not Northern, et cetera." By reversing the valences on the self/other relationship, these authors achieve two things: they expose the performativity inherent in that relationship, or the rituals in which we must engage in order to prove our identity, and they demonstrate, like many of the writers before them, how the South's and Spain's ability to be both self and other simultaneously (and uncannily) exposes U.S. and European claims to exceptionality by embodying those claims, but not quite. This in-betweenness, this liminality, no doubt haunts the modern subject and is the source of his or her melancholia. But his or her ability to thwart this relationship altogether—as seen via a Catholic Southerner and a Basque anarchist—has much to tell us about how individuals imagine national exceptionality not as one idea but as a series of acts that individuals use to both identify with a citizenry and also to alienate and oppress those that do not belong.

Chapter 4

CONTESTING NARRATIVES OF FAILED PERFORMANCE

Racial Identity and National Exceptionality

———————————————————◁▷——————————————————

An explanation of the lack of commercial appeal and critical study of African American writer Richard Wright's *Pagan Spain* emerges in the book's indeterminacy: between American and European letters, personal travelogue and anthropological study, as well as the writer's own self-identification as Western subject and black "other." Yet the book's "in-betweenness" is reminiscent of what Wright found so fascinating about Spain—the fact that he saw it as both European and not—and it very much locates Wright's own experience within global modernity. In Paul Gilroy's lengthy discussion of Wright's work in *The Black Atlantic: Modernity and Double Consciousness*, he shows how the expatriate writer understood the degree to which the American "Negro" represented the various structures of Western thought (159). For Gilroy, the transformation of the African slave into the American "Negro" involves a "splitting process" that Wright himself locates "in two connected but still independent historical conditions: being a product of western civilisation and having a racial identity 'deeply conditioned' by and 'organically born of' that civilization" (162). Gilroy's study as a whole relies on W. E. B. DuBois's conception of double-consciousness in which the individual (for DuBois, the American "Negro" in particular) is forced to see himself or herself through the eyes of others, namely, white society. For Gilroy, and Wright, the black experience points to the degree to which all identity conceived in the West is hybrid; thus not only is the individual compelled to perform an identity perceived outside himself or herself, his or her performativity will fail him or her as it relies on a myth of essential racial identity that has been "deeply conditioned" by the various political and psychological systems operating in the West.

Before Wright ever stepped foot in Spain, Harlem Renaissance poet Langston Hughes immersed himself in Peninsular culture when he served as a correspondent during the Spanish Civil War. An ardent supporter of the Republican cause, Hughes was not only interested in telling the story of the African American soldiers who had come to fight in the International Brigades but also that of the Moroccan soldiers commissioned to fight in Franco's Army of Africa. Hughes's interest in both sets of soldiers stemmed from an interest in conceptions of blackness on a global scale and particularly the "historical consciousness peculiar to black men" (Girón Echevarría 97). In his poem "Letter from Spain Addressed to Alabama," the speaker is an African American soldier who has captured a "Moor" and tries to find out why he is fighting for a cause that oppresses him. As the Moorish soldier dies, the American looks to Africa and thinks, "Cause if a free Spain wins this year / The colonies, too, are free— / Then something wonderful will happen / To them Moors as dark as me" (Hughes 22–25). The speaker's consciousness of a blackness outside of, and in some ways foreign to, his own becomes a strong desire to find kinship. Yet when he asks to shake hands with the "wounded Moor" in brotherhood, the fallen comrade dies without being able to understand what the speaker was saying. The detachment that the speaker feels—which is similar to feelings described by Richard Wright in Franco's "pagan" Spain—plucks the plight of the black man in America and in Europe and turns it into a global fight against fascism. Hughes echoed this feeling in a speech given to the Second International Writers Congress in 1937, declaring that he and his fellow writers against fascism "represent the end of race. And the Fascists know that when there is no more race, there will be no more capitalism, and no more war, and no more money for munitions makers, because the workers of the world will have triumphed" (quoted in Mullen 96). Hughes's resolve to see the "end of race" becomes emblematic of the degree to which conceptions of race are subsumed by the struggle of modernity, specifically the threat of fascism. Hughes's experience with Franco's African soldiers demonstrates the degree to which his own conceptions of race come to an "end" as communion with the wounded Moor fails on a racial level and instead finds hope in the possibility of freedom inherent in the Republican cause.

Richard Wright's later account of Spain is a story of the writer's struggle to locate the nation's perceived exceptionality in the face of Francoism. In so doing, his observations diverge from direct attack—he makes no bones about comparing Franco's "totalitarian government" to the "absolutist racist regime" of the Jim Crow South in his opening paragraph—to outright admiration and awe of the Spanish people and customs like the bullfight. The little scholarship on this book tends to see Wright's reaction to Spain as encompassing either a personal crisis with Western modernity and his own blackness or simply as his adoption of the "Black Legend," painting Spain as a barbaric colonizer that has resisted modernization. Yet what is interesting about Wright's image of Spain is the degree to which he adopts, and narrates, different roles: fascinated tourist, ethnographer, "black" outsider, "Western" insider. Even more, Wright is fundamentally aware of these posturings as he admits: "To be a functioning and organic part of something is to be almost unconscious of it. I was a part, intimate and inseparable, of the Western world, but I had seldom had to account for my Westernness, had rarely found myself in situations which had challenged me to do so. (Even in Asia and Africa I had always known where my world ended and where theirs began. But Spain was baffling; it looked and seemed Western, but it did not act or feel Western)" (228). With this realization, Wright adopts and embraces his performativity as he decides neither to accept Spain's conception of national myth being produced by the Falange nor to demonize and infantilize the Spanish populace. He chooses to accept their myths without accepting them, to walk what he calls "a mental tightrope" that, oddly, leaves him "free, in a fashion, to depict what I saw" (232).

Wright's becoming aware of the various roles he plays in depicting what he sees in Spain speaks to how he can only become aware of Spain's creation of national myths as he admits his own performance in collecting and relaying them. Meanwhile, Wright's experience as a black man understanding his own dual consciousness while describing a place that he sees as between West and non-West shows how performances of essential identity, particularly within modernity, often are linked to images of "biological" purity defined in terms of race and ethnicity—particularly as he encounters Spaniards who unconsciously link their "pure" Catholicism that historically stands as a contrast to the Moorish and Jewish "taint" on the Iberian Peninsula. Yet Wright does not have this reaction because he experiences racism in Spain. While he does receive stares in rural areas where people have never seen a black man, he still is surprised when he discovers that the first two Spanish youth he meets "have no racial consciousness whatsoever" (15). Instead, what Wright finds objectionable in Spain is the degree to which its national mythmaking is reliant upon what he sees as a pagan Catholicism— a performance of authenticity and identity that Wright believes relegates it to the periphery of Western culture. While it becomes easy to cast Wright's experience in Spain as "unique"—classifying both his experience as well as the conclusions he draws as "exceptional"—*Pagan Spain* instead represents a plurality of identity typical of modernity and present in novels from both the U.S. South and Spain. Thus my goal is not to examine Wright's personal crisis in Spain nor to judge the validity of his claims about Spanish identity—racial, ethnic, or national. Instead, I use *Pagan Spain* to contextualize what I see as transatlantic construction of racial identity within modernity in which images of biological "purity" are contested not by those who are "impure" but by those who seem to exist between racial and ethic binaries. These figures highlight the performativity inherent in racialized identities as their failure to embody the expectations of the biologically pure "self" or the impure "other" highlights the very performativity of that binary. What that failure produces, furthermore, is an uncanniness that propels the individual toward divergent paths already seen in other modern Spanish and Southern novels in this project: either a hyperperformance of racial and ethnic identity that eventually leads to death or suicide or a recognition and coping with performed identity as a means of beginning to understand one's integrated subjectivity.

In comparing the construction of racial and ethnic identities in twentieth-century Spanish and Southern culture, I am less interested in exploring or comparing the specific "races" or "minorities" within each culture than I am in how narratives of a racial or ethnic "other" figure into mythic constructions of nationhood. What this approach shows, I hope, is that while Spain's and the South's conceptions of race may differ, a similar fragmentation within that narrative of national exceptionality allows us to break down the racialized binary of "self" and "other" and how the uncanniness of figures that exist between these binaries allows us to examine and face the ghosts of essential identity that haunt us. Meanwhile, throughout contemporary Southern and Spanish artistic production—specifically William Styron's *The Confessions of Nat Turner* (1967), Ralph Ellison's *Invisible Man* (1952), Federico García Lorca's "rural" tragedies (particularly *Yerma* [1934]), and Luis Martín-Santos's *Tiempo de silencio* [*A Time of Silence*] (1962), the main characters struggle to perform an "impure" image of Spanish or Southern identity that they cannot live up to. This idea of racial "impurity"—represented by images of blood relations and graphic, bloody violence—pervades Styron's novel and Lorca's plays as the main characters are constantly asked to, and fail at, performing identities coded by an apparent biological identity. While Ellison's and Martín-Santos's novels are also concerned with the failed performance of a transgressive "other," these novels contest the idea of racial and ethnic determinacy through main characters who abandon ideas of race and ethnicity in order to understand their respective invisibility and solitude. While Ellison and Martín-Santos explore the binds of identity beyond racial and biological monikers, in the end failed performances haunt the characters in all the novels discussed in this chapter as they face ghosts of a divisive past that make them realize their own fragmented psyches—a condition that both reflects and compels their isolation and "otherness."

As these characters fail to live up to national expectations of racial identity, their failures also extend to that of gender roles and sexuality. Specifically, images of biological purity accompany images of sexuality as the sex act becomes the means by which the individual is literally and figuratively "reproduced" as pure or tainted. Richard Wright sees such a connection between female sexuality and racial identity when, as Faith Berry notes in the introduction to *Pagan Spain*, he was quick to see "the opposition between Spanish prostitutes—symbolizing the sexual abuse of black women—as against the untouchableness of the virgins, reminding him of the Southern white women of his childhood" (xii). In his book exploring Caucasian racial identity, *White*, Richard Dyer explores this connection between race and the body and makes clear that "all concepts of race are all concepts of the body and of heterosexuality. Race is a means of categorising different types of human body which reproduce themselves. It seeks to systematise differences and to relate them to differences of character and worth. Heterosexuality is the means of ensuring, but also the site of endangering, the reproduction of these differences" (20). As a site of endangering racial purity, the failed performance of racial identity usually involves assertions of failed or queer sexuality, encompassing biologically the failure imposed by national gender codes.

The degree to which racial identity becomes bound up in sexual identity and how national identity seems to articulate all of these codes at once is synthesized, for Richard Wright, in Spain's relationship to a brand of Roman Catholicism that constructed and had enforced those codes since the Inquisition. His final lines of the novel recall this memory as he describes a paganism that promoted "one Will, one Race, one God, and one Aim" and a nation that possesses a metaphysical mandate "to chastise all of those whom he considers the 'morally moribund,' the 'spiritually inept,' the 'biologically botched'" (277–88). No doubt, it is very easy to see Wright's judgments as harsh for a country he seems to really like. Yet Wright does not dismiss Spain as "barbaric" like many travelers did; nor does he completely romanticize it like Hemingway did. Instead, he finds a space where he can evaluate the role of performativity in history. Meanwhile, one observes the same process in a series of Spanish and Southern novels from the same period, and we quickly observe that the role that biological determinacy—and indeterminacy—played in Spain and the South typifies the fragmentation of national exceptionality seen throughout this project and Western modernity itself. In that sense, my reading of Wright's own performativity and that of Spain mirrors Gilroy's definition of the Black Atlantic as a space of transcultural construction that is defined "through [a] desire to transcend both the structures of the nation state and the constraints of ethnicity and national particularity" (19). In the novels and play that follow, we observe, as Wright did in Spain, the high costs of that desire as the individual can neither embrace nor reject the confines of performativity without some kind of loss—a loss that in itself becomes bound up not in the failure to produce racial codes but, as we have already observed, in the condition of modernity itself.

Within the field of Southern studies, particularly the William Faulkner industry, the subject of racial identity stands at the forefront of contemporary discussions about Southernness. In fact the specific manner in which race is often aligned with the "South" in a way that it is not with the "North" shows how Southern claims to, and Northern projections of, regional exceptionality create an image of racial identity that makes blackness into nothing more than a failed, and specifically "Southern," performance of whiteness. In *Cities of the Dead*, Joseph Roach explores this bond at length when he examines the court case that established the "separate but equal" clause that legally defined segregation in the South. While most schoolchildren learn about the *Plessy v. Ferguson* case in which an octoroon (by law, having at least one-eighth "black blood"), Homer Plessy, was arrested and fined for sitting in the "Whites Only" section of a New Orleans train, few are aware that, to even the careful observer, Plessy looked like a white man. Indeed, his transgression was one that had been planned by his colleagues in the American Citizens Equal Rights Association, including the need to reveal that he was not white to the conductor. Plessy's goal, furthermore, was not to challenge the "separate but equal" clause, but to challenge the legal assertion of race itself (Roach 235). Thus as Roach makes clear, "Homer Plessy was *not* to be distinguished from the other race by color. In order to provoke Detective Cain, the octoroon had to perform his 'blood,' first its predominate whiteness, by entering the 'Whites Only' car unquestioned, then its invisible remainder, by getting himself ejected and arrested" (236). Indeed, within the singular figure of Homer Plessy, the irrevocable bond between the performance of "white blood" and its subsequent transgression, its "blackness," was not an act of codifying the "norm" and "its difference," although that is how the U.S. Supreme Court saw it. Instead, Plessy illustrates the arbitrary and false performances of both a "white" and "nonwhite" identity, not mutually exclusive, but mutually revealing—in many ways, the image of coded exceptionality in its highest, seemingly biological, form.

One of the main reasons Faulkner scholarship is so embedded in a discussion of race is the author's interest in racial indeterminacy—evidenced by characters like Charles Bon in *Absalom, Absalom!* and Joe Christmas in *Light in August.* Contrastingly, William Styron found himself embroiled in extreme controversy because of what many saw as an essential view of blackness in *The Confessions of Nat Turner,* a retelling of a historical slave insurrection led by Nat Turner in 1831 Virginia and the published confessions that came out of the event. It is Styron's focus on what I identify as Nat's act of surrogation and subsequent performance of a transgressive blackness that caused such controversy, prompting the publication of *William Styron's Nat Turner: Ten Black Writers Respond* in 1968. The biggest complaint among these writers, as John Henrik Clarke notes in the introduction, was that "the Nat Turner created by William Styron has little resemblance to the Virgi iia slave insurrectionist who is a hero to his people. This being so, then why did William Styron create *his* Nat Turner and ignore the most important historical facts relating to the real Nat Turner?" (vii). Styron's aim, as expressed in the introduction, was to create a "meditation on history." What he narrates is a process of surrogation in which the loss of freedom that Nat's master promised him is replaced with a freedom that Nat extracts as an image of transgressive blackness that purposely contradicts the role of "good" slave that he plays throughout the novel. Nat's extreme acts of violence, however, become an uncanny recollection of the very role of "good" slave inscribed upon him by his masters as he quickly realizes that his "badness" is a performance as well. His failure comes in realizing that one image of blackness cannot replace another since both are images of "otherness" designed to either make him almost white or violently and transgressively black.

Throughout Nat's "confession" to the lawyer Thomas Gray (who collected and published the historical Nat Turner's confessions), Nat seems to enact his blackness for a white audience. Yet Nat's narration is different in its defiance of audience expectations as Gray repeatedly expresses skepticism of Nat's religious faith in light of his ability to commit murder. Nat's confession is not unlike Pascual Duarte's confession in Cela's novel as his confession becomes, in reality, a contemplation of the various manifestations of black identity throughout his life—from pampered house slave to insurrection leader. Within these various acts, furthermore, Nat considers how representations of "black" time, masculinity, and sexuality affected his actions. In other words, as Nat's images of "white" time, gender, and sex are proven illusory, he replaces them with an image of blackness thrust upon him by the white society and only escapable in the realm of memory. As Dyer's model of race "locates historical, social, and cultural differences in the body" (30), it becomes clear how Nat's apparent racial difference appears through bodily acts. As the novel's form suggests, the only means for him to escape those bonds is memory—a place where the body is not bound to performativity.

Within dreams and memory, the immense possibility of performance appears in its ability to construct narratives of integrated selfhood based on both personal experience and essentialist myths. Styron alludes to such mythmaking in the opening of *Confessions* when Nat describes a dream, "or *vision*," that has plagued him since childhood: that of the ocean that he has never seen but only heard described (4). This absence in Nat's life is representative of the sense of loss that pervades his existence, and his desire to fill this lack, this "physical hunger," becomes a license to create myths of origin when he creates "fantasies of the waves and the distant horizon and the groaning seas, the free blue air like an empire above arching eastward to Africa—as if by one single glimpse of this scene I might comprehend all the earth's ancient, oceanic, preposterous splendor" (5). Yet Nat's search for comforting, surrogate images of a mythic past, fueled by his dream of "ancient splendor," in the end becomes an image that he can neither reproduce nor live up to, and this failure becomes an uncanny image that haunts him until the novel's end.

At the forefront of Nat's failed performances in this novel is his masculinity when white society, represented by his master, emasculates him. Despite the lack of a clearly defined masculinity, Nat has a clear image of manhood when he responds to a fellow slave, Hark, who greases the master with compliments, annoying Nat by playing the role of "unspeakable bootlicking Sambo, all giggles and smirks and oily sniveling servility" (55). He later chastises Hark, saying, "You ain't a *man* when you act like that. You ain't a man, you is a fool!" (57). Yet when Nat criticizes Hark, he ignores a fundamental point: within the confines of slavery, masculinity is superseded by the role of slave. Nat reaches such a realization when one of his master's guests refers to him as slave—something that had never occurred before—and it completely floors him. Made to recognize his true status, Nat unknowingly surrenders into a performance of blackness willed by his white masters who make him their "pet, the darling, the little black jewel of Turner's Mill" (169). Only in retrospect does Nat realize exactly how his performance is constructed by his masters: "That a white child would not have been so sweetly indulged—that my very blackness was central to the privileges I was given and the familiarity I was allowed—never occurred to me, and doubtless I would not have understood even if I had been told" (169). In addition, Nat discovers that his relegation to a spoiled child becomes a feminization through infantalization as he is a "darling" and a "jewel." In acting the pet, Nat performs a surrogated identity he sees as separate from his fellow slaves as he is educated and reared in coded whiteness. What he does not realize is that he performs an emasculating failure of whiteness as those that rear him in the ways of the white world simultaneous deny the very benefits of that world to him.

Part of what makes Nat so assured in his performance is that time is on his side—he has been promised freedom. Yet Styron is clear in his novel that time is not a measure of hours and minutes for a slave, but a measure of wealth. Thus economic depression that occurred historically in Virginia during this period means that time becomes another "loss" for Nat as his master, Turner, is forced to sell his other slaves and, later, rent Nat out to another farmer in order to pay creditors. For Turner, the slaves become a measure of an obliterated past, as he admits engaging in his own masquerade when he states, "I have lied to myself night and day in an effort to believe that what I saw around me was an illusion, that this mutilated and broken Tidewater would survive in spite of itself, that no matter how wrecked and eaten up the soil, . . . Turner's Mill would forever be here grinding out timber and meal. But now it is timber and meal for ghosts, . . . and soon Turner's Mill will stand a dead hulk like the others on the landscape, and somewhere in the far South people may remember it but it will be remembered as if it were the fragment of a dream" (220–21). As Turner narrates the details of his own performative imagining of a future that will invariably not exist, Nat emerges as an uncanny reminder of that failure. Thus Nat himself begins to replicate that failure as he continues to believe that his freedom, an intangible form in the future, is guaranteed. Yet once again, Nat finds himself performing a failed notion of linear time as his freedom—like Turner's image of the South—slowly becomes the "fragment of a dream."

Throughout the novel, Nat's lack of freedom is characterized by moments of loss, particularly the innocence that keeps him blind to his own performed blackness. For example, when he witnesses his mother's rape by an overseer, he is shocked not by the act, but by the fact that sex was not "the pastime, or habit, or obsession, or something, of niggers alone" (148). Horrified, Nat attempts to flee, to eradicate the image from his mind, but as he runs from the house, he is struck by the sense of loss and immobility he faces as he suddenly realizes, "There is no place to go" (148). Similarly, when Nat later witnesses the sexual encounter between the white Emmeline and her cousin, he is shaken by this image of impure white womanhood. Again, his loss of innocence is tied to his race, as he thinks to himself, "This is what comes of being a nigger. It ain't fair. If I wasn't a nigger I wouldn't find out about things I don't want to find out about. It ain't fair" (181). As the family's pet, Nat is happy to play the role of innocent slave child projected on him by whites; yet he always alters that performance of blackness when he discovers white people playing their own specific roles. Thus as Nat discovers how his identity is bound up in white projections of race and sexuality, it upsets his sense of justice as he aims to restore his lost innocence.

Faced with the loss of freedom, Nat takes the only steps that, in his mind, are available to him. To free himself of performed whiteness, the blackness projected onto him, he will murder those who, in failing him, have caused his own existential failures. As Nat begins to gather followers and plan his insurrection, he sees his mission as one mandated by God and a "grand design" that "must include not a handful of Negroes but many, and that the blood of white men must flow on the soil of Southhampton" (336). Yet what Nat does not realize is that in trying to eradicate, to basically forget, the white projections of his blackness, he is doomed to perform a surrogated blackness that only reproduces his failure to "act" according to white demands. At no point is this failure more clear, furthermore, than when Nat murders the woman he loves, Margaret Whitehead. A young woman who believes in the emancipation of slaves and often expresses her beliefs to Nat, Margaret represents Nat's lack of freedom in that he is never allowed to express his love, and instead, performatively expresses intense hatred for her at several moments. In his effort to deny this lack of a relationship between them, however, Nat is determined to simply eradicate her completely. Yet when the insurrection begins and the moment to kill her arrives, Nat experiences a moment of pause—one that his comrades read as a failure of masculinity when Will tells him, "If'n you cain't make de *red juice* you cain't run de *army!*" (412). When Margaret flees, Nat chases after her, and when he catches up to her, his phallic sword fails to kill her. Reading this lack as a sexual failure, Nat's performance of a blackness not compelled by narratives of whiteness fails once again as he is forced to feel her gaze when he bludgeons her with a fence rail. As Nat finally has eradicated the person who most represented his loss, all he can do is circle her body and, later, sit and recall "ancient moments from childhood—warm rain, leaves, a whippoorwill, rushing mill wheels, jews-harp strumming—centuries before" (415). In grasping memories that seem "natural," Nat searches for narratives of authenticity in the past that give his life, and his actions, meaning. Yet his performances of time, masculinity, and sexual love are all existential failures; thus all he can do is resume what he describes as a "meaningless" circling of Margaret's body and, later, his insurrection.

When Nat is later questioned about his actions, he makes it clear that he has no remorse, except for killing Margaret, the actual site of his failed performance. Yet as he recalls the moment that likely caused their getting caught—letting a young woman flee into the woods—he expresses the unshakable "grief" that invariably becomes a sign of how, in eradicating whiteness, he has performed an uncanny blackness—a violent image of the black man who only lusts after white women—that pervades white Southern culture and that was the source of the most overwhelming criticism of Styron's novel. Nat thinks to himself, "I shivered in the knowledge of the futility of all ambition. My mouth was sour with the yellow recollection of death and blood-smeared fields and walls. I watched the girl slip away, vanish without a hand laid upon her. Who knows but whether we were not doomed to lose. I know nothing any longer. Nothing. Did I really wish to vouchsafe a life for the one that I had taken?" (417). As Nat becomes aware of his performance and its failures, he questions its epistemological implications. Faced with what he has lost, he questions what he can know and discovers that, ultimately, knowledge is lost when one attempts to replace loss with myth or even contrived memory.

In the end, however, Styron makes his character into neither a racial martyr nor a demon, but instead creates a novelistic form that illustrates the varying levels of performances—both black and white—that exist in this novel. In so doing, the idea of failed performance—what Roach calls "the doomed search for originals by continuously auditioning stand-ins" (3)— becomes not something that is coded racially, but something implicated in the idea of racial performance. In other words, Nat does not fail because he is black; he fails because the search for racial surrogates is bound to lead to the nothingness he encounters toward the end of the novel. Yet in the act of remembering these performances, especially just before he dies, Nat can abandon the confines of performed blackness and find both a sense of self and a love for Margaret that exist in a temporal form not bound by racial and economic concerns tied to images in the past. The willful exploration of the past therefore becomes the primary focus of Styron's novel as his "meditation on history" is told via the fragmented memories of a man's personal narrative. Not unlike Ellison's Invisible Man (as I discuss later), or even Cela's Pascual Duarte, the separation of the character as narrator and as character proves a poignant method of exposing the character's performative selfhood. As the novel closes, Nat thinks to himself that he "would have done it again. I would have destroyed them all. Yet I would have spared one" (428). Within his proclaimed lack of remorse, it becomes clear that the insurrection is not the source of failed performance. It is Margaret who compelled the performance of transgressive black masculinity; thus it is only fitting that, in the end, she is the source of his sense of selfhood and the site not of his reproduction of coded blackness, but of his realization of performance.

The ways in which images of transgressive blackness were dependent on images of whiteness—with the sexual mores such images imply—become clear in the lens of performative mythmaking. As we have already observed and Wright makes clear at the end of Pagan Spain, both Spain and the South, following their civil wars, actually engaged in a process begun long before these conflicts began in which national exceptionality materialized in terms of a racialized other. The idea of having pure Christian blood was an image of Spanish identity that persisted into the twentieth century, particularly following the regenerationist movement of Spanish national identity that followed the War of 1898. This movement, promoted by philosophers like Ortega y Gasset and Unamuno, attempted to create a "Spanish" identity that denied the religious and regional diversity in the nation. Unamuno, specifically, wrote of the idea of a pure Spanish nationality inherent in the idea of "lo castizo" [the "authentic," coming from the word "caste"] in creating an idea of an essential, and pure, Spanish character. Michael Richards explores similar images of racial purity during Francoism in his book A Time of Silence: Civil War and the Culture of Repression in Franco's Spain, 1936–1945. Here he details the slow progression of a racialized discourse of national "purity" that prevailed after 1898 and persisted as a source of Francoist oppression:

> Orteguian regenerationism and its panoply of pathological language was recycled to describe the result of Spain's "defective embryology," and to depict the workers whose "biological mission . . . to be docile" had been transgressed. Regenerationists, like Joaquín Costa and Lucas Mallada had, some years earlier, compared the Spaniards to

the indigenous peoples of Africa, as part of a racial schematization of decline. The agricultural workers and migrants of the south, often referred to as "*africanos*," were particularly viewed as genetically inferior, as a lazy and degenerate caste apart from respectable society that could not compare with the ancient, but endangered, "stratified" racial and spiritual essences found in the peasants of Castile. (48)

The loss of 1898 and the impulse to assert a racial identity are readily apparent in Falangist and Francoist propaganda, specifically the film *Raza* [*Race*] (1942), which was based on a story written by Franco under a pseudonym. This family romance traces the story of the Churrucas, specifically two brothers who find themselves on opposite sides during the Civil War. As the film's clichéd plot unfolds, the Republican brother is captured and sentenced to death, but when his brother later is captured by Republicans and can save himself by invoking his brother's name, he is true to his family, to his race, and dies with honor. The film ends with the rest of the family reunited in Madrid, celebrating the Nationalist victory at a parade presided over by the Caudillo playing himself in the film.

Like the Jim Crow South, Francoist identity irrevocably bound racial and national identity (Richards 60). Unlike in the United States, however, specific study of the degree and severity of Francoism's oppression of racialized others remains difficult primarily because of an obvious lack of documentation detailing the regime's exact policies and actions. According to Richards, there is evidence that details the creation of an office or laboratory of "'psychological investigations' charged with analyzing 'the bio-psychic roots of Marxism'" (57). While the 1938 report is listed in the Servicio Histórico Militar's archives, it has, of course, disappeared. During the early Francoist period, censorship also prevented writers and artists from directly engaging issues of racial identity. Ideas of racial purity, in part prompted by an increased interest in hygiene and cleanliness across Europe, were already appearing in works before the Spanish Civil War. Thus if we examine the rural tragedies of Federico García Lorca, the often-noted questions concerning gender also contain an implicit discourse on racial identity as the "mother" becomes the "pure" source of Spanish national identity. In many ways, Lorca is one of the first authors to directly engage the issue of a Spanish "race" as it would be conceived in the early Francoist period. While he is among the first, he is by no means the last, as the issue of a Spanish racial identity, and specifically those who do not fit within it, is a major theme in novels across the Spanish tradition—from Martín Santos to Juan Goytisolo.

The primary reasons that Lorca's "rural" tragedies, specifically *Bodas de Sangre* [*Blood Wedding*] (1932), *Yerma* (1934), and *La casa de Bernarda Alba* [*The House of Bernarda Alba*] (1936), speak so much to the issue of coded racial identity in early twentieth-century Spain is the playwright's interest in loss, and how it compels the individual to "perform" his or her identity, coupled with the transatlantic connection between the Andalusian poet and playwright and Langston Hughes. While Lorca spent time in the United States, his tragedies were not well received by critics and audiences because of their "un-modern" themes with rural characters (Smith 45). Yet Lorca found one of his most faithful translators in Hughes, also a playwright who premiered his own play *Mulatto* simultaneous to the 1935 production of *Bodas de sangre* in New York. While Hughes's translation of Lorca's play was neither published nor performed until 1992 (Smith), Paul Julian Smith locates clear connections between *Mulatto* and Lorca's tale of a bride who betrays the effort to marry her to a family of good "blood" and runs off with her lover, resulting in the death of both the man she loves as well as her fiancé. Smith notes, "If *Bodas de sangre* stages the merger of feuding lovers and dueling men, *Mulatto* dramatizes the pleasure and the danger of racial fusion—the light-skinned 'yellow' son of a white colonel and his black mistress demands entrance into white society" (59). The clear racial themes seen in *Mulatto* can be linked to Lorca's tragedies as the ideas of "purity" and "blood" dominate the relationships between men and women. While Lorca's focus on female characters and the oppression they feel has caused several critics to correctly find a gendered expression of Lorca's own homosexuality, I would posit that these readings also contain overtones that reflect the position of the "racialized," and thus transgressively sexualized, other within 1930s Spanish culture—a figure, not unlike the mulatto, who represents a hybridity that early Francoist discourse tried to erase.

While the issue of national, and I argue racial, purity, is a dominant theme throughout *Bodas de sangre*, Lorca's play about a barren woman, *Yerma*, best reflects the compulsion to perform one's "Spanishness" correctly under the watchful eyes of a judgmental rural populace. Yerma, whose name translates to "barren," has been the subject of much critical debate since her feminine resolve to have a child becomes an assertion of masculine power as she slowly takes control of her relationship, and, when resolutely denied the possibility of motherhood by her husband, Juan, she kills him. While the implications for gender and its performance are fairly clear here, I instead, following Smith's reading of the play, look at Yerma's quest for motherhood as the expression of a desire to reproduce a selfhood that reflects her own "purity," and thus that of her nation. Part of the justification for such a reading lies in the fact that Yerma, unlike the Novia in *Bodas de sangre* or Adela in *La casa de Bernarda Alba*, is not a "bad" or "impure" woman. Quite the opposite, she is very concerned with her honor and abilities throughout the play. Instead, like the well-intentioned Nat Turner, she is simply another failed performer who seeks a sense of self, yet is constantly compelled to perform her otherness for the masses.

In his study *The Theatre of García Lorca: Text, Performance, Psychoanalysis*, Smith examines *Yerma* and considers the playwright's interest in modern medicine at the time, specifically the promotion of national "hygiene" that removed childbirth from the realm of midwives and instead institutionalized it in hospitals with male doctors. Spain was by no means unique in its national efforts to promote a racialized and nationalized hygiene—the seeds of such eugenics movements were already being planted in Nazi Germany—but Smith shows how, in Spain specifically, "there is thus a structural relation between the development of reproductive technology (which doctors take care to keep out of the hands of women who are 'blind' to its monstrous potentialities), the promotion of nationalist, eugenistic hygiene (which equates family and race), and the idealization of motherhood in the face of the feminist claims to reproductive autonomy precipitated by that self-same male-generated technology" (22). By linking "motherhood" to a national "bio-power" (17), Smith illustrates, using Foucault's idea of "biopower" as a means of controlling the body in order to control the masses, what Dyer also makes clear in *White*: that "race" is irrevocably tied to the body as a site of heterosexual reproduction; thus while critics have looked to Lorca's homosexuality as a lens through which to examine gender in his plays, it also becomes a lens by which we can also examine racial identity.

Lorca's interest in Spanish identity as racial is very much a commentary on an idea of racialized "Spanishness," reaching as far back as Unamuno's ideas of "lo castizo" leading to a medical and sexual reform movement in Spain promoted by doctors and activists like Hildegart Rodriguez and Gregorio Marañon.[1] Yet in his own comments on *Yerma*, Lorca locates his protagonists' main problem in an idea of Spanish "honor" that has a much older, but still a racial, conceptualization: "Mi protagonista tiene limitado su arbitrio, encadenada por el concepto, que va disuelto en su sangre, de la honra españolísima" ["My protagonist has a limited will, connected by the concept, that runs dissolved in her blood, of utterly Spanish honor"] (quoted in McDermid 151). Within Spanish discourse going back centuries, the idea of Spanish "honor" as belonging exclusively to the "viejo cristiano" ["old Christian," that is, not a Muslim or a Jew] is nationally specific to Spain and a racial means of identifying Spanish national identity. What stands out about Yerma is, again, that she is not a "bad" woman, but one obsessed with honor and a successful performance of Spanishness. Thus her "honor" is not just an abstract ideal, but a national, and racial, identity. Yerma's desire to have children, therefore, follows Dyer's idea that race is linked to heterosexuality in that Yerma feels the need to reproduce herself in the form of children. She tells a friend who says children bring much suffering, "Mentira. Eso lo que dicen las madres débiles, las quejumbrosas. ¿Para qué los tienen? Tener un hijo no es tener un ramo de rosas. Hemos de sufrir para verlos crecer. Yo pienso que se nos va la mitad de nuestra sangre. Pero esto es bueno, sano, hermoso. Cada mujer tiene sangre para cuatro o cinco hijos y cuando no los tiene se le vuelve veneno, como me va a pasar a mí" ["Lies. That's what weak mothers say, the whiners. Why do they have kids? Having a child is not like having a bunch of roses. We have to suffer in order to watch them grow. I think that they take half our blood. But this is good, healthy, beautiful. Each woman has blood for four or five children and when one doesn't have them, it turns into poison, which is what will happen to me"] (Act I: 428). The idea that Yerma's motherhood exists in her "blood" and that only "weak" mothers woe the sufferings that result from childbearing—a process that is "healthy" and "beautiful"—suggests a clear connection between motherhood and the reproduction of a pure and clean Spanish nation. The importance of purity is even further emphasized when, at the end of the play, an old woman suggests that Yerma leave her husband and instead take up with her son, who will surely get her pregnant. Not only does Yerma adamantly refuse this idea, citing her honor, but she posits such a concept as wholly unnatural, saying, "El agua no se puede volver atrás ni la luna llena sale al mediodía" ["Water can't flow backwards nor the full moon come out at noon"] (Act III: 490). Yerma, therefore, not only seeks a child to fulfill her role as a woman, but, specifically an honorable, strong, and healthy woman whose "blood" can be reproduced for future generations.

Yet Yerma cannot fulfill her role as the ideal Spanish mother, and her loss is not just that of a child, but of her main source of personal identity. Yerma's conceptualization of a child as a sense of self emerges early in the play when she describes meeting her husband to an old woman and says, "Y me miraba en sus ojos. Sí, pero era para verme muy chica, muy manejable, como si yo misma fuera hija mía" ["And I was looking at myself in his eyes. Yes, but it was to see myself very much a young girl, very manageable, as if I myself were my own child"] (Act I: 434). In his book *Love, Desire, and*

Identity in the Theatre of Federico García Lorca, Paul McDermid asserts that Yerma's desire for a child is her quest for a "metaphysical self" as she seeks "to transcend her material being and 'reproduce' her Self on the symbolic plane of the soul" (146). While McDermid examines this search for self-hood within the lens of gender performance, I posit that the focus within Yerma's quest for self is less on gender and more on the performance of a racial surrogate—the need to the replace "blood" that does not exist in children and that, in Yerma's mind, will inevitably turn to "poison." McDermid is correct in identifying a gender reversal that occurs when Yerma leaves the domestic space, emasculates her husband by defying his wishes, and talks to people in the village streets. Yet it should again be noted the infidelity that Yerma's transgression should produce is not enacted, but perceived by the townspeople around her. Lorca's rural tragedies usually contain a chorus-like group of characters, and, in *Yerma,* one appears in a group of gossipy laundresses who talk about how ambiguous "people" have seen Yerma with another man. Yet Yerma makes clear what she is searching for when Juan confronts her about leaving the house: "Te busco a ti. Te busco a ti, es ti a quien busco día y noche sin encontrar sombra donde respirar. Es tu sangre y tu amparo lo que deseo" ["I am searching for you, for you. It's you I search for day and night without finding shade to breathe in. It's your blood and your shelter I desire"] (Act III: 478). As Yerma addresses her husband, it becomes clear that her "lack" is not exclusively feminine. If it were, she would not claim to seek her husband's "blood." Instead, her "lack" also exists in her failed performance of "honor," her failure to reproduce her blood in her children but that, instead, remains in her veins as poison. Yerma further identifies her failed performance when she blames herself while cursing her father for giving her the blood capable of producing 100 children, but that forces her to search for those children by bursting through the walls of her home (Act III: 479). Again, the failure here is not just one of femininity (though she does transgress coded femininity by leaving the domestic sphere) but also of her "honor" since her wandering around town causes the gossipy laundresses to discredit her. In addition, aside from the focus on "blood" specifically, Yerma sees this child-producing blood as only accessible from legitimate sources (her husband and her father), refusing to fulfill the role of mother if it means disavowing her honor, which is why she rejects the laundress's son.

In a play that seems to be about gender performance, gender becomes a hazy form as Yerma takes on masculine qualities and Juan appears increasingly effeminate. By the third act of the play, the androgynous nature of Yerma's and Juan's gender role-reversal coupled with Yerma's "poisoned" blood from her father suggests that the blood that Yerma sees as an eternal part of herself is instead a failure to perform her blood correctly. This failure, furthermore, is brought foreword during the *romería*, a local village event, when a masked man and woman appear and affirm the roles of the "sad" wife and the husband who "commands" her. What stands out about these figures is how the stage directions make very clear that the masks should not be grotesque in any way, but "de gran belleza y con un sentido de pura tierra" ["of great beauty and with a sense of pure earthliness"] (Act III: 485). In other words, the masks are not meant to make Yerma a transgression, but, again, a failure. What stands out here is not that Yerma is a failed woman; she is, in fact, fulfilling the role of "sad" wife according to the rural tradition of the *romería*. Instead, her failure exists on a racial level in her inability to perform her "blood" by having a child. The result is a quest for a surrogate, the maniacal search for Juan's blood, which only compels her to leave the home and engage in another role that represents failure: that of the dishonored woman.

Yerma's status as a racialized other again returns us to Dyer's idea that all concepts of race are "concepts of the body and of heterosexuality" (20), and nowhere does this idea become more true in Lorca's play than in the final scene when Yerma kills Juan. The role-reversal identified by McDermid comes to fruition here as Juan's questioning of what Yerma was searching for in the street gets turned back on him. As he tells his wife that they can live happily without children, he tenderly embraces her. As she reproaches him by similarly asking, "¿Qué buscas?" ["What are you searching for?"], he responds almost exactly as his wife, saying, "A ti te busco. Con la luna estás hermosa" ["I'm looking for you. With the moonlight, you're beautiful"] (Act III: 494). Of course, what stands out is what Juan does not seek, namely, the blood that marks sex as means of reproduction. Indeed, by proposing the idea of sex for pleasure using almost the same rhetoric that Yerma used to justify her quest for selfhood, Juan forces his wife to perform her barrenness for the entire village by compelling her to kill him—the only possible source for her child. Yerma realizes what she has done when she says, "Voy a descansar sin despertarme sobresaltada, para ver si la sangre me anuncia sin despertarme sobresaltada, para ver si la sangre me anuncia otra sangre nueva. Con el cuerpo seco para siempre. ¿Qué queréis saber? No os acerquéis, porque he matado a mi hijo, ¡yo mismo he matado a mi hijo!" ["I am going to rest without waking startled, to see if the blood delivers me another new blood. With a dry body forever. What do you all want to know?

Don't come any closer because I have killed my child, I have killed my own child!"] (Act III: 494). By declaring that she will be delivered "new" blood, and not the poison mandated to barren women, Yerma acknowledges both her performance as well as its failure, an idea C. Christopher Soufas alludes to when he says, "Yerma finally understands that, however she may be publicly judged, there can be no closure to her situation. The child was but a symptom of a deeper cycle that her violence toward Juan has allowed her to acknowledge and understand. In murdering her husband, Yerma destroys the only authorized material agent for bringing her a child under conditions that would be meaningful and, at the same time, destroys the toil of years that has reaped an abundance" (*Audience and Authority* 122). In her final act, Yerma strikingly recalls Nat Turner and his own murder of Margaret Whitehead at the end of Styron's novel. While both characters' performances contain an implicit commentary on gender roles, both the site of and the means of realizing failed performance eventually come from frustrated heterosexuality and a perceived betrayal of "blood." In the end, the artifice of gender becomes a means of highlighting something equally performative but seemingly eternal—a racial identity allegedly linked to biology, but one that is actually contrived by nations. Nat and Yerma are corporeally bound to a system that compels them to play the role of "other" by having them perform unspeakable acts of violence, with one fulfilling the role of lustful black aggressor and the other playing the part of dishonored Spanish wife. While it is at the level of the heterosexual body, and through their blood, that Nat and Yerma seem to play these roles, in reality ideas of "blood" exist as measures of discourse in which to be "white" really means to be appropriately "Southern" and being "honorable" is acting correctly "Spanish." What is most interesting about Nat and Yerma is that, at the beginning of their narratives, they almost fit those molds. Nat is a "good" slave who is "almost" set free, while Yerma is a "good" wife who seems simply unlucky in her barrenness. Only when they perform their racial transgressions for their communities, however, do they realize the roles they were playing all along and how the source of those roles existed not in the organic body but in the very community they were performing for in the first place.

Part of the tragedy of Nat Turner's and Yerma's failed performances of racial identity is that they never escape the dichotomy of "self" and "other" that compels their transgressions. While still concerned with the idea of a "failed" performance, Ralph Ellison and Luis Martín-Santos actually break down ideas of race and ethnicity through characters whose identities are fragmented into many roles, and these characters' interior monologues haunt them throughout *Invisible Man* and *Tiempo de silencio*. Indeed, Ellison and Martín-Santos themselves seem to occupy liminal spaces in these arguments as they themselves exist on the boundary of Southernness and Spanishness, with Ellison being from Oklahoma and Martín-Santos spending most of his life in the Basque region. Yet like Wright's position in Spain, this liminality allows them to expose the hybridity of their characters' identities and deny the essential underpinnings of race and biology. Both characters' inability to exemplify the qualities society places upon them leads them to a place that extends beyond racial or ethnic conceptions of identity. While the consequences of this escape are great (leading to the deaths of those closest to them and their own self-imposed exile), the result is an understanding of the benefits as well as the limitations of performed identity—and how the failed performance of the racialized other is how we realize the myths inherent in a national self.

Any idea suggesting biological predeterminacy of "blackness" has serious consequences within a discussion of twentieth-century U.S. and Southern culture since it is readily arguable that the racialized other's failed performance—and the existential crisis it produces—illustrates the personal experience of racism. Within early twentieth-century U.S. culture, the idea of "blackness" was multifaceted, and Ralph Ellison's 1952 novel, *Invisible Man*, engages the multiple performances of blackness as a complex manifestation of modernity's crushing impact on individual subjectivity. How Ellison's narrator differs from the previously discussed new man is that the "exceptional" performances of the past in response to modernity—in particular, a violent, primal masculinity—are not available to him because they would render him visible to a white culture that has cast him as invisible. Yet the narrator constantly strives for visibility in this novel, and the constant failure of the Invisible Man's various performances—as an upstanding high-school and college student, an activist for the Brotherhood, and later the trickster Rinehart—requires that he assume a new identity each time a previous one fails him.

Ironically, the problem the main character faces in this novel is not ontological, despite his constant search for selfhood. Instead, as in Nat Turner's case, it becomes epistemological since he is not aware of his various performances until the novel's end. As such, the Invisible Man's unsuccessful performances further propel his invisibility until a final, illuminating failure: his conscious wearing of a mask by pretending to be Rhinehart. As the Invisible Man struggles throughout the rest of the novel to reconcile the possibility and the dangers of performance, the implications of what it means to assume a mask in this novel prove just as ambivalent as the consequences of invisibility. What becomes most interesting about the various performances in *Invisible Man*, however, is how Ellison incorporates these questions of knowledge and visibility within his textual aesthetic as his characters assume masks within nonlinear and "unrealistic" narratives, which again question narratives of surrogated whiteness thrust upon Ellison and recall the improvisational jazz beats that influenced him throughout his career.

What Ellison achieves with this portrayal of character and use of form is an aesthetic and thematic exploration of what we see with the Rinehart episode at the end of the novel: an understanding that invisibility entails reconciling both the power and the danger of performance. What this ambivalence suggests is that performance allows for a narrative of identity that exists beyond a dichotomy of black versus white that, early on, dominates the Invisible Man's interactions with society. Instead, it describes an improvised narrative of personal history and identity that allows for a creative sense of selfhood available to all willing to perform—but, even more important, see—it. As a result, the Invisible Man turns this knowledge toward his reader—on whom he projects his vision of invisibility—at the end of his narrative when he says, "Who knows but that, on the lower frequencies, I speak for you?" (581). Once again, the narrative of performance, in its constant reformulation, does not only involve the Invisible Man's experience. It is a narrative projected onto those who rendered him invisible to begin with.

Within the various performances of blackness in Ellison's novel, there is one underlying theme that compels them all: fear—an emotion that, as Freud notes, makes the past haunt us, creating the uncanny. Indeed, the Invisible Man is haunted by the images of blackness he has been taught to portray: his grandfather's advice to him before dying that the narrator should "'overcome 'em with yeses, undermine 'em with grins, agree 'em to death and destruction, let 'em swoller you till they vomit or bust wide open'" (16) while simultaneously trying to fulfill his educational possibilities as outlined by Booker T. Washington in his famous Atlanta Compromise speech. These conflicting performances of blackness dominate the novel's famous "Battle Royal" chapter when the narrator is taken to an event where he thinks he will deliver Washington's speech and receive a scholarship. Instead, he is forced to participate in a group fistfight and scramble for fake money on an electrified carpet. Throughout this scene, what constantly plagues Ellison's narrator is how he is unsure of how he is supposed to perform; thus when he hears a white man yell that he has his "money on the big boy," he thinks, "I was confused: Should I try to win against the voice out there? Would not this go against my speech, and was not this a moment for humility, for non-resistance? A blow to my head as I danced about sent my right eye popping like a jack-in-the-box and settled my dilemma" (25). It is no coincidence that the Invisible Man's struggle with his identity is bound up in questions of performance as he "dance[s] about" and questions whether he should satisfy his audience's desires (25). Basically, he must decide whether to act the part of the Booker T. Washington he has been taught or to fight the extinct image his white audience has of him. These dichotomous images of blackness haunt him throughout the novel.

As Ellison's narrator wins a scholarship to a black college, he again struggles to perform the "coded" image of blackness set out for him, but along the way he not only fails but encounters a character that is successful at performing his blackness for a white audience. Jim Trueblood represents performed blackness in *Invisible Man* in the sense that bound up in this image are the fears of transgressive sexuality and a misplaced sense of time as Trueblood describes accidentally committing incest as a result of a dream he has. When Trueblood recounts for Mr. Norton—a trustee for the narrator's college—the story of how this event occurred, it becomes clear that he is a physical embodiment for the act of surrogation as Roach describes it—that is, a search for "satisfactory alternates" to replace a "loss" in his past (2). He describes as much when, remembering a time in Mobile, he says, "All I could hear then would be that Mobile gal—name of Margaret—she be breathin' beside me, and maybe 'bout that time she'd say, 'Daddy, you still 'wake?' and then I'd grunt, 'Uhhuh' and drop on off—Gent-mens . . . I likes to recall them Mobile days" (56). The fact that Trueblood calls the men listening to him "Gent-mens" indicates that he is aware of his white audience in Mr. Norton, and as he describes remembering the "gal" he had in his youth, he hears his daughter, Matty Lou, similarly whispering "Daddy" in her sleep. Then Trueblood describes falling asleep himself and provides details of a dream that causes him, while sleeping, to penetrate his daughter. As he awakens to what he is actually doing, his response is teemed with ambivalence as he describes wanting to possess enough agency to stop his sin—even to the point of considering cutting off his own penis—and not wanting to move since, once he is no longer inside of her, the sin is complete and real. He thus describes "having to move *without* moving" (59) and says, "Everything was happenin' inside me like a fight was going on" (60). Afterward, his wife tries to shoot him, and as he yells, "Don't make no blood-sin on account of no dream-sin," she yells back, "Shut up, niggah, you done *fouled*" (62). Indeed, Trueblood has "*fouled*" in his search for a surrogate, and instead of this failure being a conscious act to remember, which occurs before he falls asleep, his act is an unconscious forgetting as his dream distorts the image he has of the past by allowing him to commit an atrocity in the present. Thus he never hears his daughter's screams or feels her clawing at him, and he even questions whether he has sinned since he was not aware of his actions.

Jim Trueblood's act of forgetting—the painful distortion of his happy memories—does indeed take shape as part of his personal narrative and identity within the public sphere and within the particular confines of performance, to the point that he is even paid for the show when Mr. Norton gives him $100 as charity just before leaving. Indeed, Trueblood, instead of being outcast from society, has been offered help from white people, who take up for him. Although this response seems unlikely, hearing Trueblood's story—or watching his performance—makes clear the attraction whites have for this man and his family's situation. As Christopher A. Shinn notes in his essay "Masquerade, Magic, and Carnival in Ralph Ellison's *Invisible Man*," Trueblood is attractive to his white audience "precisely because he tells his story as an implicit psycho-semantic dialogue with a wide range of white and black signifying systems, strategically dislodging 'white' fears and desire within 'black' images and projections" (245). He plays the part expected of him as a black male for both white and black audiences. The narrator even notices Norton's response when he looks at Trueblood "with something like envy and indignation" (51). Trueblood to some degree even realizes the benefits of his performance since he says in the same breath how some "big white folks" from the university came and "asked me lots 'bout my folks and the kids, and wrote it all down in a book. But best of all, suh, I got more work now than I ever did have before" (53). As a result, it makes sense that Trueblood never seems terribly rattled by his circumstances when he first meets Norton: he has discovered that playing a role of blackness for a white audience will win him rewards; thus he, not unlike Homer Plessy's transgression on a New Orleans train, performs what white culture sees as his "true blood," locating white fears of sexual impurity and temporal discontinuity within the coded realm of black experience.

The idea of performing socially imposed forms of blackness for profit appears repeatedly throughout Ellison's novel, and critics like Houston A. Baker Jr. have examined it as part of the author's ambivalent engagement with the African American minstrel tradition. Although it appears that Ellison rejects the implications of the minstrel mask, Baker suggests otherwise:

"Artful evasion and expressive illusion are equally traditional black expressive modes in interracial exchange in America. Such modes, the Trueblood episode implies, are the only resources that blacks at any level can barter for a semblance of decency and control in their lives" (90). What is interesting about this scene is the utter distaste the narrator has for Trueblood, saying at the beginning of his story, "To hell with his dream!" and at the end, "You no-good bastard! *You* get the hundred-dollar bill" (69). In these scenes, the narrator's hatred can only be described as that of the failed performer who watches his successful counterpart. The problem, however, is that the narrator does not even realize he has been performing an image of blackness as well. Hence, when he returns to school, he is expelled for his actions, but when he explains that he had no choice but to take Norton where he wanted to go, to tell him the truth about Trueblood, his teacher responds, "You're black and living in the South—did you forget how to lie?" (139). In other words, did you forget how to perform your blackness in an effort to deny this white man another, opposing image that we do not want him to see?

As Ellison's character is forced to abandon his identity as the eager college student and future credit to his race, he continues on a journey in which he is compelled to perform in terms of a group ideology instead of pursuing selfhood on his own terms. In this sense, the theme of minstrelsy and the use of the mask provide a lens to explore the discourse of invisibility and its relationship to performance in this novel. The fact that *Invisible Man* concerns an individual coming to realize his invisibility by understanding the role he plays in society begs the question of how a man is supposed to obtain selfhood if he is constantly compelled to perform for others. The answer is what emerges throughout the narrator's participation in the Brotherhood—a time in which the concerns of the individual are subsumed by the ambition of a group seeking social justice. The Invisible Man plays an important role in achieving these ambitions since he is "identified with the organization both by word and image in the press" (380). Indeed, it appears as if the narrator has found a surrogate for his grandfather's image of blackness, to the point that, at one moment, he actually sees his grandfather's face in one of its members, Brother Tarp (384). What the Invisible Man has found, however, is another audience for a performance of blackness, and abandoning that for personal belief—such as what Ras the Exhorter does—becomes an act of "plunging outside of history," or, even more important, retreating into personal interest and selfhood (377). Thus when he sees his friend Tod Clifton selling Sambo dolls in the street and, later, watches him die at the hands of the police, he sees Clifton as the minstrel performer, the petty individualist. He thinks to himself, "Why should a man deliberately plunge outside of history and peddle an obscenity, my mind went on abstractedly. Why should he choose to disarm himself, give up his voice and leave the only organization offering him a chance to 'define' himself?" (438). The use of the Sambo doll only further problematizes what the Invisible Man sees as seeking individual interests when he wonders why Clifton chooses this particularly racist image to make a living. Yet once again the image here becomes ambivalent since Ellison is not interested in rejecting all folk elements of African American culture, no matter how stereotypical. As Barry Shank points out in his essay "Bliss, or Blackface Sentiment," "His use of black American folklore strove to aestheticize the mask and thereby to render it susceptible to meaningful standards, to cultural evaluation instead of outright condemnation, to political as well as philosophical debate, and to place it at the center of a national culture" (55). Indeed, this very philosophical questioning occurs as the Invisible Man ponders the epistemological implications of "plunging outside of history": "All things, it is said, are duly recorded—all things of importance, that is. But not quite, for actually it is only the known, the seen, the heard and only those events that the recorder regards as important that are put down, those lies his keeper keep their power by. But the cop would be Clifton's historian, his judge, his witness, and his executioner, and I was the only brother in the watching crowd. And I, the only witness for the defense, knew neither the extent of his guilt nor the nature of his crime. Where were the historians today? And how would they put it down?" (439). Here the Invisible Man begins to realize his participation in the process of surrogation when, like Trueblood, he realizes his unconscious sin, his doomed search for a surrogate, and admits, "I'd been so fascinated by the motion that I'd forgotten to measure what it was bringing forth. I'd been asleep, dreaming" (444). Like Trueblood, he had been trying to move without moving; meanwhile he was remembering his grandfather by forgetting what he had said, and, even more important, he had been asleep and blindly performing the whole time.

Tod Clifton's death marks the moment when the Invisible Man begins to understand his invisibility. Indeed, it seems as if he becomes committed to acts of public forgetting and the distortion of identity as he arranges a large public funeral for Clifton, where he converts him into a martyr. Meanwhile, he is chastised by Brotherhood leader Jack for this act of defiance as it is revealed that Jack has a glass eye. As Jack slams it on the table, smashing it in the name of sacrifice and discipline, the Invisible Man thinks, "So that is the meaning of discipline, I thought, sacrifice . . . yes, and blindness; he doesn't see me. He doesn't even see me" (475). As he realizes that practically none of the members of the Brotherhood see him—an integrated self—he discovers he cannot go back to performing for them and says, "Some of me, too, had died with Tod Clifton." Just as his grandfather's death leaves him searching for a new conception of blackness to follow, Tod's death and the response to his funeral find him reconciling the ambivalent view of blackness both these characters from his past represent: one that promotes personal agency and performance but does so through stereotypical and offensive views of blackness—in other words, one that grins from the mask of the Sambo doll but still "undermine[s] 'em with yeses."

The act of understanding this ambivalent performance of blackness has serious implications when the narrator assumes the mask of Rinehart near the novel's end. Almost all the Invisible Man's experiences lead up to this point of actively and consciously participating in surrogation, especially when considering Rinehart "the rascal" as an allegorical embodiment of the trickster figure within African American folklore. Once again the Invisible Man has lost the identity imposed upon him by the Brotherhood as he realizes, in conjunction with Tod Clifton's death, that such an identity is a performance to begin with. By becoming Rinehart, the Invisible Man "plunges outside of history" by taking on a stereotype-based but still subversive trickster identity (438) and, through this process, engages in an act of remembering the various forms of blackness that he has been taught and that he himself performed over the years. What is most interesting about this moment, however, is that the Invisible Man does not question his identity as Rinehart, but his knowledge of this figure and all of his characteristics as he says, "Can it be, I thought, can it actually be? And I knew that it was. I had heard it before but I'd never come so close. . . . What is real anyway? But how could I doubt it? [Rinehart] was a broad man, a man of parts who got around. Rinehart the rounder. It was true as I was true. His world was possibility and he knew it. He was years ahead of me and I was a fool. I must have been crazy and blind. The world in which we lived was without boundaries. A vast seething, hot world of fluidity, and Rine the rascal was at home. Perhaps *only* Rine the rascal was at home in it" (498). As the Invisible Man begins to understand the "possibility" and world "without boundaries" that Rinehart represents, he realizes the power of performance and sees it to be as "true as I was true." Until this point, he had been performing and even searching for a surrogate, but had never "come so close" to understanding it. The implications of this performance, furthermore, lead him to understand his own invisibility when he becomes cognizant of the fact that "*only* Rine the rascal was at home" in this new world of active, and open-eyed, performance.

While it appears the Invisible Man feels an immense sense of self and security in his new knowledge, Roach demonstrates that the search for a surrogate inevitably fails because one can never replace something lost. Thus the Invisible Man experiences the ambivalence that Roach points to as integral to surrogation. The Invisible Man identifies these emotions and again articulates them in terms of what he "knows" when he says, "I was both depressed and fascinated. I wanted to know Rinehart and yet, I thought, I'm upset because I know I don't have to know him, that simply becoming aware of his existence, being mistaken for him, is enough to convince me that Rinehart is real. It couldn't be, but it is. And it can be, is, simply because it's unknown" (498). While the narrator is entranced by the power of performance, what upsets him about Rinehart is that knowledge is not necessary for understanding this figure. He does not have to be "known" or understood to exist; there is no work involved, there is nothing behind the mask. Instead of seeking an identity based on self-knowledge, he has sought one based on nothing, on a lack of knowledge.

The result of this realization is that the Invisible Man feels compelled to ask, as he thinks of Clifton and Jack, "How much was really known about either of them? How much was known about me? Who from my old life had challenged me?" (499). In other words, he begins to question what existed behind their masks and what composed his own performance. Considering that the Invisible Man has only just come to see his mask, one can understand how these questions arise. Thus the Invisible Man's response is to wholeheartedly embrace performance, to follow his grandfather's advice of performing in an act of self-preservation. Incidentally, this act of conscious performance becomes an act of remembering (itself a performed entity) as he thinks of past humiliations: "I began to accept my past and, as I accepted it, I felt memories welling up within me. It was as though I'd learned suddenly to look around corners; images of past humiliations flickered through my head and I saw that they were more than separate experiences. They were me; they defined me" (508). By seeking selfhood through his own experience and not predefined conceptions of blackness, the Invisible Man tries to reconcile the dizzying power of the mask by realizing that he had been a resource, a suitable receptacle for various black identities. He says, "I had switched from the arrogant absurdity of Norton and Emerson to that of Jack and the Brotherhood, and it all came out the same—except now I recognize my invisibility" (508). Now that he recognizes his invisibility, he can, in his mind, effectively render the mask because he is aware it always existed. Returning to the theme of minstrelsy in this novel, critics like Barry Shank see the consequences of Rinehart as Ellison's own comment on the use of the minstrel mask. Shank notes:

> The crime of minstrelsy for Ellison was not the enactment of this trickster figure. It was not the protean liquidity of identity that followed from donning the mask. . . . Behind that mask could stand humans of the utmost sensitivity, janitors who were opera fans as well as recent European immigrants uncertain of their identity as white Americans. Ellison understood that the mask might not be a hindrance to but a means of engaging their deepest sensibilities. The institutional crimes of minstrelsy were a matter of historical record, but the techniques of the mask and perhaps even something at the paradoxical imitative base of minstrelsy could be redeemed. (58)

Although the Invisible Man realizes the possibility of performance, he does not effectively redeem the mask since he has not, to use Clifton's terms, "plunged outside of history." In other words, he consciously wears a mask but allows himself to remain invisible. As a result, he participates in a white woman's rape-fantasy, again performing a racialized and transgressive sexuality, and allows himself to be a pawn in inciting a race riot. He acknowledges, "By pretending to agree I *had* agreed" (553), but what he does not yet realize is that he still performs under the direction of his grandfather's advice. He has not recrafted the mask of Rinehart, he has simply put on the "grinning" mask his grandfather left him. Thus throughout these scenes, he has remained invisible.

What the Invisible Man must accept with the mask is not linear history, but its discontinuities, its distortions, reflected in his own disjointed experiences, including the ones that have nothing to do with "history." Thus when he falls in the hole, it is no coincidence that what he finds to burn as he tries to light his way out are the symbols of black identity that have been thrust upon him: his diploma, the remnants of the Sambo doll, the piece of paper on which Jack wrote his Brotherhood name, and an anonymous letter warning him when he had become too powerful in the Brotherhood (568). As he realizes that the handwriting on the letter and Jack's on the slip of paper are the same, he says, "That he, or anyone at that late date, could have named me and set me running with the one and the same stroke with the pen was too much" (568). This idea of being "set running" returns the reader to the

letter in the narrator's dream early in the novel that said, "Keep this nigger boy running." As he burns these images of blackness, he finally begins
to understand that they, all in one stroke, have kept him running for ages.
It is not surprising, therefore, that upon realizing his invisibility, the Invisible Man decides to assume the pen. As Jim Neighbors points outs, "Once
his invisibility is made visible, a preeminent and self-reliant self lifts out of
its confusing history in a *parousia* of self-knowledge and resolves to act or
write—conflated by this logic into the same thing—a declaration of coherent identity" (227). In other words, the narrator's sense of self arises from an
act of knowledge. This idea becomes apparent in the novel's epilogue when
he recounts what he has learned during his absence from society: "Until
some gang succeeds in putting the world in a strait jacket, its definition is
possibility. Step outside the narrow borders of what men call reality and you
step into chaos—ask Rinehart, he's a master of it—or imagination. That too
I've learned in the cellar, and not by deadening my sense of perception; I'm
invisible, not blind" (576). At this point the Invisible Man finally begins to
understand the mask's potential to allow oneself to "plunge outside of history," and outside of conformity, by changing one's vision of (and thus how
one is seen by) the world. The narrator celebrates this possibility when he
says, "Whence all this passion toward conformity anyway—diversity is the
word. Let man keep his many parts and you'll have no tyrant states" (577).
It is with this treatise of possibility and diversity that the Invisible Man can
venture back into society—as an individual and even potentially as a performer. He will just perform his own identity instead of any preconceived
notion of blackness.

As the Invisible Man arrives at self-knowledge and decides to reenter society, he is clear that his discovery of the connection between performance
and invisibility is ambivalent, and, not surprisingly, he articulates it using
the image of musical performance. He struggles between being able to wear
the mask of Rinehart and embrace possibility without using it to conform to
a static ideology. Although he admits he must emerge, he says, "There's still
a conflict within me. With Louis Armstrong one half of me says, 'Open the
window and let the foul air out,' while the other says, 'It was good green corn
before the harvest.' Of course Louis was kidding, *he* wouldn't have thrown
the old Bad Air out, because it would have broken up the music and the
dance, when it was the good music that came from the bell of old Bad Air's
horn that counted. Old Bad Air is still around with his music and his danc-
ing and his diversity, and I'll be up and around with mine" (581). Poignantly,
in these final moments the Invisible Man identifies with a performer. As he

accepts the "foul air" and rejects the nostalgia that "the good green corn" represents, the narrator understands the potential to embrace the bad air and make good music out of it. Such improvisation, in his mind, creates diversity, and the Invisible Man wants it for himself.

This final moment points to an emphasis on musical performance that has both aesthetic and thematic implications in the novel. Ellison's affinity for jazz is well documented in critical treatments of his work. It is no coincidence, furthermore, that Ellison's novel is formally characterized by its episodic nature—to the point that the Invisible Man's desire to tell his story becomes the will to create an improvised personal history. He says as much in the prologue when, after quoting Louis Armstrong's "What Did I Do to Be So Black and Blue?," he says, "Could this compulsion to put invisibility down in black and white be thus an urge to make music of invisibility?" (13–14). Indeed, the individuality of improvisation dominates this novel as the Invisible Man asks, specifically about himself, "But what did *I* do to be so black and blue? Bear with me" (14). The reader is asked to bear with him since his narrative is one that does not conform to a history of racial identity; it will keep its audience constantly guessing. As Andrew Radford says in his article "The Invisible Music of Ralph Ellison," "For Ellison jazz is poetic, elliptical, circular, and paradoxical" (44); thus constructing a narrative around this aesthetic proves as dizzying as assuming the mask of Rinehart. Radford suggests as much when he says, "The protagonist discovers how survival is dependent upon the improvised performance of identity—based upon, though not exactly imitating, Rinehart's tactics. For Ellison the essence of improvisation lies in the energy released by the pure act of invention in process. And it is this potency that, in the epilogue, keeps Invisible Man watchful and alert, cannily deferring any final judgment" (62). In addition, it is no coincidence that Ellison was particularly attracted to Louis Armstrong in articulating his aesthetic of performance since—both during Ellison's time as well as today—Armstrong has been criticized for pandering to white tastes, basically, for performing his own kind of minstrel show. Yet seeing Ellison's treatment of the minstrel makes his attraction to Armstrong all the more poignant since, again to quote Radford, "[Armstrong's] performances mocked the whole sordid panorama of American race relations. He extracted from brutal experience a near-tragic, near-comic lyricism. . . . Armstrong belongs to Invisible Man's cultural repertoire and to his process of unmasking the repression that masquerades as freedom" (50). In other words, like Rinehart, Armstrong's performances demonstrate the ability to manipulate discourse in an effort to plunge outside of history, namely, to illustrate the chaos and discontinuity that entail individual experience.

The very act of constructing an improvised, personal narrative demonstrates to the reader the capabilities—and the risks—of performance. Thus in asking what did *"I"* do to be so black and blue (14), the Invisible Man, "on the lower frequencies," speaks for "you" (581). In addition, it seems safe to assert that inasmuch as invisibility entails a public act of forgetting and distorting identity, the performance of this improvised narrative is a constructive act of memory. In addition, the act of performing in an effort to blur and forget the distortions and discontinuities of the past only further reveals these elements of the past since surrogates are doomed to failure. Roach makes this point clear at the end of his study, furthermore, when, like the Invisible Man, he embraces diversity and chaos: "Genealogists resist histories that attribute purity of origin to any performance. They have to take into account 'he give and take of joint transmissions, posted in the past, arriving in the present, delivered by living messengers, speaking in tongues not entirely their own. Orature is an art of listening as well as speaking; improvisation is an art of collective memory as well as invention; repetition is an art of re-creation as well as restoration. Texts may obscure what performances tend to reveal" (286). It is this very kind of performance, furthermore, that Ellison delineates and articulates in his novel. It contains elements of the past (his grandfather's advice), is delivered by a messenger in the present (Louis Armstrong), and speaks in a voice and language that are foreign (those of Rinehart). Yet through it all, it creates a discourse of improvisation that trumps any static discourse of race or racial identity. Instead, it is nondiscursive, exists on the "lower frequency," and thus speaks for us all.

While Ellison's Invisible Man reflects various images of blackness across modernity, his character in many ways reflects the milieu of modernist characters like Joyce's Leopold Bloom and Faulkner's Quentin Compson. This figure not only inspired Luis Martín-Santos's main character, Pedro, in *Tiempo de silencio*, but the indeterminacy of his identity informs Martín-Santos's conception of race in relation to nationalist ideology during the Francoist period. Among the countless studies of this novel, scholars are quick to point out how Martín-Santos criticizes the essentialist, and racial, myths of Spanish from the likes of Ortega. Yet only Jo Labanyi, in her book *Myth and History in the Contemporary Spanish Novel* (1989), links the essential "myth" to biological conceptions of race, pointing out how Spanish conceptions of racial purity date back to the Inquisition. Thus Labanyi argues,

"The biological and botanical analogies with which the 1898 writers and Ortega adorned their racial theories are turned upside down in the novel to show that Spain's backwardness is not naturally determined, but is the result of man-made conditions that have led to the abandonment of civilization for nature" (*Myth and History* 64). Indeed, as Pedro the young scientist studies a specific strain of cancer found in rats, he finds hope in the fact that the cancer may not be hereditary, and fated by biology, but instead brought on by a virus, which doctors could use to develop a vaccine. It is Pedro's effort to study these rats and the biological source of their illness that drives what I identify as his various performances in the novel. Neither a member of the upper class like his friend Matías nor a poor man living in the *chabolas* ("shacks") outside of Madrid, Pedro finds himself constantly navigating people's expectations of his class and gender just as he navigates the city streets. At every turn he seems to fail in some way, and these failures to perform accurately cause him to lose everything he knows, thus propelling him to assume a new role. In the end, he flees Madrid not in escapism, but, like the Invisible Man, into a realm of unconsciousness in which embracing performativity lets him understand it and thus free to determine how it will shape his identity.

Given the role that biology played in the conceptualization of Spanish purity, it seems logical that Martín-Santos, as a doctor and psychiatrist, took an interest in race as a determining factor in identity. Yet Martin-Santos's interest in configurations of racial identity stemmed from the author's interest in William Faulkner, particularly his novel *Light in August* in which a young man's ambiguous racial identity causes a personal crisis for him but also cultural crisis in the small Southern town of Jefferson (Townsend 106). Martin-Santos's interest in this type of blurred identity appears in *Tiempo de silencio* when Pedro, drinking in a café with various writers and artists, declares the importance of the American novel, praising its qualities: "Olas que vienen y van. Mareas de espíritu. Pepinvidálides de Egipto. Hay situaciones en que el atolladero es total. Evidentemente, sí, evidentemente. Hay que leer el Ulysses. Toda la novela americana ha salido de ahí, del Ulysses y la Guerra civil. Profundo Sur. Ya se sabe. La novela Americana es superior, influye sobre Europa. Se origina allí, allí precisamente" ["Waves that come and go. Spiritual dizziness. Pepinvidálides from Egypt. There are situations in which the impasse is total. Evidently, yes, evidently. One has to read *Ulysses*. All American novels have come from it, from *Ulysses* and the Civil War. The Deep South. You already know. The American novel is better, it influences all Europe. It comes from there, from there precisely"] (79). While many have pointed to (and at times down-played) the role Joyce's novel played on Martín-Santos's aesthetic, one can also not deny Faulkner's influence, which had been ubiquitous in Spain (and Latin America) since the translation of *Sanctuary* just before the Civil War. Yet in terms of novelistic form, what Martín-Santos employs specifi-cally is the "dizziness of spirit" that characters like Joe Christmas feel as they are suspended between images of "pure" and "impure" racial, and thereby national, identity. For Pedro, his own role in the performance of racial identity only becomes clear as he remains at an "impasse" between the world of high class and culture and the shanty underworld because of his failure to perform accurately in either.

Like the Invisible Man, Pedro's quest to perform well begins with his education and a desire to please his supervisor at the lab. When the mice he is investigating die, he follows his friend Amador to the shantytown where a man, Muecas, has been successful at breeding the mice by placing them under his daughters' breasts for warmth. Pedro's trip to the shantytown, like the Invisible Man's trip with Mr. Norton to the countryside, both fascinates and astonishes Pedro. Clearly mocking early twentieth-century ideas of the strength of the Castilian race, Martín-Santos shows a dazzled Pedro, who comments, "¡De qué maravilloso modo allí quedaba patente la capacidad para la improvisación y la original fuerza constructiva del hombre ibero!" ["What a marvelous method lay clearly there of the capacity for improvi-sation and original constructive force of the Iberian man!"] (50). Yet after Pedro meets Muecas and the narrator describes the mice reproducing in a room in cages where he and his daughters sleep, the novel's perspective changes. Like the Invisible Man who sees Trueblood's black performance for white tastes and resents it, the narrator intimates that Muecas's success is not biologically related to the strength of the "Iberian" race, but of his own opportunism. Martín-Santos mocks this idea further as he declares that Muecas's condition in the *chabolas* cannot be attributed to the "accidente (tan confortablemente accidental) del color de la piel y de las proporciones relativas entre la fibra muscular y la tendinosa de la pantorrilla, correspon-diente a individuos de dos razas biológicamente bien definidas" ["accident (so comfortably accidental) of skin color and of the relative proportions of the muscle fiber and the leg tendons, corresponding to individual of two biologically well-defined races"] (69). Thus the narrator calls Muecas a "príncipe negro y dignitario" ["Negro prince and dignitary"] whose status in the world is related not to his skin color but to his royal and political status. In fact, he shows Muecas as inventing a myth in which he and his opportunistic counterparts are lucky to have black skin that differs, relaying their own "black science" to the white man. The bold move that Martín-Santos makes in linking opportunism to race in this scene becomes the means by which he deconstructs conceptions of race and instead links a person's condition and identity to class and his or her environment. It is how he or she performs in that environment—much like Pedro's mice, which can only reproduce themselves in warm comfort—that determines fate.

Pedro's encounter with Muecas unfolds a chain of events where he wanders through Madrid experimenting with identities that he has never assumed: dashing playboy/intellectual who drinks in cafés and visits brothels with his friend Matías, and coy lover who drunkenly seduces the young granddaughter of his boardinghouse's matron. As all of these events occur in one night, Pedro finds himself hungover and disoriented, worn out by the consequences of a performativity that does not suit him and leads to a failure to act that drives the action for the rest of the novel: the death of Muecas's daughter, Florita, after a botched abortion to rid her of her father's child. What is most interesting about this scene is that, until this moment, Pedro has managed to keep up appearances in cafés and consummate his relationship with Dorita. However, Pedro realizes his performativity with Florita's death, much like the Invisible Man does with Tod Clifton's death. Meanwhile, he becomes even more aware of his posturings as he sees how Matías drags him along in his plans, that Dorita's "seduction" is a plan by her mother and grandmother to marry the girl well, and that Florita's death was more or less certain before he ever arrived. Yet what is most important about this scene is that Florita, the "little flower," becomes the vessel by which both Muecas's performance of success and Pedro's security in his medical training fail both characters. Again, the failure for Pedro is linked not just to biology as he performs a uterine scrape on an almost-dead girl, but to his own performance when he thinks to himself afterward, "La segunda vez lo haré mejor" ["The second time I'll do it better"] (131). In trying to scrape clean the site of Muecas's sin, Pedro attempts to return Florita to a "natural" state—to recover her lost "flower." What Pedro does not realize is that no such primal state ever existed to be soiled by the taboo of incest. What Florita's body becomes then is not a natural vessel soiled by sin and scraped clean, but a liminal space that shows how people reproduce images of purity onto itself. This state is only further represented in the novel as Pedro's forgetting to sign the death certificate puts Florita's body in limbo, buried vertically, later exhumed for an autopsy, and held until the circumstances surrounding her death can be solved.

Pedro's failure to sign the certificate for Florita's death also suspends him between the role he thinks he has in her death and what he actually did, all of which becomes compounded by the fact that Pedro is put in prison for killing her. Meanwhile, this loss, as Labanyi shows, begins a cycle for a return to maternal origins for the rest of the novel as Pedro takes refuge in a brothel, whose mistress, Doña Luisa, embraces and protects him (*Myth and History* 70). Labanyi argues, "Even in prison Pedro attempts to turn his forced passivity into a 'Return to the cradle. To a womb' (219). When he claims he is more free in prison than in the outside world, he is confusing freedom with the liberation from responsibility that is the other side of dependence" (*Myth and History* 70). Playing the role of murderer, Pedro finds comfort in wearing this mask as it has the power to assuage his guilt. Like the Invisible Man donning the mask of Rinehart, Pedro listens to the inspector weave a narrative of suppositions that incriminate him and decides to accept them, saying, "Los hombres deben afrontar las consecuencias de sus actos. El castigo es el más perfecto consuelo para la culpa y su único posible remedio y corolario. Gracias al castigo el equilibrio se restablecería en este mundo poco comprensible donde él había estado dando saltos de títere con la cabeza de humo mentiroso" ["Men should face the consequences of their actions. Punishment is the perfect consoler for guilt as well as its only possible remedy and corollary. Thanks to punishment, equilibrium would reestablish itself in this hardly understandable world where he had been jumping like a puppet with a head of lying smoke"] (237). It is the moment that Pedro decides to be a "puppet" that he realizes his performativity up to that point and accepts its consequences. Thus Pedro's realization of his performance means that the loss of biological essentialism must be replaced by something else. So, like the Invisible Man, he chooses to accept performativity as the only thing essential and willed by nature and is willing to suffer the consequences of that fact.

Although Pedro seems content to wear the mask of murderer, the very feminine, "natural" forces he seeks are those that deny him the mask when Florita's mother proclaims his innocence, releasing him from jail. As he departs, however, he still returns to feminine protection, running into Dorita's arms and playing the role of dutiful fiancé. Thus faced with the loss of Florita, he replaces that loss with another mask: loyal lover to a pretty, sweet young woman. Martín-Santos highlights this fact when the final scene has Pedro taking his mother-in-law and Dorita to the theater and, afterward, to an amusement park. Instead of a light and happy tone, the scene is filled with dark, uncanny posturings as Dorita begs Pedro to hammer the catapult to show his strength, but he can barely hit it. Despite the fact that Pedro seems content to accept his fate, he is clearly not thrilled with the role he plays. Yet like the Invisible Man, Pedro discovers that the costs of performativity are high when Cartucho, a violent street thief who claimed Florita as his own, stabs and kills Dorita as revenge for believing that Pedro impregnated Florita and botched her abortion. Pedro is not present for the murder, nor does he see Dorita's assassin, but as the narrator points out, Pedro discovers upon seeing her body that vengeance proves that "no hay plazo que no se cumpla ni deuda que no se pague" ["there is no deadline that is not met nor any debt that is not paid"] (276). As Pedro copes with the loss of Florita and Dorita, there seems to be an emphasis on fate as the controlling factor in his life, which he has stoically chosen to accept. Yet one realizes that Pedro is paying for sins that are not his—instead, he is suffering the consequences of playing the roles of saving doctor and dutiful fiancé when he is not capable of fulfilling those roles. In other words, essential ideas of masculinity, class, and biology haunt this character throughout the novel as he fails to live up to any of their implications; thus Dorita becomes an uncanny memory of previous failures that are literally transposed onto her body.

This failure, furthermore, deconstructs the historical myth of a racially determined national identity in the novel as biological determiners determine nothing and instead are subsumed by the same performative myth-making that goes on throughout the novel. Pedro himself finally begins to realize this fact when he realizes his creation of a surrogate femininity—the eternal mother and source of life—with Dorita following Florita's death. He says, "Claro está que ella está igual que la otra también. Por qué será, cómo será que yo ahora no sepa distinguir entre la una y la otra muertas, puestas una encima de otra en el mismo agujero: también a ésta autopsia. ¿Qué querrán saber? Tanta autopsia; para qué, si no ven nada. No saben para qué las abren: un mito, una superstición, una recolección de cadáveres, creen que tiene una virtud dentro, animistas, están buscando un secreto y en cambio no dejan que busquemos los que podíamos encontrar algo" ["Clearly she's the same as the other one too. Why can it be, how can it be that I don't know how to distinguish between the two dead women, put one on top of the other in the same hole: also this autopsy. What could they possibly discover? So much autopsy; for what, if they don't see anything. They don't know why they open them: a myth, a superstition, a recollection of cadavers, they believe that they have virtue inside, animists, they are looking for a secret and, in turn, they don't let those of us look who just may find something"] (278). Realizing that there is no eternal knowledge to be found by opening the female body, Pedro retreats to the countryside to become a rural physician. While it seems as if he is escaping into another performance, his retreat is instead like the Invisible Man's, and, this time, he accepts performativity open-eyed as he feels "vacío, porque me han pasado una gamuza y me han limpiado las vísceras por dentro, empapando bien y me han puesto en remojo, colgando de un hilo en una especie de museo anatómico de vivos para que perciba bien las cualidades empireumáticas e higiénicas, desecadoras y esterilizadoras, atrabiliagenésicas y justicieras del hombre de la meseta" ["empty, because they have passed me through a sieve and have cleaned my insides out, soaking me well and placing me in a jar, suspended by a thread in a kind of anatomical museum of the living so that one can well observe the empyreumatic, hygienic, evaporating, steril-izing, splenetic, and righteous qualities of a man of the meseta"] (280). As he goes to the Castilian countryside, his performativity becomes linked to his racial identity as he knows his flesh will be dried out and he will allow himself to be castrated without cries of protest or pain. While Pedro accepts performativity, he no longer links it to his body, to his racial identity, as he accepts the disintegration of his flesh and, more important, the removal of his reproductive abilities. As Pedro begins to imagine his new life, he chas-tises himself for thinking at all (285), realizing that he has no knowledge and plunging into unconsciousness as the only means of understanding his place in the world.

Again like Ellison's Invisible Man, at the end of the novel Pedro ends exactly where he started—at Madrid's Príncipe Pío train station—and he has plunged outside of history as a means of understanding the relationship between performativity and racial and national identity. Pedro proclaims that he would enjoy being part of a primitive "negro" tribe so that he could dance himself to ecstasy, but declares, "Pero no somos negros, no somos negros, los negros saltan, ríen, gritan, y votan para elegir a sus represent-antes en la ONU" ["But we are not negroes, we are not negroes, negroes jump, laugh, shout, and vote to elect their representatives to the UN"] (283). Instead, Pedro declares that his is a time of silence (283) in which the per-formance of a mythic racial identity has dried up the collective imagination and political sovereignty—something available to his black counterparts. While I do not agree with Labanyi's reading of the novel's end as Pedro's unheroic acceptance of a facile existence and his determination to remain blind to unpleasant truths (*Myth and History* 78), I do agree with how she regards the two functions of silence in the novel, which exist in how "the characters use language to silence truth. [And the] narrator, by making the reader aware that meaning must be sought in what the words do not say, turns silence into a critical instrument" (87). Pedro himself sees the possibility of silence—and performativity—being critical tools when, in the novel's final moment, he sees the palace and monastery, El Escorial, on the landscape. The project of Felipe II, the sixteenth-century king who made Madrid Spain's capital and greatly strengthened the power of the Inquisition, the monastery was built in honor of St. Lawrence, whom Pedro compares to himself. Like the saint who was roasted over the coals, Pedro admires that the saint "era un macho, no gritaba, no gritaba, estaba en silencio mientras lo tostaban torquemadas paganos, estaba en silencio y sólo dijo—la historia sólo recuerda que dijo—dame la vuelta que por este lado ya estoy tostado . . . y el verdugo le dio la vuelta por una simple cuestión de simetría" ["was a man, he did not shout, he did not cry, he was in silence while the pagans tortured him, he was silent and only said—history only remembers that he said—'turn me over as I'm done on this side'. . . and the executioner turned him over as a simple question of symmetry"] (286). Much like the Invisible Man's admiration of Louis Armstrong—who appears to play to white tastes while refuting them—Pedro sees in San Lorenzo the subversive possibility of performance and the degree to which silence and performance resist myths of essential identity. As Pedro looks at the monastery that represents the place where Spanish national authenticity was perhaps most constructed, he realizes he can do nothing about the building. It does not move, but what he can do is embrace the supposed actions of St. Lawrence because, as Pedro tells us, history can pretend to remember what he said, but only his performance recalls to us what was left to silence.

The themes of darkness and silence in the novel are augmented by the disjointed narrative in which Pedro's voice is intermingled with that of an omniscient narrator that relays the perspective of other characters. The result is that one overarching voice never dominates the novel, and this fragmented narrative relays Pedro's own fragmentation, what he calls his drying up or "roasting" like St. Lawrence, at the end of the novel. Thus as Labanyi notes, Martín-Santos creates an "ironic novel—and an anti-mythical novel—in that it describes a world where there are no certainties but only ambiguities, for truth resides in silence and night" (*Myth and History* 89). Indeed, the novel's narrator focuses on ambiguities at length in the novel, and nowhere is this more clear than when he describes bullfighting. As the narrator points out that the sport was popularized and institutionalized at the moment when Spain's imperial splendor was coming to an end, he shows "que el acontecimiento más importante de los años que siguieron a la gran catástrofe fue esa polarización de odio contra un solo hombre y que ese odio y divinización ambivalentes se conjuraron cuantos revanchismos irredentos anidaban en el corazón de unos y de otros no parece dudoso" ["that the most important happening of the years that followed the great catastrophe was this polarization of hatred against one single man and that this ambivalent hatred and divinization combined together to countless amounts of unredeemed vengeance that nested in the heart did not seem doubtful"] (218). The fact that Martín-Santos uses bullfighting as the example of performative mythmaking of history speaks to how those myths lend themselves to narratives of essential identity and blood—the strong, brave matador faces the primal animal in the ring (as he allegedly has done for centuries) and is willing to shed his Castilian blood for the honor of fighting the bull in front of the masses. It was this essential quality of the bullfight that attracted Hemingway, hence the reason he gives it a primal, sexual allure in *The Sun Also Rises*.

Martín-Santos's description of the bullfight, however, returns us to Richard Wright's *Pagan Spain*. Although Wright's encounter with the bullfight is different, he is no less fascinated by the spectacle, declaring early on that the matador "in his bright suit of lights was a kind of lay priest offering up mass for the thirty thousand guilty penitents, I sighed, realizing that, in Spain, all things were Spanish" (114). Following his first fight, Wright seems to abandon his essentialism slightly, observing the young matador, "I had the feeling that the boy did not quite believe in the value of what he had done, or maybe did not thoroughly understand it, and harbored some rejection or doubt about the Niagara of applause that deafened his ears. Anyway, he seemed detached from, and consciously outside of, it all" (132). Here, and throughout his account, we see Wright walking his "mental tightrope" of accepting what is "Spanish" and remaining outside of it. Indeed, the feeling he observes in the young bullfighter encompasses the ambivalent hatred and divinity projected onto the bullfighter, and Wright, in many ways, understands the disconcertedness that such double-consciousness entails. The bullfighter thus represents the liminal space between self and other that characterizes the inevitable "failure" of concrete racial identity. We want the young hero to kill the bull, but we also relish the goring (as evidenced by the countless images of such events on television in Spain when they occur). The only recourse for the bullfighter—like all the characters in this chapter—is to embrace the performativity, to continue to wear the suit of lights and posture for the crowd. The cost of that acceptance is no doubt high—the danger of the bullring becomes the perfect metaphor for that sacrifice—and it invariably contains loss of life. But it is in that moment before the fighter kills the bull, the moment where the man himself can still be killed, that all the possibility of that performativity lay before the fighter as well as his audience, and it is that possibility that embodies, and allows us to see simultaneously, the myths and realities of how modern nations shape even the bloody, biological identity of the individual.

Chapter 5

BEING "BAD" AND OBJECTIFIED WOMANHOOD

Transgressive Femininity in Spain and the South

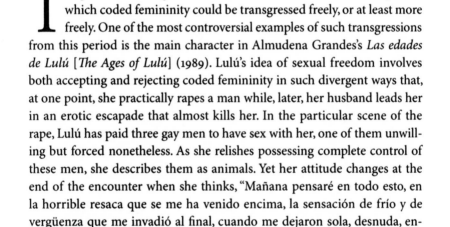

The period following the death of Francisco Franco created a space in which coded femininity could be transgressed freely, or at least more freely. One of the most controversial examples of such transgressions from this period is the main character in Almudena Grandes's *Las edades de Lulú* [*The Ages of Lulú*] (1989). Lulú's idea of sexual freedom involves both accepting and rejecting coded femininity in such divergent ways that, at one point, she practically rapes a man while, later, her husband leads her in an erotic escapade that almost kills her. In the particular scene of the rape, Lulú has paid three gay men to have sex with her, one of them unwilling but forced nonetheless. As she relishes possessing complete control of these men, she describes them as animals. Yet her attitude changes at the end of the encounter when she thinks, "Mañana pensaré en todo esto, en la horrible resaca que se me ha venido encima, la sensación de frío y de vergüenza que me invadió al final, cuando me dejaron sola, desnuda, encima de la mesa, y sólo podía pensar en que tenía que pagarles" ["I'll think about all of this tomorrow, about the horrible hangover that came over me, the sensation of cold and embarrassment that invaded me in the end, when they left me alone naked, on the table, and all that I could think was that I had to pay them"] (178). In many ways, what Lulú faces the next morning is not the horror of her badness per se, but its contrast to the "good" version of her that exists in the light of day. The vow to "think about it tomorrow" suggests erasure of memory that not only seeks to dispel the horror, but that ironically recalls one of the most famous Southern "bad" women of the twentieth century.

While no doubt a very different figure, *Gone with the Wind's* Scarlett O'Hara, like Lulú, shows how national exceptionality is bound up in gender roles as she embodies sexual power attributed specifically to the Southern belle while also being her family's protector and savior during the Civil War. If one were to examine images of femininity over the course of the twentieth century, some of the most pervasive images no doubt come from Spain and the South: the devout, purely Castilian mother dominated Spanish Nationalist ideology, and the image of the white, pure belle, while a nineteenth-century image, also pervaded Jim Crow conceptions of Southern femininity. Yet though disparate in most ways, characters like Lulú and Scarlett still show how ideas of female "goodness" and "badness" become performatives that must be proven by actions that these characters can never achieve. Thus throughout both Margaret Mitchell's and Grandes's novels, these women are both innocent virgin and evil seductress, mother and child (both their husbands infantilize them), victim and violent aggressor. My particular interest in female "badness" exists in the fact that, in Spain and the South, it became an uncanny form that haunted these cultures with the possibility for their own "badness," particularly during Francoism and Jim Crow. Even more, "bad" femininity can only exist as a transgression of "good" femininity; thus each performance is reliant upon the other—just as the South exists only in contrast to the North or Spain in opposition to Europe. It is playing the role of the "bad" woman, furthermore, that exposes the discursive power of the "good" woman since the performance of "badness" is necessary to realize that "goodness" is also a construction. That realization causes the fears represented by the "bad" woman to be let go, thus creating an environment in which a populace, particularly a population of women, can move away from coded gender roles, and with it, coded nationality.

Gender as a performed entity—that is, "constituting the identity of what it is purported to be" (Butler, *Gender Trouble* 24)—is a well-known assertion of Judith Butler, whose *Gender Trouble: Feminism and the Subversion of Identity* (1990) and *Bodies That Matter: On the Discursive Limits of "Sex"* (1993) inform most scholarship on performance and gender studies. Butler's reliance on speech-act theory and psychoanalysis in relation to performativity returns us to the dividing line within performance studies: following the Butlerian line or focusing on theater and ritual. Even within Butler's model, the two are not completely amiss, as she points to the importance of iterability, or the continual repetitive nature, of performance, thus linking it to ritual, albeit in a different way than Roach (*Bodies That Matter* 95). Meanwhile, in *Gender Trouble*, she cites Foucault's assertion that juridical systems of power inevitably produce the very subjects they come to represent as a means of showing how sex and gender emerge out of those same systems (2)—articulated as what Foucault mockingly calls a "truth" of sex. Here Butler relies on Foucault's idea of a "will to truth," expressed in his essay "Discourse on Language," which evokes Roach's discussion of surrogation and performance as it is precisely the "will to truth" that prompts the desire to replace the loss of something "original" with something else. I posit, therefore, that the particular conditions of Jim Crow and Francoist ideologies (no doubt juridical systems of power) represent a very specific, and maniacal, "will to truth" that stems from a perceived loss of national authority in war that, in turn, produces not just performatives of gender, but ones that get bound up in nationalist ideologies via very specific images like the Southern belle and the Spanish "mamá." What is interesting about these particular performatives of gender is that the "will to truth" that produces them is not contested by their opposite—that is, "bad" women—but instead emerges in the liminality of gender performatives—figures like Scarlett O'Hara and Lulú whose goodness and badness are contested by their inability to live up to either expectation.

Foucault's idea that systems of power produce the subjects that they claim to represent becomes key when observing the production of femininity as a performative since these same systems actually convert femininity—and the women that embody both good and bad versions of it—into objects. Thus in the inability to live up to constructed ideas of femininity, the Spanish and Southern woman's experience within modernity is defined by a figurative loss that translates into a literal one in many novels of the period. For example, both Laurel in Eudora Welty's *The Optimist's Daughter* (1972) and Andrea in Carmen Laforet's *Nada* [*Nothing*] (1944) lose their parents when Laurel's father dies as she still mourns her mother and the orphaned Andrea is sent to Barcelona to study. Similarly, Flannery O'Connor's short story "Good Country People" (1955) involves a young woman who has lost her leg, while Carmen Martín Gaite's novel *El cuarto de atrás* [*The Back Room*] (1978) is framed around Franco's death—Martín Gaite herself began it the day after Franco died. While these novels all address the idea of loss in different ways, the manner in which these bad belles and picaronas cope with loss is to invest inanimate objects with a desire for "good" femininity. By objectifying the feminine in this manner, the characters in these novels and stories not only reveal the discursive power of the feminine, but they also reveal how these gender roles are performed. By transferring coded femininity to an external object, these characters can simultaneously realize its performativity and let it go. While it seems that "letting go" means a disappearance of coded Spanish and Southern womanhood, writers during post-Francoist Spain and the "New" South reclaim these codes as a way of queering them, removing the idea of authenticity from concepts of gender and nation and extending them to issues of sexuality and race.

The assertion of a relationship between femininity and nationality has a lengthy history within Spanish and Southern letters, and examples of "bad" women as alluring but dangerous exceptions to such a rule abound. In the period immediately following the Spanish Civil War, the ideal of the perfect Spanish woman was so rigid it seemed unattainable, as Carmen Martín Gaite describes in her creative nonfiction work *Usos amorosos de la postguerra española* [*Courtship Customs in Postwar Spain*] (1987): "La única que a una muchacha de postguerra le permitía, con el consenso de la sociedad, desobedecer" ["The only thing allowed for a young girl in the postwar era was, with the consensus of society, the right to disobey"] (37). Here Martín Gaite shows how the demand for "good" womanhood creates a figure I term the "picarona" (a feminine version of the Spanish picaresque hero). In the postwar period, women became the source of Spanish rejuvenation given that, with huge population losses following the war, it was the Spanish mother who could literally give birth to the new nation. Falangist discourse even coded such an ideology by establishing the "Women's Section" of the Falange headed by Pilar Primo de Rivera, the daughter of Franco's predecessor, José Antonio Primo de Rivera, and sister of the Falange's founder. While Pilar did indeed serve as the paragon of Spanish womanhood throughout Franco's dictatorship, she remains a unique figure in the sense that she herself never fulfilled the role of Spanish wife and mother, despite an attempt to marry her off to Adolf Hitler (Bowen 191). Martín Gaite discusses the odd figure of Pilar in *Usos amorosos*, and while she by no means paints her as a feminist figure, she does acknowledge the quasi-masculine power and influence she possessed in Spain. Similarly, while I will not go so far as to posit Pilar as a "picarona," her unmarried status does demonstrate the coded womanhood that Spanish political discourse deemed "exceptional" within the European mold. Her own exceptionality to this mold, furthermore, only solidifies the degree to which Spanish womanhood was a performance in the first place and how Pilar herself became an uncanny manifestation of Falangist values in her possession of masculine political power (that, in many ways, lasted longer than Franco's) by performing a subservient and innocent code of femininity.

In a similar manner, Southern women, who always had major social and political power in Southern culture, only gained influence following major population loss after the U.S. Civil War. This power produced a subsequent fear of "unsexing" women, creating a figure in nineteenth-century fiction that Betina Entzminger calls the "bad belle," namely, a character "who manifests these writers' discontent with the domestic structure they outwardly defended" (2). For Entzminger, the "bad belle" is a specifically sexual being who uses her exotic allure to manipulate and destroy men for her own self-serving means. While I largely agree with Entzminger's depiction of the "bad belle," I believe the figure's importance lies outside of her seemingly essential sexual allure, and instead I view her as an uncanny figure who represents twentieth-century Southern fears of Northern industrial domination, dishonor, and, above all, the abandonment of a mythic past. In representing such uncanny fears, the figure of Scarlett O'Hara represents a modern manifestation of Southern exceptionality in the sense that she highlights its construction by defying that rule. While it seems that the Southern belle archetype should have faded by the 1930s, in reality threats against the "exceptional" Southern white woman and her honor were among the most common justifications for the lynching of black men during the Jim Crow era (Cooper and Terrill 525). As she drives her "good" counterpart off such a high pedestal, the "bad belle" persists as a figure well into the twentieth century, as femininity becomes so prominent within the definition of place and region that the figure of the woman is still invested with the national implications for, and particularly the fears of, an impending modernity.

As coded femininity causes women to "act" correctly or transgress the codes they have inherited, the ability to construct viable sources of memory becomes impossible as the "will to truth" hides a personal engagement with the past. Specifically, Carmen Laforet's *Nada* (1944) presents vain efforts to remember within a domestic space of female domination, as the novel's protagonist, Andrea, finds herself suspended between her family's antiquated (and intensely Catholic) ideal of feminine propriety and her friends' desires for comfort and freedom. As Andrea wanders through the streets of Barcelona, she discovers what the novel's title implies: nothing, and the story ends in a manner almost identical to the way it began. What happens in between, however, is an exploration of female experience that constantly questions what makes this experience "feminine." Thus a paradox emerges that Gustavo Pérez Firmat identifies when he says that "Andrea is a narrator whose language insistently calls attention to itself but who is equally insistent in covering up or dissembling the acts of narration" (28). While it is commonly asserted that Laforet is coming out of the same "tremendismo" (violent, grotesque) tradition as Cela, I question that label since it fails to acknowledge the performed nature of regional exceptionality that occurs in

both novels. In fact, while Pérez Firmat sees the links between Cela's and Laforet's novels, he acknowledges that a fundamental difference is that Laforet
does not detach the character from an external narrator. Yet by employing
a female voice, the act of narration is detached from the act of experience
in a manner that, like the extreme violence in *La familia de Pascual Duarte*,
sees both the act of narration and the codes of nation and gender that the
character follows to be equally performed. What often stands out in this
novel is the manner in which Andrea follows a set of maxims, particularly
from her aunt, which she constantly questions and defies. Her actions and
her thoughts are often set against each other in a manner that questions
which role is she playing, good girl or bad.

What is striking about Andrea's year in Barcelona is that female forces
dominate her life, specifically her aunt Angustias and her friend from the
university, Ena. Both women represent the two sides of Andrea's world—
her home and her education—and both sides also present a very different
view of the city in which she lives. Throughout the novel, Andrea is en-
chanted by the city, but her access to it is impeded when Angustias informs
her that she cannot leave the house without her permission and says, "La
ciudad, hija mía, es un infierno. Y en toda España no hay una ciudad que se
parezca más al infierno que Barcelona . . . eres mi sobrina; por lo tanto, una
niña de buena familia, modosa, cristiana e inocente. Si yo no me ocupara de
ti para todo, tú en Barcelona encontrarías multitud de peligros" ["The city,
my dear, is hell. And in all of Spain, there is no city that is more hellish than
Barcelona . . . you are my niece; therefore, a girl of good family, well brought
up, Christian, and innocent. If I didn't worry myself about you, you would
find a multitude of dangers"] (26). For Angustias, whose name translates to
"anguish," her house on Aribau Street is a domestic space that represents
a prewar Spain that she struggles to preserve, as her family, fairly affluent
before the war, has now fallen upon hard times. Angustias's embodiment
of the nation at times even emerges in her appearance, for example, when
at one moment she gets angry and her cheeks turn red and yellow in the
pattern of the Spanish flag. A subtle exception to her male counterparts,
Laforet does not describe the streets or the city in narrating the devastating
effects of postwar Spain, as Cela does in *La Colmena*, but instead the domestic sphere dominated by oppressive women and occupied by prostrate
men. The house becomes almost a grotesque manifestation of a roman-
ticized Spanish nation with marked walls that "conservaban la huella de
manos ganchudas" ["conserved the marks of hooklike hands"] (19); thus
the home becomes a haunting reminder of Andrea's lack of freedom within

a home whose hands hold her in accordance with Angustias's pure image of Catholic womanhood.

If there is a character that gives Andrea a different, and "bad," view of Spanish femininity at the time, it is Ena, the daughter of a bourgeois Catalan businessman who befriends Andrea while they are at the university. Throughout the novel, Ena represents all that is possible in Barcelona: she and her family are blonde and beautiful and live in a comfortable apartment in one of the city's most affluent neighborhoods. Ena's family relays a tale of prosperity that Nationalist propaganda wanted to portray, but within Ena's personality, there is a sinister side that relishes her ability to control those around her, particularly men. She admits as much to Andrea, saying, "Porque a mí me gusta que los hombres se enamoren, ¿sabes? Me gusta mirarlos por dentro. Pensar . . . ¿De qué clase de ideas están compuestos sus pensamientos? ¿Qué sienten ellos al enamorarse de mí? La verdad es que razonándolo resulta un juego un poco aburrido, porque ellos tienen sus añagazas infantiles, siempre las mismas. Sin embargo, para mí es una delicia tenerles entre mis manos, enredarles con sus propias madejas y jugar como los gatos con los ratones" ["Because I like that men fall in love, you know? I like to look at them on the inside. Thinking . . . What kinds of ideas compose their thoughts? What do they feel upon falling in love with me? The truth is rationalizing it is a kind of boring game because they all have their infantile enticements, always the same. But, for me it's a delicacy to have them in my hands, to capture them with their own traps and play with them like cats with mice"] (128). When Ena claims that she loves to "capture" men in their own knots, she describes an appropriation of masculine power that is utterly characteristic of a picarona. In addition, her desire to see inside men's thoughts converts her into a kind of female spy out to infiltrate the male psyche for her own opportunistic ends. Yet as with almost all picaronas, Ena's "badness," and the force of will it gives her, remains intensely attractive both to Andrea and to the reader throughout the novel. Yet at the same time, Ena's complexity as a character remains available to the reader because her "badness" is not exposed by a man who it destroys, but by a woman who desires it for herself.

Andrea's desire for Ena's life possesses a homoerotic tone as she finds herself in a state of perpetual envy that permeates every facet of her life. Thus Andrea's existence is not dominated by the search and capture of male affection, but female. As a result, Andrea reconfigures experiences meant to establish and assert masculine authority by having those experiences represent female desire and self-worth. She does this by taking an inanimate object, a handkerchief given to her by her grandmother for her first communion, and investing it with female desire when she gives it to Ena as a Christmas gift. Indeed, the "panuelo" itself contains great symbolic force as it represents Andrea's adolescent acceptance of God's existence, which in itself asserts a masculine authority over not just Andrea's life, but that of Spain itself. In addition, the handkerchief points to its traditional role as the typical female "token" given to a male admirer during chivalric times. By giving this as a gift to Ena, Andrea repositions the masculine desire for the female object and passive acceptance of God's authority and instead expresses her own form of desire and assertion of authority among her peer group. Andrea admits as much when she gives the gift and relishes Ena's response, saying, "Esta alegría suya me unió a ella más que todas sus anteriores muestras de afecto. Me hizo sentirme todo lo que no era: rica y feliz. Y yo no lo pude olvidar ya nunca" ["Her happiness tied me to her more than all her previous expressions of affection. It made me feel like everything I wasn't: rich and happy. And I could never forget it"] (67). In trying to make herself rich and happy, Andrea tries to replace the "nothingness" that pervades her life in postwar Barcelona with a feeling of feminine desire and self-worth. In addition, by saying she could never "forget" the feeling, she transforms the memory of masculine authority in her life—her first communion—into a memory of female power. Thus while it becomes easy to see Ena as the picarona for her sexual allure and manipulative power, in reality Andrea is the true transgressor by performing a femininity that is "exceptional" from the oppressive force of prewar Catholic womanhood represented by Angustias and postwar bourgeois conformity represented by Ena and her family.

Andrea's repositioning of personal experience within coded expectations of gender persists throughout the novel as she tries to fill the sense of "nothingness" with an act of comfort and happiness. For example, when she gets a small allowance to provide for herself, she spends it by eating in a restaurant a few evenings and basically starving the rest of the month. Yet the "lack" that pervades Andrea's life persists and stands out most when she experiences what is generally perceived as a major moment in a young girl's life: her first kiss. Yet when it occurs, the focus is again not on male desire, as Andrea's commentary on the moment compares it to her first menstrual period. Particularly, Andrea recalls being sat down by a nun at her school who told her that she was no longer a little girl, but a woman, and that what she was experiencing was not a sickness, but something natural willed by God. Andrea thinks of the kiss: "De modo que este hombre estúpido me ha

besado por primera vez.... Es muy posible que esto tampoco tenga impor-
tancia" ["In the same way that this stupid man has kissed me for the first
time.... It is very possible that this too has no importance"] (137). By denying the importance of a feminine function "willed" by the masculine force
of God in comparison to being the object of male desire, Andrea repositions
both her memory and her experience within the realm of coded Spanish
womanhood. Even more important is the degree with which she links the
experience to a supposed moment of biological origins—the moment she
"becomes" a woman. Yet within the repositioning of memory, both her first
period and her first kiss lose their essential allure. The presence of religious
authority in both these scenes is not an accident as the church became the
ultimate enforcer of Francoist oppression; thus in very subtle recountings
of "female" experience, Laforet questions the large ideas of what is feminine
and national by having her protagonist experience both as encounters with
"nothing."

    With her existential main character, Laforet challenges the discourse
of feminine exceptionality in much the same manner as Cela questions
codes of masculinity in *La familia de Pascual Duarte*. In other words, as
the authors of *A New History of Spanish Writing: 1939 to the 1990s* point
out, "Where *La familia de Pascual Duarte* enacts matricide as an existential
necessity for its male protagonist, Carmen Laforet's *Nada* subtly substitutes
the mother-daughter bond and female friendship for the various relationships with men that were supposed to characterize a good Falangist woman
and bring her contentment: paternal authority followed by submission to
her husband and the production of the prized male heir" (86). Thus Andrea's transgression is not necessarily an opposition to or control of masculine authority, but instead the desire to remove masculine desire from
her memory and experience. Yet Andrea soon realizes that she cannot effectively eradicate the past. Instead, all that is left is loss, both of memory
and of any sense of an integrated self. Such lack is what Andrea faces by the
novel's end as she finds herself following Ena's family to Madrid in a cycle
that eerily recalls the novel's opening pages that describe Andrea's arrival in
Barcelona. The end of *Nada* is ambivalent in the sense that Andrea seems
to find freedom in leaving Barcelona, but it seems she does so by seeking
paternal care from a "good" family who returns her to the nation's political
center. Such ambivalence is by no means new within modernity and modernist art, but what Andrea's "badness" achieves is a transgression that does
not simply replace the "nothingness" she feels, but deconstructs it in a manner that makes the feminine not a measure of opposing masculinity, but of

oppressive feminine power that itself becomes representative of national authority.

Throughout twentieth-century fiction by women, there is an often-noted failure to foreground feminist themes, and writers like Laforet and Carmen Martín Gaite have at times rejected the label of "feminist" throughout interviews and articles. Yet women writers did explore the representation of the feminine within cultural discourse, representations that were bound to change following the death of Francisco Franco in 1975.

Carmen Martín Gaite stands out among women writers of her generation since her career spanned the length of Francoism, and she devoted much of her creative nonfiction to exploring the idea of woman as national discourse—specifically in *Usos amorosos del dieciocho en España* [*Courtship Customs in Eighteenth-Century Spain*] (1972) and *Usos amorosos de la posguerra española* [*Courtship Customs in Post-War Spain*] (1987). Yet her most famous novel, *El cuarto de atrás* [*The Back Room*] (1978), uniquely blends personal experience and an experimental narrative form in a manner that reconstructs both the ideal of womanhood and, like Laforet's *Nada*, what constitutes female experience, especially post-Franco. Martín Gaite claimed she began the book the day Franco was buried, but annoyed with the plethora of memoirs that followed his death, she abandoned her own project and instead decided to write a fantasy novel, influenced by Todorov. What she produced in *El cuarto de atrás* merges the two genres as her autobiographical narrator, C., during a night of insomnia, receives a visit from a man dressed in black who interviews her. As she relates details of her life, including details of the Civil War that were previously banned, pages of a book begin to appear on the desk of the back room. When her daughter awakens her later, the man has gone, but the book remains. As C. begins to question whether the interview actually happened, we as readers question the events of her life as this reconfiguration of personal narrative explores the dialogic relationship between the individual and her nation in a manner that more or less equates both with fantasy.

The conversation between C. and the elusive man in black seems to create a situation in which womanhood is again juxtaposed with a primal masculinity as the narrator relates "female" experience to a "male" source. Yet the gender of this sometimes pushy interlocutor proves as hazy as the figure itself, and his continued presence, marked by the increasing number of pages on the desk, gives him a discursive function as he both challenges and is challenged by the narrator. Indeed, what marks the narrator's contemplation of gender in this novel is similar to Andrea's reconfiguration of her own memory through feminine experience. For example, when C. recounts her experiences of post–Civil War oppression and her family's anti-Francoist leanings, she expresses them not through the guise of large historical moments from male figures like Franco himself, but through women's hairstyles. As C. describes seeing Franco and his family in Salamanca as a child, what stands out to her is not the caudillo, but his daughter, Carmencita, who seemed to her like a locked-up princess. When asked if she envied Carmencita Franco, C. replies no—her family was not Francoist—but that she did admire her hair. As C. recalls the various hairstyles of film stars of the period, she also remembers Carmen Laforet receiving the Nadal Prize for *Nada* and notes that "lo que más me revolucionario me pareció, aparte del tono desesperanzado y nihilista que inauguraba con su novela, fue verla retratada a ella en la portada del libro, con aquellas greñas cortas y lisas" ["what seemed most revolutionary to me, apart from the desperate and nihilist tone her novel engendered, was to see her on the book's cover with those short and plain tresses"] (60). Again, the mark of female transgression in this novel is not an opposition to masculine authority, but the performance of coded femininity through hairstyle. Thus C., through the guise of Carmen Martín Gaite, exposes the discursive nature of gender performance in this novel by presenting two different versions of national femininity. In other words, these two disparate Carmens elicit the singular performance of womanhood as it pertains to C.'s personal narrative.

While Martín Gaite's novel differs greatly from the dark existential narrative of Laforet's Andrea, the degree to which the protagonists in both novels feel the overwhelming need to transgress an oppressive femininity and reconfigure their experience through memory demonstrates a clear link between post–Civil War and early post-Francoist narrative. Martín Gaite asserts this connection at the end of the novel when C. is awoken by her daughter who has stayed out all night with friends and enacts the kind of freedom not available to the previous generation. While it seems inconsequential, this daughter is not "bad" because of her actions. Instead, the narrator C. herself has subverted dominant historical discourse by reconfiguring it through so-called feminine experience. As the authors of *A New History of Spanish Writing* point out, "Experience is shown to be mediated through discursive practice and the heterogeneity of the discourses invoked, transformed, and reinscribed in the novel serve [sic] to call into question authoritative, hegemonic discourse with its claim to the metanarratives of history and truth" (65). Thus as C. describes a personal narrative of gender and nation, the only thing that is concrete within history is her experience of it, which emerges as nothing more than pages on the desk—an inanimate object—which is the novel we are reading.

The idea that personal experience can be refigured in the gift of a handkerchief or with the pages of a novel suggests the manner in which women's writing is itself a transgression of gender and memory. These externalized objects, furthermore, reveal the degree to which the "will to truth" determines their existence not by denying "truth" per se but by existing between truth and fiction, myth and reality—all of which is made more complicated by the fact that both Laforet's and Martín Gaite's novels have autobiographical elements. In addition, images of cultural objects, and not experience per se, constantly figure in Martín Gaite's creative nonfiction and novels like *El cuarto de atrás* as she reconfigures objects like speech, hairstyle, magazines, and film as cultural artifacts that stand between her own experience of Francoism and the public memory of the period itself. In a very similar manner, such cultural artifacts—as well as a keen interest in photography—define the works of U.S. Southern writer Eudora Welty, who has been noted often for her attention to speech, accent, and social custom in her stories and novels. Given her extraordinary attention to seemingly minute cultural details, critics have devoted exhaustive energy to locating a feminist, or simply a political, voice in her fiction, especially since part of her career occurred at the height of the civil rights movement. What one observes in a novel like *The Optimist's Daughter* (1972), however, is a subtle reconfiguration of female and national exceptionality that shows a semiautobiographical main character who, like Laforet's Andrea, also exists between two imposing female figures, each of whom represents a different facet of Southern culture. Again, while there is an apparent "bad belle" in her sexually alluring and manipulative stepmother, Fay, Laurel's reconfiguration of personal memory proves the true transgression within coded female exceptionality as she shows how gender and nation are masks we wear to cope with the uncanny effects of memory and our personal tendency toward nostalgia.

As Robert Brinkmeyer Jr. notes in his article on Welty's novel, "New Orleans, Mardi Gras, and Eudora Welty's *The Optimist's Daughter*," the author gives a major indication of just how performativity demands adherence to social codes as well as their transgression when she opens *The Optimist's Daughter* in New Orleans during Mardi Gras. Her protagonist, Laurel, has come from Chicago to help her father, Judge McKelva, see the doctor about his eye. As Laurel struggles to cope with her father's illness, which requires surgery, while contending with her father's new wife, Fay, Laurel finds herself in a world that is foreign from both the life up north she had with her now-dead husband and the life she knew in the small Mississippi town, Mount Salus, where the Judge and Fay still live. When her father dies Mardi Gras night, Laurel observes the drunken people in costume, the bands playing: "She heard the crowd noise, the unmistakable sound of hundreds, of thousands, of people, *blundering*" (43). While Laurel is horrified by the revelry, and equates it with Fay, Brinkmeyer asserts that a Bakhtinian "carnival spirit," even in its absence in Laurel, is a shaping force of the novel as carnival is about transgressing social codes, allowing us to reposition them, which is exactly what Laurel must do by the novel's end. Yet in this early moment, even when she has not done so, the role of carnival and New Orleans shows that Laurel must detach herself from the past in order to understand it. Thus Laurel must return home after her father's death and reconfigure her relationship to her region as well as its gender codes. What Laurel finds upon her return, however, is not a world dominated by a masculine, and national, ideal of oppressive womanhood, but a domestic sphere haunted by the uncanny memory of her dead mother, Becky, while simultaneously infiltrated by the shallow presence of Fay.

What is simultaneously striking and subtle about Welty's depiction of her native Mississippi is its juxtaposition with female characters who are from very different, and in some ways questionable, versions of the South. For example, Laurel's mother, Becky, is from West Virginia—a state whose existence arose from its refusal to secede from the Union before the Civil War. Meanwhile, Fay is from Texas, a state that did join the Confederacy but whose independence from the United States to this day compels its citizens to imagine itself as somehow separate. Yet throughout the novel, Becky and Fay serve as opposing forces upon Laurel's conception of her home, thus herself. Becky, in almost every way, serves as a prototype for pure Southern womanhood and stoicism whose actions are constantly juxtaposed with Laurel's, for example, when we discover that a fifteen-year-old Becky piloted a raft on an icy river in order to get her father to a hospital and also failed to save him. As the citizens of Mount Salus recall "Miss Becky" to Laurel, Welty's protagonist mourns a figure very different from her father's second wife, and despite the fact that her mother has been dead for ten years, Laurel's return home, to the domestic space she has always known, is to reencounter her own grief and nostalgia for a code of Southern femininity that she rejected by leaving, but whose loss she still feels.

The character of Fay has born the brunt of some very harsh criticism, some of it from Welty herself,[1] and Entzminger characterizes her as a "bad belle," a "symbol of 'evil,' not of feminine 'evil,' but of the evil society enacts against women through such silencing clichés as Fay herself" (136). Yet not unlike the calculating Scarlett O'Hara, Fay utterly represents a shallow performance of so-called New South capitalist success, which Fay flaunts with her symbolic green high heels that she buys to match her earrings early in the novel. When Laurel returns to her childhood home, she is aghast at the peach satin with which Fay has covered her parent's mahogany headboard, and Welty depicts the subtly asserted but profoundly present disapproval of her that the citizens of Mount Salus express. Yet within their disapproval of Fay is the community's censure of Laurel for leaving Mount Salus to begin with. As one woman says at the judge's funeral, "Laurel is the one who should have saved him from that nonsense. Laurel shouldn't have married a naval officer in wartime. Laurel should have stayed home after Becky died. He needed him somebody *in* that house, girl" (115). Even Fay criticizes Laurel for her actions early in the novel when she lies and says that all her family has died and bitingly asserts, "Oh, I wouldn't have run off and left anybody that needed me. Just to make a lot of money and call myself an artist" (28).

In her decision to seek selfhood through art, Welty creates what is truly a "bad belle" in Laurel, and her badness stands out inasmuch as it is highlighted by both old and new vestiges of Southern womanhood. Meanwhile, with the death of her father, Laurel feels a sense of loss that she struggles to fill throughout the novel. Like Andrea, however, she only encounters a lack as she searches her father's desk for letters her mother wrote and suddenly remembers: her father never kept letters from anyone. Instead, what Laurel finds is a nail polish stain left by Fay. The nail polish on the desk is all that remains of human life, and even it is only an item used to cover and decorate the female body. Attempting to fill the void that she feels, "Laurel studiously went to work on [the nail polish marks]; she lifted them from the surface of the desk and rubbed it afterwards with wax until nothing was left to show of them either" (123). As Laurel struggles to eradicate Fay from the domestic space, she wishes to castigate her even more than the town does—to hear her admit her role in her father's death, essentially, to admit her "badness." Yet as Laurel recalls how her father's death so mirrored her mother's, she "saw the horror. Father, beginning to lose his sight, but who am I at the point of following Fay? Laurel thought. The scene she has just imagined, herself confiding the abuse to her mother, and confiding it in all tenderness, was a more devastating one than all Fay had acted out in the hospital. What would I not do, perpetrate, she wondered, for consolation?" (132). As Laurel attempts to fill the void left by her grief, she realizes that her adulation for her mother's femininity, her "consolation," is no less a performance than Fay's cries and false tears in the hospital. In other words, just as Fay's "badness" is a construction mandated by an Old Southern conception of womanhood, Laurel begins to realize that her own Southern lady socialization is contrived by the same mode that sees one as "good" and the other as "bad," that her eradication of the nail polish on her father's desk is an act meant to deny Fay's version of "badness" when that cannot really be achieved.

Laurel's realization that Fay's performance equals her own reveals a subtle truth in Welty's novel that Julia Eichelberger exposes in her book *Prophets of Recognition: Ideology and the Individual in Novels by Ralph Ellison, Toni Morrison, Saul Bellow, and Eudora Welty*, when she notes how the criticism of Laurel's badness from manifestations of both the old and new South "demonstrates that class, race, and gender distinctions in *The Optimist's Daughter* are not preexisting facts, but social constructions that require constant maintenance and upgrading. For a hierarchy to have meaning, boundaries must be observed; Welty's characters sense that if differences dissolve, their own status as better than someone else, which to them is the equivalent of their human worth, will be threatened" (143). Yet before Laurel can finally reconcile her own identity and its relation to her Southern lady socialization, she must position both within the confines of her memory. This moment occurs in her final confrontation with Fay and her discovery that Fay has marred a breadboard made by Laurel's husband as a gift to her mother by cracking walnuts on it with a hammer. As Laurel tries in vain to express what the board meant to her—her mother's comforting bread, her husband's act of love and care—it is all pitifully lost on Fay, who declares that she "belong[s] to the future" (179). Despite her initial desire to take the board, clean it, make it new, Laurel abandons the board in the house and leaves as she realizes that "memory lived not in initial possession but in freed hands, pardoned and freed, and in the heart that can empty but fill again, in the patterns restored by dreams" (179). In these lines near the novel's end, Welty sees in memory what Joseph Roach sees as the role of performance in surrogation. It is not in the past that memory or performance exists, but in the uncanny present, the "patterns restored" by similarly uncanny "dreams" that persist. As a result, Laurel does not need her mother's breadboard in order to restore an image of womanhood in the past. She can instead assert a selfhood that "can empty but fill again," and thus remain unique to her personal experience. While Fay may remain in her childhood home and represent a pervasive New Southern womanhood, this brand of womanhood is just as contrived and performed as Laurel's breadboard, Andrea's handkerchief, and C's manuscript—all invested with personal, though no less constructed, meaning.

At the end of *The Optimist's Daughter*, with Laurel's exile from her home to the devices of Fay's shallow sense of self, it seems as if Welty, almost like Laforet, has exiled her protagonist and filled the sense of loss with a highly ambivalent sense of self. Yet in both novels the constructive, and performative, power of memory becomes a feminine force as it provides a manner of coping not just with loss in the past (Becky), but with an increasingly image-filled present (Fay). Although she engages such an issue in a wildly different manner, Welty's contemporary, Flannery O'Connor, uses a more fantastic form as she fills her stories and two novels with tricksters, misfits, and false intellectuals who become vehicles of salvation for both themselves and other characters. Because of O'Connor's intense Catholic faith and its juxtaposition with evangelical Protestantism throughout the rural South, critics often correctly locate her use of a gothic aesthetic within the author's personal and philosophical struggle with the issue of faith versus knowledge within her fiction. Within such a struggle, the implications for gender seem hazy, and Katherine Prown, in her book *Revising Flannery O'Connor: Southern Literary Culture and the Problem of Female Authorship*, emphasizes this idea by pointing to significant changes to manuscripts in which the presence of strong female characters emerges only to be cut in a novel's or story's final version. Prown attempts to explain these changes when she notes, "O'Connor's ambivalence toward femininity . . . suggests that [her] identification with the powerful masculine forces in her works resulted in large part from her association with the Southern New Critical establishment and her struggle to adopt an aesthetic founded on the opposition between the female body and the male intellect" (156). While O'Connor seems to share the detachment from feminist sensibilities pointed to in Welty— and in Laforet and Martín Gaite, for that matter—in reality her ambivalent engagement with coded female exceptionality points to its performance in a manner that makes the body, especially the female body, a site of constructed meaning as a response to intense loss.

O'Connor's allegorization of the female body is most striking in her short story "Good Country People," in which her main character's transgression of coded female exceptionality—that is, not being "good country people"—is revealed to be a performance no different from the rural Southern code of behavior she so disdains. Joy-Hulga Hopewell, a thirty-two-year-old Ph.D. with a wooden leg, is one of many of O'Connor's false intellectual characters, but, despite her education, she is by no means a feminist hero. In fact, there are few heroes in this story, and O'Connor makes this point clear by filling it with characters that operate only through performance and communicate via clichés like "Everybody is different" and "It takes all kinds to make the world." As the narrator describes Joy-Hulga's mother, "Mrs. Hopewell had no bad qualities of her own but she was able to use other people's in such a constructive way that she never felt the lack" (264). Yet simultaneously, Joy-Hulga fills the "lack" of clichéd discourse with a performance of "bad" femininity by changing her name to something intentionally "ugly," calling it her highest "creative act" (267). We discover that, for Joy, "one of her major triumphs was that her mother had not been able to turn her dust into Joy, but the greater one was that she had been able to turn herself in Hulga" (267). Indeed, Joy relishes in her performance throughout the story as she sees it as the only means to assert selfhood in the face of clichéd femininity. Where Joy flounders is in thinking that selfhood and performance are the same thing, that she is filling a "lack" with an identity that is self-generated when it is a social construction by virtue of being a willful denial of her Southern lady socialization, placing Joy-Hulga into a category of characters that O'Connor called "interleckchuls" (Coles 111).

Ironically, both Joy and her mother suffer from the same "lack," which for each seems to be filled with the arrival of a young Bible salesman, Manley Pointer. As "Manley" infiltrates the world of feminine performance occupied by Joy-Hulga and her mother, he exploits both by declaring to Mrs. Hopewell that he is "good country people" and expressing interest in Joy-Hulga. Joy-Hulga does not see this interest as a love opportunity, however, but as an opportunity to convey her atheism to the "inferior mind" of the young salesman. She agrees to meet him, for example, but imagines "that she very easily seduced him and that then, of course, she had to reckon with his remorse" (276). When she and Pointer finally meet in a barn loft, Pointer slowly exposes Joy-Hulga's performance to her when he makes her declare love for him by taking off her wooden leg. Suddenly, he opens his briefcase of Bibles to reveal whiskey, condoms, and playing cards with naked women on them. Just as Joy-Hulga starts to realize her folly, screeching for her leg, Pointer says, "I've gotten a lot of interesting things. . . . Once I got a woman's glass eye this way. . . . And I'll tell you another thing, Hulga, . . . you ain't so smart. I been believing in nothing ever since I was born!" (283). As Pointer runs off with the wooden leg, Joy-Hulga's attempt to fill what she sees as a void of intellectual scrutiny results in profound personal loss as she is left helpless, alone in the barn.

Throughout "Good Country People" the perceived lack of meaningful communication that produces the need for performance finds a continuous symbol in Joy-Hulga's wooden leg. This wooden leg gains meaning among characters whose discourse and speech are meaningless as they all try to either placate or deceive one another. O'Connor herself saw the leg as a meaningless object that acquires symbolic force as the story progresses (Desmond 148), but the leg also possesses a gendered implication for the performance of coded femininity. Joy's missing leg, coupled with a heart condition that forces her to live with her mother, is perceived as a feminine lack by her mother, who thinks, "It was hard for Mrs. Hopewell to realize that her child was thirty-two now and that for more than twenty years she had had only one leg. She thought of her still as a child because it tore her heart to think instead of the poor stout girl in her thirties who had never danced a step or had any *normal* good times" (266). In other words, the lost leg becomes a mark of womanhood whose loss Joy fills with a performance of transgressive femininity, namely, intellectualism. When the leg is stolen, it is almost a rape of her mask for the "bad" femininity she has performed. The exposure of that performance, as we see in Welty as well as in Laforet and Gaite, comes through the reconfiguration of a seemingly feminine object— a breadboard or a handkerchief, for example. By giving Joy-Hulga's wooden leg such discursive profundity and forcing its reconfiguration within per-formed womanhood, O'Connor has gone a step further in that she has not just shown the feminine to be a discursive form, but the female body as well.

Viewing the female body as a discursive form, the particular, stereotypi-cal images of Spanish and Southern femininity become, to borrow from Roach, cultural effigies that "provide communities with a method of per-petuating themselves through specially nominated mediums or surrogates" (36). Particularly, figures like the Southern belle or the Spanish mamá become the means by which images of Southern and Spanish femininity are dissected, particularly in the period that followed Jim Crow and Fran-coism. Such dissections find their most ironic turn in the web site for the Catalan film troupe La Cubana. Upon entering the site (in Spanish, Cata-lan, or English), a woman appears dressing behind a screen. As she narrates her clothing, including "los blummers," her process of dressing highlights her objectification, particularly in the context of waiting to enter a web site (something that one expects to be able to do immediately). When the woman appears, she defies expectations of Spanish femininity for several reasons: she is a black mammy, and she makes the spectator aware of the shock she produces when she asks, "¿Qué pensabas encontrar? . . . Una página erótica? . . . o lindas cubanitas desnudas en el Malecón?" ["What did you expect to find? A porn site? Or pretty, naked Cuban girls on a promenade in Havana?"]. As the mammy declares that those things are not to be expected, the web site (actually a Flash-based animation) asserts that the spectator has gotten a computer virus, converting to a black screen with text and making ominous noises. Asserting that the medium by which we view the web site is somehow sick or debilitated, La Cubana's actual web site takes us to a page where the mammy is center, and her arms, like those on a clock, allow you to navigate the site. On various pages, black children with cornrows sit in the audience. The choice of a Catalan comedy troupe to use a mammy as the embodiment of their aesthetic (the mammy in the introduction declares she is "La Cubana") speaks to the manner in which images of essential identity—particularly offensive, evocative ones—can be externalized in a way that allows the deconstruction of essential identity, in both the Spanish and Southern contexts. La Cubana's use of the mammy speaks to the manner in which the troupe seeks to deconstruct images of "ideal" Spanish, and particularly Catalan, identities, by opposing them with a stereotyped, and even offensive, image of another essential identity. Such destabilizing of identities particularly exists in La Cubana's 1992 television show *Teresines, S.A.*, and it also illustrates a process that we have seen in the novels already discussed—that is, how the externalization of objectified images of femininity not only allows for their deconstruction but their reconfiguration as well. Thus within various images of the "New" South and democratic Spain, artists like Pedro Almodóvar and various Southern performance artists have rethought these codes of femininity—while at times, even running the risk of nostalgically asserting them—to show exactly how performance leaves a space not only for personal expression but also for collective memory.

As contemporary Spain moved into its postdictatorship phase in an increasingly globalized Europe while mainstream U.S. culture encountered the "New" South, both cultures began to protagonize regional female exceptionality in manners that seemed to combat the loss of narrative that accompanies postmodern fragmentation. While in many cases the response to this new kind of loss is a form of rampant nostalgia, in reality regional female exceptionality also became a tool used particularly by contemporary filmmakers as a means of queering both feminine and regional exceptionality. Nostalgia, it seems, proves most apparent in the medium of television, but even early 1990s shows that have women as their protagonists—for example, La Cubana's show, *Teresines, S.A.* (1991–92), and the U.S. program

Designing Women (1986–93)—renegotiate ideas of Spanish/Catalan and Southern femininity while still relying on gender and social stereotypes. In particular, scholars writing about both shows note the conflation of public and private spaces within each program as both involve a group of women who engage in business activity within the space of the home. *Teresines, S.A.*, for example, concerns three sisters all named Teresa (for different saints) who make objects that correspond to "traditional" holidays in the "modern" Catalan capital, Barcelona. This merging of "traditional" and "progressive" modes of regional femininity is heavily promoted in *Designing Women* as four diverse, yet still "Southern," women run an interior design business in Atlanta—the center of New South urbanity. Again, what proves most interesting about these shows is their efforts to remain between spaces of "tradition" and "modernity," public and private, gay and straight, as both shows utilize transvestism to highlight the blurry lines between these dichotomies that contemporary Spanish and Southern culture continually negotiate.

Josep-Anton Fernández's discussion of *Teresines, S.A.* not only highlights how the program's attempts to marry "tradition" and "modernity" are at the center of Catalan culture, but they also allow him to reject positioning the show within other female-oriented situation comedies in the United States (he cites *The Golden Girls* specifically). What separates *Teresines*, Fernández posits, is the degree to which it "opens up a space for the values and norms to derived from tradition to be discussed and reformulated, so that the articulation between public and private spaces, between social norms and everyday practices, can be examined and called into question" (152). This process allows that essential ideas of identity are based on fictions; yet Fernández notes that within the context of the show's marriage of "tradition" and "modernity," these myths of identity can "be simultaneously disavowed and tolerated" (152). Indeed, he points to this idea when describing an episode when the Teresines gay upstairs neighbors, Rafa and Pepe, create a lavish hoax to convince Rafa's brother, unaware of his brother's sexuality, that the two lovers and the Teresines are a "traditional" family. While the trick fails (as they almost always do in television sitcoms), Rafa's brother, though angry, accepts his brother's sexuality. In the episode's final scene, Rafa and Pepe, having been "straight" for a day, watch television and remark on the performance in front of them:

RAFA: Ay, siempre me ha gustado, a mí, esta canción.
PEPE: Ai. sí.
RAFA [singing]: Amado mío . . . te quiero tanto . . .

PEPE: Ai, aquesta és d'aquella pelicula de la Rita Hayworth, de la Gilda.

RAFA: No, que ésta no es la Rita Hayworth, Pepe.

PEPE: No, ja ho sé, home. Si aixo és un home!

RAFA: No es un hombre, es una mujer. Lo que pasa es que va muy bien maquillada.

[RAFA: Oh, I've always loved this song.

PEPE: Oh, yes.

RAFA [singing]: My love . . . I love you so . . .

PEPE: That one's from the Rita Hayworth movie, *Gilda*.

RAFA: No, that's no Rita Hayworth Pepe.

PEPE: I know! That's a man.

RAFA: It's not a man, it's a woman. What happened is that they made her up too well.]

As Rafa and Pepe proceed to discuss and laugh hysterically at the day's events, the reversal of gender and societal expectations at the end—not unlike what occurs on La Cubana's web site—shows how performativity (in this case on the television screen) allows a space where exaggerated femininity can belong to a man, but in fact is still attributed to a woman. It is that possibility that the Teresines represent, as even their theme song asserts being a "Teresina" és una fauna que es troba per tot el món / no es pas qüestió d'etat ni sexe / és mes profund i més complexa" ["is a group that exists all over the world / it's not a question of age or gender / it's more profound and complex"]. Meanwhile it is a possibility that the show extends to its audience that the same song ends, "Som unes Teresines i potser . . . tu també!!!" ["We are the Teresines and maybe . . . so are you!!!"]. The idea that the ability to be a Teresine extends beyond the world of television and into the audience again suggests the degree to which the liminality of performance creates a space that is capable of diffusing the boundaries created by systems of power: those between public and private; between the young, postdemocratic Catalan youth and an older Spanish populace; and even those between ideas of gay and straight identities.

The presence of gay neighbors in *Teresines* allows for a perpetual queering of traditional gender roles, and the same space exists in *Designing Women* in the character of Anthony. An African American ex-convict hired by the women as their stockroom worker and later a partner in the business, Anthony, as Tara McPhereson notes in her discussion of the show in *Reconstructing Dixie: Race, Gender, and Nostalgia in the Imagined South*, becomes a liminal figure as a black man who at times participates in "girl" talk yet often offers the women a "man's" perspective on various issues; meanwhile, he is both the "help" earlier in the show and later an equal. McPhereson identifies this liminal space for Anthony when she describes him "moving in and out of the women's daily lives, destabilizing firm oppositions between insiders and outsiders, masculinity and femininity, and, in brief moments, black and white" (183). Anthony does navigate these spaces, themselves not always clearly delineated, since, as in *Teresines, S.A.*, the women work out of the stoically Southern (yet vehemently liberal and feminist) Julia's home. Again like La Cubana's program, the show also uses a moment of questioned transvestism to highlight the liminal spaces at play in the entire show. In the episode "Blame It on New Orleans," the beauty-queen character, Suzanne, has denied that a drag performer she saw is actually a man. When another character, Charlene, brings the performer to a restaurant, complete with the man's driver's license, Suzanne remains unconvinced, declaring that he must "prove" his gender. When the man responds by taking off his earrings and wig, Suzanne declares, "Oh, that doesn't prove diddly!" and removes her own wig as well. Like Pepe and Rafa discussing the performer on television, the former Southern beauty queen comparing herself with a drag performer shows how gender codes can be put on or taken off, like makeup or a wig, and these very moments of gender indeterminacy reveal that fact. As Suzanne drags the man to the lady's room to really determine his gender—and afterward shrieks in horror that there is a man in the women's bathroom—we observe again how gender, and racial, codes are both deconstructed and tolerated in the show as a means of incorporating "tradition" and "modernity." Meanwhile, like the opening of Welty's *The Optimist's Daughter*, New Orleans provides a carnivalesque atmosphere that allows these codes to again be externalized and examined. While at times *Designing Women* allows for Old South nostalgia in a New South setting— an almost unavoidable occurrence within the twenty-five-minute space of a sitcom episode—both it and *Teresines, S.A.* reveal how the blatant use of gender stereotype as a performative allows for these codes to be externalized—even, at times, dangerously objectified—as a means of providing a space where they can be navigated and explored not only as a means of providing a space to reinvent gender codes but to let the old ones go in order to effectively remember them—a phenomenon apparent as Spain and the South entered the twenty-first century.

While the medium of television has always been a venue for cliché, other artists have used stereotypes of Southern and Spanish women as a means of detaching these forms from coded ideas of gender and nationhood, instead exploiting the performativity of these images as a means of destabilizing essential ideas of gender, sexuality, and even race and ethnicity. Some of the most compelling reconceptualizations of gender have occurred in Pedro Almodóvar's films, particularly *Todo sobre mi madre* [*All About My Mother*] (1999) and *Hable con ella* [*Talk to Her*] (2002). Almodóvar's engagement with so-called Spanish identity in order to resignify what that national moniker means has been pervasive throughout his body of work, and his means of questioning what it means to be "Spanish" has gone hand in hand with questions about gender roles. In *Todo sobre mi madre* in particular, Almodóvar even utilizes the Southern belle stereotype by having his film unfold and be juxtaposed against Tennessee Williams's play *A Streetcar Named Desire*. As Huma, the actress who plays Blanche in the play, echoes her character's mantra, "I've always depended on the kindness of strangers," the film continues by exploring the multiple roles women play. In addition, the story of Manuela and the search for her dead son's father leads her to become the eternal mother figure in Spain's political and cultural capitals, Madrid and Barcelona, as she mourns this loss by becoming assistant/caretaker for Huma, helping a nun pregnant by Manuela's former husband and her son's father, and receiving the colorful commentary from her transvestite friend, Agrado. As Samuel Amago notes in his article "Todo Sobre Barcelona: Refiguring Spanish Identities in Recent European Cinema," Almodóvar is aware of the connections he is making throughout this film; thus the Argentinean exile Manuela becomes a maternal crossroads for different, and competing, versions of Spanish femininity. Almodóvar's film also questions the idea of an eternal Spanish identity by setting the film in Barcelona, thus subtly inscribing the city's cosmopolitan quality by his use of African extras and the song "Tajabone" by Senegalese singer Ismael Lô. As Amargo notes about this presence in the film, "In this way, filmic form follows function: *Todo sobre mi madre* is all about bodies, heredity, family inheritance, identity formation, art, film, authenticity, and its very structure reflects those themes. While the viewer enjoys a Nigerian Senegalese folk/blues/M'balax song in a filmic sequence that could very well appear on MTV Europe, the main characters converge in Barcelona from their various points of origin: Madrid, Argentina, and the Canary Islands" (17).

While Manuela as the eternal mother in many ways composes the core of this film's thematic and aesthetic form, the transvestite Agrado, and her monologue late in the film, most conceptualizes the reconfiguration of the female body within Spanish national identity. As she informs an audience of theatergoers that the evening's production of *Streetcar* has been cancelled, she promises to entertain them with the story of her life. Agrado's "story" is not just a history of self-fashioned femininity, but of contrived authenticity. Indeed, not only does she tell the audience that she is "muy auténtica" ["very authentic"], but the audience is reminded of her expressed hatred of drag queens earlier in the film when she declares that they have confused transvestism with a circus. In Agrado's mind, she is not "acting" like a woman; she *is* a woman. As Agrado takes account of what "authenticity" has cost her in the form of plastic surgery, she asserts, "cuesta mucho ser autentica, señora, y en estas cosas no ha que ser rácana porque una es más autentica cuando más se parece a lo que ha soñada de sí misma" ["it costs a lot to be authentic, honey, but with these things, you can't be stingy because one is most authentic when she looks most like what she has dreamed herself to be"]. While Agrado seems to deny an idea of an "authentic" gender or nationality, Almodóvar instead repositions the idea of "authenticity" itself, suggesting that mainstream Spanish culture's claims to authenticity are no different than Agrado's. Meanwhile, again by objectifying various modes of femininity, Almodóvar (aside from bearing the brunt of many a feminist attack for doing so) creates a space where they can be examined not just by the audience but by the characters themselves, as questions of "authenticity" are broken down as a means of reconstructing them as the characters all attempt to cope with the various losses suffered at the end of the film: Huma of her lover (who leaves her), Manuela of her ex-husband and the pregnant nun for whom she cares (both die of HIV).

With Almodóvar's use of *Streetcar* and, at the end, a Federico García Lorca play, *Todo sobre mi madre* foregrounds performance in a manner that is repeated in *Hable con ella* as the film's opening shot is the curtain opening on a stage. Like *Todo sobre mi madre*, this film is also about connections between bodies, particularly the lifeless bodies of comatose Alicia and Lydia, as the men who care for them form a friendship that forces both to question the nature of love and relationships. Yet at the forefront of this film is the national sport of bullfighting, and Almodóvar focuses specifically on its ritualized aspects—the elaborate dressing ceremony, the order of events during the fight—as a means of aesthetically mirroring the performativity of gender. In his female-bullfighter character, Lydia, Almodóvar blends masculine and feminine stereotypes, making Lydia into an androgynous figure (the actress who plays her has a boyish figure and looks, yet she is almost always dressed in designer dresses). Questions concerning masculine, feminine, and sexual identities abound in this film as Benigno's colleagues constantly debate his sexual orientation, the stoic Marco unexpectedly cries at things that "move" him, and Alicia lays comatose, dressed by Benigno like a little girl in a nightgown and pigtails.

What this ambiguity of gender and sexuality points to in *Hable con ella* is a "loss" of coded femininity, and what stands out most in this film is the manner in which the male characters find ways of coping with the loss of the feminine in their lives. For Lydia's current boyfriend, Marco, his response is to seek out the friendship of the effeminate Benigno, Alicia's nurse. Benigno's response to female loss (first of his mother and then Alicia) is to become both halves of an imaginary relationship with Alicia, whom he only met once. Marco's and Benigno's responses to their feminine "lack" perhaps manifest themselves most in Benigno's narration of a silent film he saw about a man who takes a nutritional supplement and shrinks to a few inches, breaking up with his girlfriend as a result. When he and his lover are reunited, Benigno recounts their love scene to Alicia as the audience watches the silent film itself. Compensating for his lack of size, the shrunken man plunges himself inside his lover's giant vagina. This comic moment echoes a theme throughout the film of intense male desire to literally plunge into the feminine. For Benigno, this desire means that, aside from attending the films and dance performances Alicia likes (as if he were her), he also plays the role of male love interest/aggressor when he rapes her, resulting in her pregnancy. In the end, the film asks the viewer for sympathy for Benigno— an act that has drawn much criticism. Ultimately, Benigno and Lydia, the characters whose gender roles were most androgynous and transgressive, die. What occurs here is similar to what we observe throughout the twentieth century: it is only through the recognition and understanding of "bad" femininity that one can understand the performativity of "good" femininity. In other words, one is completely reliant upon the other, much like Spain and the South exist as "transgressive" examples of European and American identities. The knowledge of that relationship in Almodóvar's film, furthermore, causes a resuscitation of the other two characters, Marco and Alicia (who is now no longer comatose). Almodóvar alludes to this idea in the final scene when Marco and Alicia begin to talk to each other, suggesting that the only means to let go of coded gender roles is to accept their loss, realize their liminality, and engage in dialogue.

Pedro Almodóvar's use of the Southern belle stereotype is by no means new in contemporary, and even international, culture. As McPhereson describes in *Reconstructing Dixie*, the Southern belle stereotype is alive and well in mainstream films and television, and films like *Steel Magnolias* (1989) in particular use melodrama as a means of giving a narrative to nostalgic forms of white Southern womanhood (158–68). McPhereson quotes Truvy, a character in the film played by the stereotypically flamboyant Dolly Parton, whose assertion that "there is no such thing as natural beauty" almost makes the performed quality of Southern femininity into a farce by having come from a woman who has made millions promoting her "down-home girl" persona. What proves most interesting about this statement, however, is that it comes from a singer/actress whose flamboyant appropriation of Southern femininity has not only made her famous, but is consistently appropriated by drag queen and transvestite culture as a means of making the performance of coded femininity stand out even more.

In *Reconstructing Dixie*, McPhereson documents the appropriation of white Southern femininity by drag queens across the United States. In particular, McPhereson cites RuPaul, whose autobiography, *Letting It All Hang Out* (1995), details how she learned the art of femininity after she moved to the South and that when she migrated back to the North, what she found in the drag culture there was a "slice of Georgia in New York City" (quoted in McPhereson 194). While McPhereson does not go as far as to say that drag culture is a specifically Southern phenomenon, she is clear that "it does resonate in the region. It can be seen as a response to the excessively performative nature of southern femininity, a relation already mapped out in popular discourse when [*Designing Women's*] Suzanne Sugarbaker compares wig styles with a drag queen. Drag modalities repurpose white Southern femininity, modeling new ways of being southern that can sometimes break free from a tired old recycling of the myths of lady and belle" (194). While McPhereson is correct in highlighting how the "recycling" of old "myths" can serve a constructive and redemptive function, she fails to acknowledge how this "new" mode of Southernness still relies on "old" vestiges of Southern femininity. Thus the same political agenda that promotes a figure like RuPaul is utterly rejected by the uncanny opposite that it inevitably produces, namely, the figure known as Shirley Q. Liquor.

The stand-up comic Chuck Knipp is a middle-aged gay man who has become the center of a huge controversy surrounding his performances as Shirley Q. Liquor—an obese, African American welfare mother with nineteen children who describes trips to "K-mark" in a highly stereotypical Gulf Coast black dialect. As Knipp smears on brown makeup (complete with large wig, garish lipstick, eye shadow) each evening, he is usually greeted by protestors at his performances who see him as a modern-day blackface performer, simply reproducing stereotypes for the benefit of his white (and gay male) audiences. Shirley Q. Liquor also asks audience members to empathize with the plight of poor blacks in contemporary U.S. culture, yet, as Knipp has made a career in gay clubs throughout the South and now the rest of the United States, there emerges a serious question about whether people laugh with Shirley or at her. Even Knipp is aware of this issue when he admits in an interview with *Rolling Stone*: "Wealthy white people are starting to hire me for private parties where I play the raisin in a bowl of oatmeal. . . . From the way they interact with me, I can see that my being there as Shirley makes them feel it's acceptable to openly mock black people in a way they otherwise would not, and that does cause me to have second thoughts. If what I am doing is truly hurtful, then I need to stop" (*Rolling Stone*, May 31, 2007).

Yet Knipp has not stopped, and, despite boycotts and protests, he has also received immense support from fellow performer RuPaul, who is African American. Knipp also performs an alter ego to Shirley in the form of Betty Butterfield, a white, pill-addicted Southern woman, but she has not taken off in quite the manner as his original character. Within Knipp's seemingly racist performance, however, there is a stark ambivalence to his appropriation of womanhood in the sense that he is a Quaker deacon who is one of the only preachers in the South who will preside over same-sex marriages, citing that most of his clients are black lesbians in the Mississippi delta (*Rolling Stone*, May 31, 2007). While Knipp may not know what to make of the ambivalence of his performing what is certainly a transgressive/racist form of Southern femininity, it is not surprising that the appropriation and renegotiation of white Southern femininity by drag culture would produce the same uncanny "badness" that we have seen throughout modernity and postmodernity. Thus while it seems easy to separate white Southern femininity from its uncanny opposite, in reality the fact that both are compelled into existence renews both the assertions but also the fears of regional exceptionality by prescribing it to so-called queer sexualities.

The degree to which Almodóvar's films both question and, at times, embody quintessentially Spanish ideas of femininity coupled with Shirley Q. Liquor's questionable implications for racist embodiments of Southern womanhood demonstrate the degree to which ideas of the feminine possess nationalist implications even as these images reach international audiences—from RuPaul having his slice of Georgia in New York to Almodóvar seeing a genealogy between Tennessee Williams and Federico García Lorca. Within these images, it is clear how the various manifestations of "bad" womanhood are not detached from, or are simply benign opposites to, the "good" woman. Instead, these figures inform one another and compel the other into existence, and writers have used the discursive power of the feminine to explore similarly "othered" narratives and voices, specifically, those of African Americans and Catalans. In other words, just as society wants to see a "bad" woman as wholly different to the "good" woman, the same hierarchy is employed when describing alternate forms of "Southern" and "Spanish" identities; thus, again, the lens of gender informs the representations of place not by prescribing labels of "exceptionality" but by creating dialogic narratives of gender and nationhood.

As both Almodóvar and Knipp have come under attack for their representation of gender and racial stereotype and shows like *Teresines, S.A.* and *Designing Women* at times show nostalgia as they exalt a type of old-world femininity, there are lingering questions about how the externalization and objectification of Southern and Spanish gender stereotypes create a space to remember the past—particularly an inhospitable one. Yet as we observe in the novels that emerged during the Jim Crow and Francoist periods—a time when memory was controlled and coded by these systems of power—the externalization and investment of female codes in Andrea's handkerchief, Laurel's breadboard, C.'s manuscript, and Joy-Hulga's wooden leg not only allow these characters to let go of these female codes, but allow them to externalize the memories inherent in them as well. Robert Brinkmeyer Jr. identifies this very element in Laurel's breadboard in *The Optimist's Daughter* when he sees it as her symbol of the "solid past" and that Laurel, "rather than worshipping an unchanging image of the past, her memories hardened into icons to be idolized, . . . understands that she must continuously reinterpret her memories according to her present needs and perspectives, thereby making memory 'vulnerable to the living moment'" (440). In a democratic Spain and a "New" South, the use and even objectification of these same codes represent a move from a kind of memory that uncannily haunts toward a view of gender that does not equate it with melancholic loss and instead moves toward a place of mourning—a place where regional female exceptionality can be let go as a means of constructively remembering the role it had in shaping identity. What stands out over time is the degree to which transgressive femininity has served to provide alternate narratives of gender as they have been put forth by supposedly exceptional, and highly coded, Spanish and Southern nations. My interest in women authors in particular stems from the fact that, in the act of writing, women perform transgressive and surrogate femininities by taking up the so-called masculine pen—Anne Bradstreet's notion of a phallic plume. Again, what proves striking about the various female characters discussed here is how there is consistently a perceived "loss" that provokes the reconstruction of self, gender, and nation. In so doing, female writers may take a different path than their male counterparts, but the modes of performance remain the same.

While women writers have played varied roles in debunking the myths of regional female exceptionality, this history of "bad" women in Spain and the South has been accompanied by insinuations of "bad" feminism throughout both traditions. For example, in her essay on the controversial and problematic implications of Grandes's *Las edades de Lulú*, Alison Magin states that "female expression, and in particular sexual expression, is at a different stage for women in those countries that have enjoyed democratic traditions" (printed page 13). Similarly, critics of Southern culture, while admitting the denial of the Southern belle myth in contemporary fiction, still, like Barbara Bennett, identify the "precarious position" of Southern feminists in that "they had to defend their region as unique, but also they needed to suggest that some things had to change for the betterment of all" (441). What seems to be ignored in such efforts to contextualize women's writing with contemporary feminist movements is that the renegotiation of gender, particularly its exceptionality, within culture invariably involves a subsequent rethinking of nationhood itself. In prescribing a "difference" to Spanish and Southern feminist movements—often a variant term for what is seen as "backward" or "inferior" to mainstream European and U.S. feminists—critics and scholars ultimately reinstate the very modes of oppressive essentialism they attempt to shake. Such assertions are evidenced in efforts to assert "exceptionality" within Spain and the South themselves, suggesting insurmountable differences between women of different races and languages. Yet from writers like Alumudena Grandes to Eudora Welty, leading to the transvestite images of Spanish and Southern femininity, there emerges an intense desire to expose the various manners that ideas of the feminine both make claims to but ultimately question the idea of regional exceptionality and how we remember it. In so doing, it becomes readily apparent how establishing connections between seemingly exceptional nations and identities, instead of asserting essentialist differences, becomes a means of exposing not just the methods of establishing exceptional ideas of gender and nation, but the uncanny fears, desires, and conflicts that such imaginings produce.

Chapter 6

EXCEPTIONALITY AS LEISURE

Tourism and Urban Planning in the New South and Democratic Spain

W hile Spain and the South have always possessed warm weather, beaches, and "exotic" culture available to any traveler, the middle of the twentieth century marked a dramatic change in each tourist culture. In Spain, this change occurred when the Spanish government intensified efforts to promote tourism, culminating in the devaluation of the peseta, which created an increased purchasing power for European tourists. In the United States, postwar economic prosperity, coupled with President Dwight D. Eisenhower's passing legislation to begin the construction of what became the Federal Interstate System, created a more mobile U.S. traveler. Consequently, both Spain and the South became even more attractive within the already-rampant spread of tourist culture as the factory worker from chilly climates in, for example, Berlin or Detroit could (for a price and with air-conditioning) experience the "exotic" food and music stereotypically representative of Spanish and Southern culture. Realizing such an appeal, Spain and the South represent specific examples of locations that market claims to exceptionality, which, in Spain, was famously heralded by the 1960s tourist slogan, "Spain is different." Yet concurrent with the tourist boom in Spain and the South remained two cultures that were operating under concrete, and oppressive, ideas of Spanishness and Southernness. As Francoism's hold on Spain softened and the civil rights movement brought integration to the South, tourist culture in both places took on performative elements as tourist sites became venues for selective forgetting. For example, visitors to Granada's Alhambra or one of the many plantations along the coastal South could enjoy each site's "unique" architecture while ignoring the history of the Inquisition or slavery that many of these monuments recall. In the end, tourist culture in "democratic" Spain and the "New" South reflected a performativity that we have observed throughout this project as tourist infrastructure—and city planning meant to support it—enacts an idea of Spanishness and Southernness that means to be inclusive and international while it is still exclusive and nationalistic.

While a discussion of tourism in Spain and the South goes beyond the project's proposed scope of Francoism and Jim Crow, this chapter demonstrates the degree to which tourist culture selectively remembers specific moments in what many consider to be a tarnished history. This relationship with memory solidified as Spain and the South became major tourist destinations into the 1970s and 1980s, and their attempts to capitalize on exceptionality caused each to chip away at their essential allure by promoting a selective re-remembering, thus forgetting, of the past. Put simply, in offering up their unique qualities to the highest bidder, Spain and the South diluted their "exotic" appeal by promoting a jazzed-up, untarnished, and universally accessible understanding of their shared national and cultural experience, and particularly their imagined history. It is for this reason that, again, tourists can visit Barcelona's Montjuïc without ever being made aware of it being a popular execution site during the Spanish Civil War. Similarly, visitors to Georgia's Stone Mountain State Park never discover that it was the site of the reemergence of the modern Ku Klux Klan. With these sites in mind, Barcelona and Atlanta—because of each city's hosting of the Olympic games—become exemplary models for how such touristic performativity greatly influences urban planning. In the construction of public spaces, both cities have attempted to transform themselves into "international" locales that simultaneously claim to be particularly Spanish (or in the case of Barcelona, Catalan) and Southern. While the desire to promote their international and universal elements seems like a sharp departure from the assertion of a masculine and essential nationalism during Francoism and Jim Crow, contemporary filmmakers José Luis Guerín and John Sayles show that these new, and similarly shiny, narratives of nationhood are no less constructed and no less subject to acts of erasure. Thus by exposing and exploiting the tourist image and showing how that image is reproduced in city planning, this chapter links tourism, urban space, and performance in a way that shows how the desire to exoticize culture enables a forgetting of the past that involves the same claims to authenticity observed throughout this project—despite claims to diversity and inclusiveness that "public" leisure and "communal" spaces seem to imply.

The discussion of tourism as it relates to urban planning brings this project full circle since the desire to return to a mythic past offered by places like Spain and the South returns us to the desire—exhibited both by the Agrarian and the Generation of '98 writers—for an authentic sense of national self. In the introduction to their book *Spain Is (Still) Different: Tourism and Discourse in Spanish Identity*, Eugenia Afinoguénova and Jaume Martí-Olivella cite Dean MacCannell's assertion that tourism represents a "quest for an escape from the separation of work from leisure and the compartmentalization of land, a search for an experience that would allow one to touch the 'authentic' in order to 'reconstruct a cultural heritage or a social identity,' now removed in time (to history) or in space (to natural, 'primitive' or exotic destinations)" (xi–xii). As I discussed earlier, the performance of exceptionality entails the construction of an essentialized "other," and ironically, this figure appears prominently in images of Spanish and Southern tourism, in particular, the Andalusian "gypsy" figure and the romanticization of the primitive mountain hillbilly.[1] Within both of these images, the combination of the essential and the exotic is a key element as tourists seek to participate in what they imagine as a shared mythic ritual representative of an exceptional culture that they are never asked to fully understand. Thus while a traveler cannot actually become a gypsy or mountaineer, he or she can experience the image of that lifestyle and, even more important, take home artifacts of that experience in the form of the souvenir—"folk" art, crafts, and music. Unable to find authentic experiences at home or abroad, tourists thus attempt to own evidence of the act of having partaken in the mythic rituals of a culture they neither know nor want to know. While there are many types of tourism in both places—gastronomical, ecological, historical, and sports-related—even those seemingly modern manifestations of Spanish and Southern culture are pared down by the tourist into an "experience" or an "excursion" that can be packaged and marketed to an audience.

In attempting to achieve an authentic experience of an exotic or primitive locale, tourists who visit Spain and the U.S. South participate in a worldwide shift from travel to tourism, identified by Daniel Boorstin in his influential 1961 book, *The Image: A Guide to Pseudo-events in America*. For Boorstin, the modern tourist really seeks "pseudo-events" and "has come to expect more strangeness and more familiarity than the world naturally offers" (79). Such pseudo-events have become synonymous with images of postmodernity as Boorstin identifies a shift from individualized experience in favor of communal consumption of the same packaged "adventure." Although neither the gypsy nor the hillbilly could ever have authentically existed in the manner their culture imagines them, such an attempt to perform a neutered image of them for consumerist demands, while simultaneously asserting authenticity, proves particularly dangerous. Dean MacCannell alludes to this danger in a 1989 introduction to his 1976 book, *The Tourist: A New Theory of the Leisure Class*. While MacCannell examines tourism as a product of postindustrial modernity, when work no longer became the center of social life and created a subsequent space for increased leisure (7–8), his revised introduction considers the array of experiences available to the modern tourist and asks: "Does tourism and/or postmodernity, conceived in the most positive possible way as a (perhaps final) celebration of distance, difference, or differentiation, ultimately liberate the conscious or enslave it? Is modernity, as constituted in the system of attractions and the mind of the tourist, a 'utopia of difference,' to use Van den Abbeele's energetic phrase? Or does it trap consciousness in a seductive pseudo-empowerment, a prison house of signs?" (xx). MacCannell makes it clear that his project does not offer a concrete answer, and his questions become more complicated when the idea of "difference" becomes an essential quality of a specific tourist culture, like Spain or the South. In many ways, both are examples of tourist cultures that have become "prisons" of difference with geographic spaces that reflect such stifling in their resolve to echo a tourist refrain seen in countless advertisements and brochures, that is, to offer "something" for "everyone."

Indeed, contemporary Southern and Spanish tourism does not rely exclusively on "exotic" exceptionalism. While the image of "diversity" and "variety" seems like a new one within Spanish tourist culture, Sasha D. Pack notes in her book *Tourism and Dictatorship: Europe's Peaceful Invasion of Franco's Spain* that despite assertions of Spain's "difference," "much more important was a return to the theme of national regeneration, which had dominated public discourse during the first decades of the century. Advocates of tourism in this period regarded it as a means to reassert Spain's international presence and reduce, not reinforce, prevailing beliefs in Spanish exceptionalism within and without" (4). Pack notes how images projected to tourists were ones of a "modern" Spain with an infrastructure and amenities attractive to visitors. The result today is a nation with a major tourist infrastructure designed to give visitors an image of Spanish "difference" without addressing any elements of its contested history. For example, the web site for Granada, the city that houses one of Spain's most visited destinations, the Alhambra, allows potential visitors to download an itinerary that mimics the route of Washington Irving, a nineteenth-century U.S. traveler, through the city. Irving's book *Tales from the Alhambra* is still used in tourist discourse (and readily sold at gift shops) to promote the "orientalist" gaze of the Western tourist, while the palace's description on Granada's web site gives a brief history of the palace without ever mentioning the fact that it fell out of Muslim hands during Spain's Christian "Reconquest" (yet it does mention, without explanation, that the site was "abandoned" in the eighteenth century). Even more emblematic of the desire to gloss over Spanish history are the lack of sites that directly recall Francoism and the Spanish Civil War. Even the Valle del los Caidos ("Valley of the Fallen"), the mammoth cross on a mountain that marks the basilica where Franco is buried, proves fairly difficult to get to for the average tourist, with a small-town bus that goes there only once a day—a surprising lack of service in a country that has, based on personal experience, one of the most developed and useful tourist infrastructures in Europe.

The similar gloss of history in contemporary Southern tourism has received much attention from scholars like McPhereson in *Reconstructing Dixie*, whose tour of plantation homes along the Mississippi River produces a narrative of history in which slavery is conveniently streamlined or simply forgotten (41). In addition, the role of performance here is key since, similar to the orientalist gaze of the Western tourist on "Muslim" Spain, Southern historical tourism has a specifically coded white, Northern audience that seeks an exotic culture that is "almost" American, but distinctly different. Plantation tours echo the kind of "pseudo-events" that characterize tourist culture by ignoring the parts of the story that make an audience uncomfortable. Such is the homogeneity of contemporary Southern tourism, which Ted Ownby details at length in his essay "Nobody Knows the Troubles I've Seen, but Does Anybody Want to Hear about Them When They're on Vacation?" As Ownby points out, "Today the dominant trope of southern tourism is variety.... Guidebooks and travel brochures always say that tourists can find what they expect to find: land, mountains or beaches, old houses, Civil War sites, rural stuff to see and buy, local music. On the other hand, they also stress that tourists can find things they didn't expect: things not so old and not so stereotypically Southern" (247). Again, however, what stands out here is what is notably absent in these narratives of Southern homogeneity. In other words, the history of oppression and poverty disappears in the universalized narrative, more or less repeated at various tourist sites, of gentlemen and belles who presided over their grand estates or untouched mountain land presided over by a simple, innocent people. Yet such narratives still seem authentic and exotic as they rely on an image of the South as "other" while ignoring a history that can be included in not just a uniquely "Southern" history, but a U.S. one as well.

Central to creating a tourist culture is creating an infrastructure, and, time and again, the Olympics have provided an opportunity for cities to highlight their "unique" qualities while promoting an image of international cooperation and appeal. In particular, Barcelona's (1992) and Atlanta's (1996) hosting of the Summer Olympics provide two prime examples of how these two cities utilized the games as means of transforming their cities from prototypes of modernist progress to what Boorstin sees as sites of post-modern leisure—chock-full of nationalistic pseudo-events that ask visitors to examine only certain elements of the two cities' culture and history. At first glance, both Barcelona and Atlanta already seem to occupy a singular space within Spanish and Southern history given the role each played in their respective nation's civil war. Barcelona was, along with Madrid, a major Republican stronghold throughout the war, and its Catalan heritage and liberal culture have always (and in many ways still do) set it apart from the rest of Spain. Similarly, Atlanta has always had an industrial base that separated it from the largely agrarian South, and the rapid growth it experienced following the Civil War and its burning during Union general William Tecumseh Sherman's "March to the Sea" set it apart as an early Southern metropolis (and today, the South's preeminent example of suburban sprawl). Yet by the 1990s both cities had become the center of Spanish and Southern "progress"—evidenced by their being used as settings in programs like *Teresines, S.A.* and *Designing Women*—and each used the Olympics as a means of promoting both national exceptionality and "international" appeal. The implications of such a dichotomous enterprise—the same erasure of history and the displacement of people who do not fit the "universal" mold already observed in tourist culture—remain in the contemporary urban landscape as both cities still venture to draw more and more visitors each year.

The 1992 Summer Olympics in Barcelona are still regarded as the prototypical example of what hosting the games can do for both a city's international reputation and its economy. For Barcelona, the Olympics, coupled with Spain's hosting the 1982 World Cup, was a definitive announcement that the city and nation had fully entered democratic Europe. Yet in several ways Barcelona was reinstituting a process begun before the Spanish Civil War. In the early twentieth century, Barcelona had posited itself as a paragon of modernity and liberal thinking, beginning with its hosting of the International Exposition of 1929 and continuing to its Olimpiada Popular in 1936, a response to Hitler's racist Berlin games that were interrupted by the coup that began the Civil War. Although, at the outset, it seems that Barcelona attempted to preserve this history by renovating sites that held these

events, critics like Manuel Vázquez Montalbán, in his 1992 book on architecture, *Barcelonas*, instead point to the widespread gentrification that has
resulted from such redevelopment. Within the realm of "renewal," architects
and city planners enact a performative of national identity as they search
for an "original" city by "renewing" an old one that seems to replicate the
original, but, instead, reveals the discontinuities and contested memory of
that "original" image. For example, the Olympic Ring that would have held
the 1936 Olimpiada Popular was redesigned for the new games, conserved
but expanded greatly to later become a focal point of a real-estate empire,
complete with concert halls and sports facilities (Vázquez Montalbán 8). In
addition, the Olympic Village, designed to reflect nineteenth-century socialist design, ironically was constructed on land appropriated by the government, and, despite promises to subsidize the apartments in the Village, practically all were sold on the open market, in a very unsocialist manner, for
prices around 375,000 U.S. dollars (40 million pesetas). By 2002 the value
of these apartments had multiplied two-and-a-half to three times, making
them among the most expensive real estate in the city (Carbonell 4). What
developers during this period sought was an image of Barcelona that was
"lost" after the Spanish Civil War, and it is because that past was "lost" that
they can claim that is essential and thus worthy of "renewal." The fact that
renewal comes at the expense of those who cannot afford to participate in
this kind of memory is, for Vázquez Montalbán, not a desire to remember, but to "clean up" and erase the past as a means of making a profit. It is
this rush to such progress that he questions in his preface to the English-
language edition of *Barcelonas*, saying, "Few will wonder if it all might not
have been handled differently. The same attitude will prevail towards the
Olympic Village, the ring roads, the telecommunications towers and the redevelopment of the old *barrios*. For the citizen of the future, a meaningful
assessment of the old and the new, of conservation and improvement, will
be impossible" (8). The reason it will be impossible, in Vázquez Montalbán's
mind, is that the emphasis is really only on the new and entails a need to
make the "old" authentic so that "new" claims to national exceptionalism
can go uncontested in an effort to return the public to a space's "traditional"
function—a move that again returns us to the "regenerationist" movements
of the early twentieth century and, even more important, tourist discourse
in Spain during the 1950s and 1960s.

　　If there is a site that demonstrated the kind of performativity seen in
tourism, and by extension, urban planning, it is Monjuïc: a hill from which
the best views of Barcelona can be had and the site of a tower that was

initially designed to repel Spanish troops in the seventeenth century and later served as a prison and popular execution site during the Spanish Civil War. It was here that the wartime president of Catalonia was shot in 1940, and the main Olympic Stadium was named for him in 1992. The hill's transformation into an entertainment and tourist district is perhaps most famously mocked at the end of Juan Goytisolo's *Señas de identidad* when his protagonist visits the site of his own father's Civil War death and bemoans the lack of memory, the pseudo-experiences, that accompany the area's touristic commodification. In particular, the Palau Nacional (National Palace) and the Font Màgica (Magic Fountain) both represent spaces that were created as part of Barcelona's early twentieth-century modernization, which were later reappropriated in the postmodern zeal to promote international appeal. For example, the Palau Nacional was constructed as the centerpiece of Barcelona's many projects during the 1929 International Exposition, having been designed by architects Enric Català i Català and Pedro Cendoya Oscoz to resemble palaces that housed royalty throughout Europe. Coupled with the city's wide, almost Parisian boulevards, and the various Art Nouveau buildings designed by Antoni Gaudí, which have become synonymous with images of Barcelona, the Palau Nacional became a symbol of European design as well as, in 1934, a home for the National Museum of Catalan Art. Similarly, the Font Mágica was built to be emblematic of new technology at the time by illustrating the innovation of filtered electric light. In almost every detail, Barcelona's hosting of the 1929 exposition desired to show, as the city would attempt to do again in 1992, that Barcelona represented everything that a liberal and particularly a modern city should offer its citizens.

Given Spain's entrance into civil war and a major economic crisis during the early dictatorship, it is unsurprising that these buildings were neglected and fell into major disrepair by the late twentieth century. The Palau Nacional specifically underwent a major renovation for the 1992 Olympics, but even attempts at restoration have taken on a notably homogenous tone as the National Museum of Catalan Art, beginning in 1995, began the acquisition of Romanesque and Gothic art from throughout Europe in efforts to make itself an "international" museum. As its English-language web site boasts, "The Palau Nacional is situated in a unique setting: Montjuïc, the mountain of museums, leisure and sport, well on the way to becoming an area of culture and life. The institutions you will find spread around the park, of renowned international prestige, make Monjuïc the museum *par excellence* in Barcelona, with a diverse, complete offer." In this bold statement, the desire to identify a "unique" setting by identifying its "diverse, complete offer" perfectly exemplifies the manner in which postmodernity, pace Boorstin, commodifies exceptionality by promoting homogeneity masquerading as diversity. Again, the effort is not to remember or even experience something, but simply to consume. Such has become even the fate of the Font Mágica, which today is illuminated every summer evening in thirty-minute intervals to classical music and movie soundtracks—representative of nothing more than universal recognition for a tourist audience (one that is actually *so* touristy as to attract locals seeking kitsch)—as children buy plastic trinkets and eat carnival-type food that could be found at a U.S. state fair as easily as it could in Barcelona.

The particular examples of the Palau Nacional and the Font Mágica are not highlighted to discount the various positive impacts of Barcelona's redevelopment. In addition to the renovation of various buildings from the early twentieth century as well as the eventual completion of Antoni Gaudí's Temple of the Sagrada Familia, the dockyards of Barcelona, allowed to lay dormant as industry moved out, have experienced amazing renewal. Instead, what these examples, and this chapter, illustrate is that while postmodern redevelopment seems to entail a different performance of nationhood—one that promotes diversity, not essentialism—in reality it actually promotes universality and consumption in a manner that is still nationalistic. Antonio Sánchez, in his article "Barcelona's Magic Mirror: Narcissism or the Rediscovery of Public Space and Collective Identity?," sees Barcelona's redevelopment in a more positive light while still acknowledging a postmodern aesthetic in spaces like the old dockyard Moll d'Espanya. Now the site of a glittering shopping mall with a cinema and covered in a reflective surface, Sánchez reads such architectural innovation as a form of urban narcissism, a desire for the city to see itself—clean and shiny—in the image reflected by the building's surface (303). Such an idealized image, Sánchez suggests, leaves out various "undesirables" as it promotes a safer, cleaner self-concept—a concept that does not diverge from the clean and exceptional image of Spain observed throughout this project.

The desire to chronicle the narrative of the "undesirables" that Barcelona's redevelopment leaves out emerges in José Luis Guerín's 2001 film, *En construcción* [*Work in Progress*]. Consisting of two-and-a-half years of footage chronicling the reconstruction of an apartment building in Barcelona's Barrio Chino (also known as El Raval), Guerín's film straddles the line between documentary and narrative film as his "actors" are real people who followed a basic plot given by Guerín a year into shooting (San Cornelio 202). On the surface, *En construcción* is very much a commentary on real-es\.ite development in present-day Spain, and, in particular, Barcelona's effort, particularly post-Olympics, to "renew" its dockside neighborhoods. Yet within this critique, Guerín aesthetically interrogates the idea of "renewal" as the camera blurs concrete divisions between the "new" and "old" spaces, the "old" and "new" residents. Indeed, the Barrio Chino, as a dockside area, has always been a transient space within Barcelona's history, having been home to large immigrant populations, most of whom lived there as workers in the various dockside industries. Guerín's film is very much interested in this liminality as his own film becomes a work in progress while he films it—existing in between documentary and narrative film and exposing the performativity inherent in making a supposedly "authentic" and "old" space new again by exposing, through the artifice of the camera, the "construction" that it entails—a construction that mirrors how tourist discourse makes the old "new" in the eyes of the foreign visitor.

Critical work on *En construcción* often notes how the film is about displacement—of people and of concrete ideas of time and space. As Abigail Loxham notes in her article "Barcelona Under Construction: The Democratic Potential of Touch and Vision in City Cinema as Depicted in *En Construcción* (2001)," Guerín's film "refuses to create dichotomies or reinforce binary oppositions; instead it highlights the advantages of blurring and the importance of heterogeneity in the contemporary urban environment" (34). Throughout the film, Guerín blurs ideas of concrete time by juxtaposing images of clocks, watches, and life cycles (we see a resident's baby born over the course of the film) with the progression of the construction itself, which takes place during the two years of filming. The juxtaposition of real time and diegetic time appears throughout the film (Marsh, par. 5). Yet as Gabriel Cabello notes in his essay "Construyendo tiempo: Los ensayos cinematográficos de José Luis Guerín" ["Constructing Time: The Cinematographic Essays of José Luis Guerín"], the juxtaposition of these two ideas of time serves to blur them, and the best of example of this moment comes when construction of the building slowly obscures the Romanesque San Pau Church, one of the oldest in Barcelona. As the church slowly fades from the screen as an apartment is built right next to it, Cabello observes, "La iglesia de San Pau irá pasando desde su condición original de ser el edificio que preside todo el espacio urbano y el telón de fondo sobre el que discutir la grandeza de una construcción humana, a convertirse en una mera «vista», muerta ya como referente de la acción humana, para los inquilinos que llegan con la obra finalizada" ["The San Pau Church will go passing from its original condition of being the building that presides over all urban space and the background for a discussion on the greatness of a human construction to being converted into a mere 'vista,' already dead as a referent for human action, for the tenants that arrive with the finalized product"] (III, par. 4). What Cabello describes here is the conversion of the "old" into an image, a view that is "dead" and has no referent to any concrete past. What Cabello unwittingly describes is a conversion often seen in tourist discourse as described by Boorstin—the transformation of something "old" into an image for the new tenants, foreigners of sorts to the neighborhood. Yet concurrent with the conversion of the "old" into a "new" image of history is an interrogation of what is authentically old. If this church can be so easily converted into a dead "vista" with no reference to the past, then the question remains of how to effectively remember that past when its image has been renewed.

Guerín's film is very much a contemplation of memory, and the film opens with archival footage of El Raval during the 1950s that aesthetically illustrates the construction of the past into a "renewed" image in the present. As the film chronicles the development of a neighborhood conceived as different, part of Barcelona's underbelly, Guerín also repeatedly returns to a sign proclaiming how the redevelopment is possible because of funds available from the European Union. With these two images of past and present, Guerín highlights the ambivalence inherent in urban renewal. In many ways, these projects—much like tourist discourse—rely on a space's "exceptionality" while they aim to "universalize" a specific area, forgetting and blotting out specific elements of its past. Indeed, there is a deep ambivalence within these projects as they often displace lower-income residents from their homes (which also occurred when other buildings in this neighborhood were demolished for the Olympics) while these projects also replace decaying and dangerous buildings and improve city services by providing cleaner water and better sanitation.

Part of exposing this ambivalence for Guerín comes not just by blurring ideas of "old" and "new" but also of insider and outsider in terms of the neighborhood—roles that also correspond to those of tourist and native. There is a difference in the way Guerín shoots the buildings' original inhabitants and the potential buyers of the new apartments. The original inhabitants are almost always placed in the frame with tight shots. For example, a young couple, Juani and Ivan, share intimate moments as Juani puts on makeup in preparation to work as a prostitute and support them. Earlier in the film, the camera tightly shoots a construction worker flirting with a woman hanging washing as we later see a woman pointing things to her baby out of a window. The focus here is on these characters' interactions, and they are directly juxtaposed with long, tracking shots of the potential buyers, who comment on the fact that the neighbors hang washing on the balconies, noting that it is important that the neighborhood look "good" ["guapo"]. There is a blurring between insider and outsider as these characters are linked not by their connection, or lack thereof, to the building, but by their interactions with one another. All of the people in this movie are from somewhere else, including the various construction workers, most of them Moroccan migrants, who also fill the frame. Here Guerín plays with the idea of who inhabits, or "owns," a space, showing all the characters in the film to be both insiders and outsiders, depending upon the process of construction. Before the project is completed, people like Juani and Ivan are the "natives," that is, until the Barrio Chino's exceptionality becomes "kitsch" for the "tourists" who invade it. As Cabello points out, where Guerín succeeds in these scenes is in showing how these characters are invisible to one another, but rendered visible to us by the aesthetic of the film (III, par. 14). Indeed, the juxtaposition here serves not to create a binary between insider and outsider, but to blur those distinctions as the delineations between insider and outsider, tourist and native, are shown to be reliant upon the construction of old into something new.

Within efforts to "renew" the past in the present, Roach shows us how such performativity becomes an uncanny search for "origins," and Guerín highlights that search early in the film when a Roman burial ground is discovered at the construction site. What is most interesting in this scene, as Loxham notes, is the director's decision to never show us the bones that are unearthed; instead, we only see the faces and hear the conversations of people discussing the discovery. In various languages, local residents ponder whether the bones are Roman or Catalan, with one man suggesting that they are looking at a mass grave from Civil War murders. While Loxham reads Guerín's decision to replicate the character's "frustrated" view of the bones for the spectator and reads it as a complex depiction of the various frustrations these characters feel, I would extend this reading to include the frustrated attempt to search for national origins—the very origins that become uncanny when they are enacted in the present. Thus throughout efforts to "renew" the past, one will always be haunted by a contested history that construction allows us to build over but that, quite literally, we are always doomed to dig up.

Guerín's film highlights the, at best, questionable implications of a nation's, region's, or city's efforts to reconstruct itself and what that means for one's sense of "community." While the idea of nationality logistically no longer exists in postmodernity, the idealized image that Barcelona projects onto itself and onto the world through its urban planning and tourist discourse suggests otherwise. As Vázque Montalbán aptly defines the "cultural perplexity" of postmodernity at the end of *Barcelonas,*

> Por una parte, inseguridad respeto a "la continuidad" del patrimonio, por otra, duda metódica entre no aceptar ningún modelo y aceptarlos todos y, finalmente, instalación en un eclecticismo que utiliza todo lo sabido y asumido según convenga. Para algunos ese talante postmoderno significa la instalación en el final de la historia, en el fin de su sentido dialéctico: toda la oferta histórica ya está hecha y empaquetada en el supermercado de las conductas y los gustos, basta escoger los productos más adecuados para cada momento, sean acciones, creencias, ideas moralidades. . . . Al antiguo conservadurismo a la defensiva que ha caracterizado los últimos cincuenta años de conciencia burguesa, le sucede un conservadurismo agresivo y ratificado por la supuesta evidencia de la inutilidad de toda utopía. Es más: ¿acaso las utopías no han creado siempre finales infelices?
>
> [On the one hand, (it consists of) insecurity about "the continuity" of its heritage and, on the other, methodic doubt about whether or not to accept unconditionally all those models bequeathed by its past, and finally arrival at an eclecticism which uses all knowledge and assumptions as needed. For some, this postmodern mood means the arrival of history's end, in its dialectical sense: the entire historical product already is made and packaged in the supermarket of channels and pleasures, it is enough to choose the most adequate products for each moment, be they actions, beliefs, ideas, morals. . . . Traditional conservatism, now on the defensive after half a century of bourgeois consciousness, has produced a new aggressive conservatism, vindicated by the supposed evidence that all utopias are useless. More to the point, haven't they always had unhappy endings?]
> (230)

While Barcelona may have a distinct Catalan identity, its "evolution" into an Olympic city attempts to present a history of coded nationalism that we have observed throughout this project. In the end, the assertion of either national exceptionality or universal appeal represents an effort to perform an authenticity that lacks crisis, victims, or danger when, in the end, performativity—the creation of an image that Guerín's filmic aesthetic replicates—actually exposes those very things.

While *En construcción* focuses on a particular building in El Raval, the redevelopment in this area was sparked by the Olympics. While the games allowed Barcelona to become a model for international appeal and progress, the 1996 Summer Games in Atlanta did not receive quite the same praise. Nonetheless, the city's preparation for the event proved similar to Barcelona's, with attempts at making itself into a city that was still authentically "Southern" but that could still attract and entertain visitors from around the globe. In so doing, Atlanta converted many of its historical sites—some of which possess a controversial history—into venues of homogenous leisure, producers of pseudo-events. The fact that Atlanta was capable of making such a transformation should come as little surprise given the city's long history as a railroad hub and industrial center in the largely agrarian post–Civil War South. As in Barcelona, officials in Atlanta in the late nineteenth and early twentieth centuries were interested in making it a city that was emblematic of modernity; thus it hosted expositions in 1881, 1887, and 1895. The largest, the 1895 Cotton States and International Exposition, was an event of weighty proportions by including a Negro Building—with exhibitions showing the progress of African Americans in the South—as well as Booker T. Washington's famous speech (mocked at the beginning of Ralph Ellison's *Invisible Man*) in which he more or less accepted segregation while promoting black education and economic advancement (Newman 216). Leading into the nineteenth century, Atlanta used its status as a railroad hub and more "modern" reputation as a means of becoming a popular convention site—a business it continues today. As Jim Crow laws segregated the South, Atlanta strove to attract black and white tourists and convention-goers by providing hotels, restaurants, and clubs in different neighborhoods that could serve both populations separately (Newman 218). By the 1960s Atlanta became more eager than most Southern cities to promote desegregation as the policy became bad for business, thus causing Mayor William B. Hartsfield to declare that Atlanta was a city "too busy to hate" (quoted in Newman 218).

Such was the image that Atlanta aimed to put forward in its attempts to become an Olympic city. Yet not surprisingly and similar to Barcelona's, Atlanta's redevelopment of urban space in order to build venues was plagued by gentrification that displaced African American communities from the city center. For example, the construction of the Olympic Village caused the demolition of the Techwood Homes public housing project, displacing

1,000 residents, of which only 100 returned to the post-Olympics community (Newman 225). In addition, the Atlanta Committee for the Olympic Games (ACOG) entered into another lower-income community to build the Olympic Stadium only steps away from the Atlanta–Fulton County Stadium—home of the Atlanta Braves Major League Baseball team—where two major interstates also pass through the area. Faced with protests by the community, the ACOG agreed to demolish the old stadium and reconfigure the new one for the Braves (Newman 224–25). While ACOG honored its promise, the area around what is now Turner Field has experienced widespread gentrification as condos and townhomes, owned by private investors, now fill an area once slated for urban renewal.

The influence of private investment in Atlanta's hosting of the Summer Olympics greatly affected how the international press perceived the games and their "success." In addition to a heavy corporate presence by Coca-Cola and AT&T, which set up stages in Olympic Park, the city also leased out booths to food and souvenir vendors on city streets, giving the Olympics a carnival atmosphere. The initial desire of the ACOG was to have as much private funding of the games as possible, and the committee fell quite short of this goal. The lack of funds meant that Olympic venues were not built with design in mind, and the press noted their architectural lackluster (Newman 226). Yet for all of the uniformity of the Olympic venues, the closing ceremony was a "Southern Jamboree" that featured local music, including Little Richard. For all of Atlanta's efforts to fulfill the image of the "international" city of the New South, its efforts, combined with several logistical problems, led International Olympic Committee president Juan Antonio Samaranch (a Catalan from Barcelona) to declare the games "most exceptional" and not the "best ever" as he had at the close of the four previous Olympics (Newman 233). Yet while Atlanta's efforts were not as well received as those of Barcelona, the same effort to transform the "modern" city into an image of international cooperation produced the same postmodern commodification of Southern exceptionality—making it into a homogenous site of leisure that continues to be performed in the marketplace.

Among the various public sites that cooperated with the ACOG, including several universities in the area, perhaps the most compelling example of the marketing, and resulting dilution, of Southern exceptionality occurs at Stone Mountain State Park. The site for three Olympic events, Stone Mountain also contains the three tenets of Southern tourism: nature, history, and an amusement park. The "mountain" is actually an exposed dome of granite—one of the largest east of the Mississippi River. It is carved with the largest high-relief sculpture in the world meant to be the Confederate version of Mount Rushmore, featuring the images of General Thomas "Stonewall" Jackson, General Robert E. Lee, and Confederate States of America (CSA) president Jefferson Davis. While the amusement park predates the Olympics, Stone Mountain has certainly transformed itself into a site with a controversial history of Southern exceptionality to a site where people can experience homogenized Southern pseudo-events that deny the mountain's own "tarnished" history. The result is a prototypical example of how commodifying exceptionality chips away at it in a manner that causes a tendency toward the denial of memory in favor of amusement that again promotes consuming culture instead of experiencing it.

Visitors to Stone Mountain today are not denied history per se—there is a very large relief sculpture that obviously promotes it. Yet the history given to park visitors leaves out the detail that the mountain was the site of the 1915 reemergence of the Ku Klux Klan, the fraternal organization founded to promote white supremacy in the South. Originally founded by Confederate general Nathan Bedford Forrest during Reconstruction, the organization had more or less disbanded by the twentieth century, that is, until D. W. Griffith's film *Birth of a Nation* (1915) brought the Klan back into public consciousness. The revival of the modern Klan in the South is credited to William Joseph Simmons, a minister whose desire to reinstate the Klan involved an extensive effort to reconstruct its "original" form. Simmons made sure to include Nathan Bedford Forrest's grandson to link his Klan to the "original" organization's founder, carefully researched other fraternal organizations to understand their traditions, and incorporated the cross-burning custom—something the original Klan never did but that was derived from the novel *The Clansmen* (1905), on which Griffith's film was based. The choice of Stone Mountain for the organization's reemergence seemed a logical one given that the relief sculpture memorializing the Confederacy had been conceived and was in progress. Simmons's Klan even helped raise funds for the memorial, which had to be abandoned and was only finished in 1972 after the state of Georgia purchased the mountain and surrounding land in 1958.

Despite Stone Mountain's association with the Ku Klux Klan and the desire of early neo-Confederates to make it the Mount Rushmore of the Confederacy, the contemporary visitor to Stone Mountain Park quite obviously finds no evidence of this link. Instead, visitors find a series of attractions and events that celebrate a "universalized" and carefully constructed Southern history designed not to offend. For example, the Antebellum Plantation and Farmyard is a collection of pre–Civil War buildings from around the state of Georgia; thus, in having no specific referent to the past, they cannot be directly linked to the trauma of Southern history. In addition, the *Tall Tales of the South 4D Movie* that "celebrates the South's love of storytelling" gives visitors an image of Southern culture in a package that is accessible and comical to all (Stone Mountain Park web site)—not unlike the park's universalized "country stores" where visitors can make their own candles and soap in a setting that is almost more western (thus more accessible) than Southern. Stone Mountain also offers attractions that are specifically not Southern, in particular its Sky Hike, a roped obstacle course through the park's trees. What is most striking, however, about Stone Mountain's construction of Southern exceptionality while offering a "wide variety of family fun activities" is just how successful it has been in converting a controversial historical site into one of consumption and leisure. This conversion is evidenced by the fact that, unlike other Confederate monuments, such as plantations and battlefields, Stone Mountain enjoys a diverse crowd of visitors, including a large number of African Americans. Thus in its successful conversion to a leisure site, Stone Mountain shows how the New South's assertion of universality entails a similar erasure of memory and the same performance of nationhood that we saw with its claims of exceptionality.

Within the desire to promote a neater and safer image of national identity there exists a level of narcissism, identified by Antonio Sánchez in his study of Barcelona's Moll d'Espanya, in which the image of itself that a city projects to the world becomes self-fulfilling as it promotes this ideal to its own citizens. Yet as such images are constructed narratives of national authenticity, especially since it is usually a historic site that is "reclaimed," they are subject to the same kinds of discontinuities and fragmentation that all narratives of imagined nationhood experience. A prototypical example of such redevelopment is Underground Atlanta, a previously abandoned commercial center that was deemed a historical site in the 1960s and experienced a brief boom with the Olympics and following the 1990 opening of the World of Coca-Cola, the company's museum that has since moved. The space that is now Underground Atlanta was originally a series of buildings built during Atlanta's post–Civil War railroad boom. By the early twentieth century concrete bridges connecting the railroads led many store owners to move their businesses to the upper levels, causing the "underground" portion to be mostly abandoned. While the area's rediscovery in the 1970s caused an initial boom as an entertainment site, recent renovations of the area as a shopping mall have been relatively unsuccessful, with the city of

Atlanta having to more or less financially support the project. Part of the problem that Underground Atlanta faces, however, is one of its own history of segregation in that downtown Atlanta has always been occupied either by businesses (whose workers leave at 5 P.M.) or African Americans, who have populated the area since Jim Crow demanded there be separation of the races within the city. Realizing this fact, club and restaurant owners in Underground Atlanta are now trying to specifically attract an African American clientele—an action that has not been well received by Underground Atlanta's owners who still envision the area as a tourist site. Thus while city planners may want to imagine themselves as immune to history, sites like Underground Atlanta show quite definitively that such a desire is unrealistic. Again, in trying to selectively forget a city's history, one runs the risk of literally digging up an uncanny past as Atlanta's "underground" struggles to find a place in the city's renewed image.

The construction of renewed Southern spaces is at the center of John Sayles's satirical film *Sunshine State* (2002). Focusing on a small town on Florida's northern coast resisting further development by a real-estate company, Sayles's dark comedy, though very different from Guerín's *En construcción*, also explores the ambivalence inherent in trying to remold geographic spaces with tourist infrastructure in mind. What is most compelling about *Sunshine State*, however, is that, again like Guerín's film, it avoids easy contradictions between the North and South, past and present, progress and gentrification, as the film showcases stereotypical elements of Southernness—the stoic belle, the Civil War reenactor, and the racist restaurateur—but utilizes these characters in unconventional manners by making the belle a liberal crusader who runs a nonprofit theater, the reenactor a first-generation Greek American who tells his ex-wife (while in Civil War–era uniform) that "you can't live in the past," and the restaurateur a blind old man who is more or less ignored by those around him and shoves off desegregation as inevitable and "not so bad." In so doing, Sayles uses "types" of Southernness and reconfigures them as inverse parallels of touristic images and promises of growth that come with real-estate development. In other words, Sayles shows how seemingly essential elements of Southern culture are constructions while simultaneously showing how redevelopment of the Southern landscape is no less constructed or exclusive than the exceptionality that tourist sites market to their visitors.

Sunshine State connects its various characters in Delrona Beach, Florida, as some welcome and some protest the onslaught of developers. While the film clearly has a political agenda in showing the perils of real-estate development in the coastal South, it also defies the idea that this contemporary community has any authentic origins in the film's opening shots. The first scene shows a youth burning a pirate ship that we later discover is the main float for the annual "Buccaneer Days," a poorly attended series of events meant to celebrate the area's pirate history for a tourist audience. Its organizer, Francine Pinkney (Mary Steenburgen), admits that her attempt to homogenize and clean up the beach's torrid history of pirates, slavery, and Native American killings has been to no avail when she cries to her husband the town does not "know how difficult it is to invent a tradition." As a juxtaposition, the film's second scene features a group of retirees golfing as they walk the golf course and Murray describes their "discovery" of the naked swampland: "In the beginning, there was nothing. . . . Endless raw acreage, a land infested with crocodiles— . . . Crocodiles, alligators—if you're talking retirement bungalows, that's not a selling point." Yet as another golfer points out, they bought "nothing" because they knew they were not selling land, but "dreams," a "concept," and "sunshine." When Murray describes their appropriation of "nothingness," however, he explains a contradictory process of asserting exceptionality (with its essential allure of a mythic origin) while creating universally enjoyed sites of leisure like resorts, retirement communities, and golf courses. Such a contradiction, however, proves elusive to the golfers, as Murray proudly identifies what they created: "Nature on a leash."

Between the "Buccaneer Days" tourist event and Murray selling "sunshine dreams" to certified public accountants from Toledo who "don't want to spend their golden years trekking through slush," *Sunshine State* clearly links tourist infrastructure and urban planning as it shows the effects that homogenized development specifically has on how individuals interact within communities. In particular, the film points to Lincoln Beach, an African American community typical of many in the New South that, formed in the 1930s and 1940s as a result of Jim Crow, is threatened with displacement and dilution by the aptly named Plantation Estates development—a gated community selling its own image of Southern tranquility for a predominantly white audience. As the community's self-proclaimed defender and spokesman, Dr. Lloyd (Bill Cobbs) explains the area's slow decline to a younger African American visitor who asks, "So what happened?" He responds, "Civil Rights happened. Progress. Used to be you were black, you'd buy black. Jim Crow days, you need your shoes shined, wanted to ride a taxi to the train station, wanted some ribs, a fish sandwich, chances are a black man owned the place you got it in. Now the drive-thrus will serve anybody. But who owns them? Not us. All our people are doing is wearing paper hats and dipping out them fries. The only thing we have left are funeral parlors and barbershops." As the young man protests, claiming that now African Americans can do anything, Dr. Lloyd chuckles but acknowledges, "Them that can get over do fine. Them that can't are in a world of trouble." Here the audience hears an alternative narrative to the "progress" and "harmony" of the New South and, in particular, the role that the touristlike infrastructure of shopping malls and restaurant chains plays in that process. In addition, while Dr. Lloyd seems to be advocating a Jim Crow–like system, instead what he is rejecting is a forgetting of history and, more important, the fragmentation of a community's interaction that inevitably comes with the kind of progress brought by redevelopment. For Dr. Lloyd, if artifacts of struggle are left to die, then that loss elicits the inevitable question of why that struggle existed to begin with as they camouflage the dangers caused by new types of struggle.

The subtlety with which *Sunshine State* encapsulates the elements of "Southernness" in manners that highlight their performative nature proves almost too nuanced to make citing specific examples profitable.[2] Yet what stands out about performed Southernness in this film is that it becomes isolated to elements that illuminate how communities form and individuals interact with one another, and, for Sayles, it is such interaction, and not any abject idea of Southernness per se, that is threatened by the kind of development that seeks uniformity via consumption. In this respect, *Sunshine State* proves ironically similar to Guerín's *En construcción*, and what is most striking about these two films is that ideas of community in both are questioned most with the discovery of an ancient burial site. As such, despite protests from present communities who stake their claims to the landscape, a Native American burial ground stops the Plantation Estates development at the end of *Sunshine State*. Thus despite the golfers' claims that "in the beginning there was nothing," Sayles shows that, within the realm of "development" and "progress," the image of a naked landscape is nothing more than a dream that can be sold to the highest bidder.

Though Sayles's film seems to assert an authentic origin to Native American culture, again his film makes no easy assertions of authenticity since the construction worker who digs up the bones is himself a Native American who discounts his coworker's idea that he has access to some eternal "lore" and instead describes his parents' business selling lawn ornaments to tourists. Instead, Sayles uses the same set of golfers that opened his film in its closing to show how the idea of essential origins is a sellable image and how even that image has been tarnished in the era of postmodern homogenization. Describing how Spaniards came to Florida looking for gold they never found, killing countless Native Americans in the process, Murray the golfer bemoans, "What do we have today where you can strike it rich like that, transform your life in an instant?" Countered with a man who won the Florida lottery, he declares, "It lacks poetry." Murray's main issue, however, is that people do not even seem to want such authenticity any more, instead opting to appear on quiz shows and date supermodels. Finally, when told there may be gold on the moon, he finds mystery and wonder in the idea of "prospecting in outer space" just as the Spanish did in Florida. The camera moves from him to his golf ball being hit into open traffic on a boulevard filled with strip malls and burger joints, ricocheting off a sandwich shop sign and almost hitting a tourist (played by director John Sayles). As one of the other golfers asks, "But what will we do for Indians?," the screen fades to black as the viewer is left to consider the ever-present costs of asserting an "essential" right of a person to take land and change his or her life—whether it be Spanish sailors seeking gold or Northeast retirees lusting after sunshine and palm trees. What Murray and his golfing compatriots describe, however, is not just real-estate development, but the creation of an imagined community that, in Boorstin's image of a postmodern world, usually originates from a diluted version of an already-imagined nation, hence the creation of Plantation Estates. Thus while it seems that coastal development becomes an inclusive, diverse enterprise—with shopping malls and drive-thrus that "serve anybody"—it actually involves the same assertions of authenticity that we observe with performed exceptionality. For this reason, resorts and real-estate developers can successfully market the idea of "something different for everyone" when they are usually selling the same thing to a privileged few.

As Dean MacCannell describes when quoting Boorstin, it is very much in vogue to bemoan tourism—a fact echoed in a common Southern bumper sticker, quoted by Richard Starnes in his anthology on tourism in the South, "If It's Tourist Season, Why Can't We Shoot 'Em?" (1). Yet exploring tourist discourse and how it emerges in city planning shows that, as cities seek to make the "old" authentically "new," the difference between tourist and native is blurred as both are asked to accept uncontested images of coded nationhood. The degree to which tourism reflects performance emerges in tandem with J. L. Austin's idea that to "say" something is to "do" something else. As tourists, when we "do" something on vacation, we are actually *not* "saying" something else; that is, to ride the gondola up Stone Mountain is to ignore the space's contested history and accept a benign version of that history that the mountain's sculpture relief represents. While I am not saying that people avoid such tourist sites, I am suggesting that the relationship between tourist and native is one that goes back to Homi Bhabha's idea of colonial mimicry, the desire for an "other" that is almost the same but not quite. Tourists often strive to do what the "locals" do only to find themselves enacting an image of cultural exceptionality—such is the fate of the tourist in New Orleans who wears Mardi Gras beads when it is not carnival season or the unwitting tourist in Spain who eats bad paella in a region where it is not a typical dish. It is that difference that allows so-called natives to make the tourist into an other when recent urban planning and real-estate projects, as both Guerín's and Sayles's films show, make us all into tourists who want our geographic spaces to "say" something about us as citizens. Exploring the performativity in tourist discourse and urban planning, furthermore, breaks down the relationship between "insider" and "outsider," "self" and "other," by exposing how we simultaneously exoticize and obliterate the past not just as a means of constructing concrete ideas of nationhood, but in how we do something seemingly universal: just have fun. Thus as planners construct tourist sites and urban development projects, they unwittingly consider not what people want to "do" when they live and play, but how they want to "act" to the outside world.

CONCLUSION

From Tourism to Time Travel

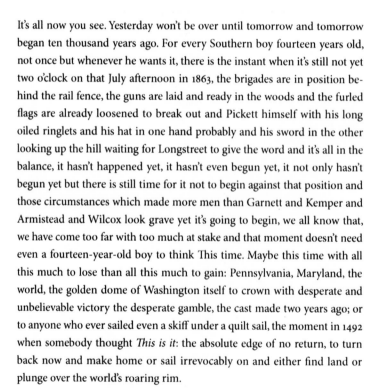

It's all now you see. Yesterday won't be over until tomorrow and tomorrow began ten thousand years ago. For every Southern boy fourteen years old, not once but whenever he wants it, there is the instant when it's still not yet two o'clock on that July afternoon in 1863, the brigades are in position behind the rail fence, the guns are laid and ready in the woods and the furled flags are already loosened to break out and Pickett himself with his long oiled ringlets and his hat in one hand probably and his sword in the other looking up the hill waiting for Longstreet to give the word and it's all in the balance, it hasn't happened yet, it hasn't even begun yet, it not only hasn't begun yet but there is still time for it not to begin against that position and those circumstances which made more men than Garnett and Kemper and Armistead and Wilcox look grave yet it's going to begin, we all know that, we have come too far with too much at stake and that moment doesn't need even a fourteen-year-old boy to think *This time*. Maybe this time with all this much to lose than all this much to gain: Pennsylvania, Maryland, the world, the golden dome of Washington itself to crown with desperate and unbelievable victory the desperate gamble, the cast made two years ago; or to anyone who ever sailed even a skiff under a quilt sail, the moment in 1492 when somebody thought *This is it*: the absolute edge of no return, to turn back now and make home or sail irrevocably on and either find land or plunge over the world's roaring rim.

—WILLIAM FAULKNER, *INTRUDER IN THE DUST*

It is often said that being a tourist makes us appreciate home, and it is with a conception of a particularly "Spanish" or "Southern" home that I choose to conclude this study. Yet what is interesting about tourism, being a product of an industrial modernity that separates the individual from the means of production and the product of work itself, is how it attempts to return us to a primal existence on a beach, in the mountains, or in a museum discovering our "roots." As we observed in chapter 6, however, what ultimately happens is something in between: never allowed to fully access "nature" or "the past," we remain suspended within the realm of the packaged tour that allows us to leave home while having all of its creature comforts. While there is much to criticize in contemporary tourism, the performativity inherent within it reveals a great deal about how we self-conceptualize identity in relation to nationality, exceptionality, and both collective as well as personal memory. Nowhere is this relationship more apparent than in the works of Thomas Wolfe and Juan Goytisolo. Both self-imposed exiles from the South and Spain, respectively, Wolfe and Goytisolo present scathing attacks against tourism as events that fragment human experience and memory, only further detaching the individual from the means of marking his or her identity. While emotionally painful for both the authors and their autobiographical characters, the experience of exile allows them to examine the performativity inherent in efforts to self-identify with national exceptionality. Thus the concept of "home" for these authors ceases to exist as an essential component of their identity as its meaning becomes lost to them, forcing these domestic tourists to reconceptualize "home" in relation to their own memory of it, both good and bad.

The liminality and ever-present possibility inherent in their image of tourism as well as their own exile takes us to the epigraph above: William Faulkner's assertion in *Intruder in the Dust* that every young Southern boy can return to the moment in July 1863 just before the Battle of Gettysburg, and the U.S. Civil War itself, was lost to the Confederacy. When he says, "It's all in the balance, it hasn't happened yet, it hasn't even begun yet, it not only hasn't begun yet but there is still time for it not to begin," he illustrates how that moment exists in the past to be renewed, and enacted, in the present. It is not without consequence that Faulkner compares this moment to the beginning of Spain's imperial enterprise: Columbus's 1492 voyage. In this passage, Faulkner makes a key connection between the renegotiation of defeat and loss and how that renegotiation is linked to impending discovery. With that connection in mind, my goal with this project has been to examine the various manifestations of perceived loss within twentieth-century Spanish and Southern culture and how the renegotiation of that loss entails a performance—articulated and enacted via Francoism and Jim Crow—in which to call yourself a Spaniard or a Southerner was to participate in a selective remembering, and forgetting, of the past. While Faulkner's assertion seems romantic, in reality it speaks to the manner in which trying to re-create a seminal moment in history itself becomes a moment of psychic tourism that allows us to displace ourselves from the present in a manner that, when understood and examined, allows us to construct memory—a conception of "home"—in a manner that compels discovery instead of erasure, diversity instead of monolithic systems of power.

It is the spirit of discovery that dominates the ends of Wolfe's *You Can't Go Home Again* (1940) and Goytisolo's *Señas de identidad* [*Marks of Identity*] (1966). In their engagement with the tourist experience, both authors reposition the idea of "home" as an uncanny form that haunts their main characters with the very space each has sought to escape. By being uncanny, "home" is neither completely recognizable nor completely foreign; thus the result of home becoming "uncanny" is that both Wolfe and Goytisolo reduce it to a series of fragments that can be let go and reimagined via their own relationship to the nation-state. In so doing, Wolfe and Goytisolo make the idea of home into an entity that must be performed. Put differently, the act of escaping and/or returning "home" becomes a ritualized act in which to call a geographic space "home" involves the act of clinging to, or recoiling against, a specific language, customs, and history. It is not a coincidence, therefore, that Wolfe's and Goytisolo's main characters, George Webber and Álvaro Mendiola, enact their complex relationships with home by both leaving it and coming back. With this apparent escapism and clinging, they reveal a melancholia by self-identifying with a lost home they still hate, eventually absorbing that hatred into their own psyches. Within both writers' aesthetics, home is a ritualized act that is imagined in tandem with the self, and just as home becomes a purely semiotic form, both writers use their own autobiographies in the same manner since their novels are not efforts to provide an established narrative truth. Quite the opposite, Wolfe and Goytisolo take only fragments of their own life as pieces of their fragmented narratives, rendering the self as uncanny as home itself. This detachment allows for a careful examination of the performatives of "self" and "nation" in a manner that allows us to understand the relationship to the other.

Like George Webber in *You Can't Go Home Again*, Thomas Wolfe was horrified by real-estate speculation and tourist commodification in Asheville, North Carolina—depicted as Libya Hill in *You Can't Go Home Again* and Altamont in *Look Homeward Angel* (1929). George Webber's description of his sleepy mountain town is of one that is full of "madness" as he observes: "On all sides he heard talk, talk, talk—terrific and incessant. And the tumult of voices was united in variations of a single chorus—speculation and real estate" (104). As George tries to acclimate to being "home," all he feels is homelessness as his town and its inhabitants become fragmented into mere voices; meanwhile, space suffers the same fate as every piece of land changes ownership almost daily. Indeed, George comes to equate any concept of home with destabilization—hence the novel's title. In Wolfe's case, as Louis Rubin notes, the only meaning the author could give his native Asheville was "that of change," which is why "once he had described the process of alienation he could not return there artistically. He never came home again, physically or spiritually, save for short visits" (71). Yet for both Wolfe and his George Webber, trying to find a new home in Nazi Germany, and their experience there as tourists, is what culminates their perpetual exile from any attempts at rootedness but also allows them a space for real evaluation of their relationship to a "primal" sense of nation as both Wolfe and George Webber seek solace in the "spirit" of the German people as their own nationality and regional affinity only make them feel "homeless."

Like Thomas Wolfe, the young writer George Webber experiences great success and personal satisfaction in Germany. Yet George's trip to early Nazi Germany slowly becomes an effort to negotiate the obvious signs of Nazi oppression with his personal love for German culture. Based upon a similar experience Wolfe had in pre-Nazi Germany in 1929, the novel's final pages relate George's train ride out of Germany when a Jewish man in his compartment trying to flee the country is caught by the Gestapo and arrested. Before this moment, George simply had enjoyed the company and communion of his four fellow travelers—themselves fragments of humanity that, by chance, happened to coalesce in the one space and time. George admits as much when he says that he and the others felt ashamed after the man was dragged away: "They all felt as if they were saying farewell, not to a man, but to humanity; not to some pathetic stranger, some chance acquaintance of the voyage, but to mankind" (659). For George, this moment has less to do with Germany or fascism as much as it has to do with how five individuals—fragments in the cloth of humankind—came together in time and space only to have a piece torn away from them, making them all feel exiled within their own perceived sense of community.

This profound feeling of exile, furthermore, propels George to arrive at the conclusion that titles his novel when a German woman in his train car admits relief at being "out" of Germany. As George contemplates what it means to be "out" of a place that could once have been so dear to a person, he realizes that indeed "you can't go home again—not ever. There [is] no road back" (664). In realizing that there is no path back toward a collective unconscious as he leaves Germany, George in many ways embodies the suspension between competing ideas of nationality that allows one to explore them honestly by being able to discern the fragments and see its place within a whole, not making the fragment into the whole itself. As such, he looks "outward, outward toward the rich and life-giving soil of a new freedom in the wide world of all humanity. And there came to him a vision of man's true home, beyond the ominous and cloud-engulfed horizon of the here and now, in the green and hopeful and still-virgin meadows of the future" (664). As George returns to the United States, he is armed with a newfound freedom, which he exercises by leaving his editor (echoed in Wolfe's real-life abandonment of Maxwell Perkins) and making a proclamation also echoed by Wolfe: his resignation from the Lost Generation. George proclaims that while he was lost as a young man, he is by no means lost anymore, and there is a masculine tone to his newfound freedom. What George (and to a large degree Wolfe) denies by rejecting membership within a "Lost Generation" is the escapist tendencies of what George calls the "sensitive man of talent, the young genius, crucified by life, misunderstood and scorned by men"— in many respects, the image of the modern subject described throughout this project. George describes this figure in perpetual conflict and escape from life, which he characterizes as wholly negative since it creates men who are "deficient in the vital materials and experiences of life" who think of themselves as "exempt from the human laws that govern other men" (682). What George claims to realize is that "humility and tolerance and human understanding" are the means to selfhood, to understanding the fragment that connects him to humanity as a whole (617). Thus he is not "lost" as a fragmented exile himself, but instead he moves forward in a narrative of which he sees himself a part.

In rejecting the idea of being "lost," George also denies the "exceptionality" that brands him an exile as well as the "exceptionality" that defines his Southern heritage. Yet the South seems to remain within George's consciousness—yet another fragment that, pace Eliot, is the sum of his experiences. As such, George describes himself as someone whose sense of self is rooted in the past. He says about himself, "No man that I have known was ever more deeply rooted in the soil of Time and Memory, the weather of his individual universe, than was I" (700). He continues to describe this contemplation of identity being Southern in origin when he admits, "That was a giant web in which I was caught, the product of my huge inheritance—the torrential recollectiveness, derived of my mother's [Southern] stock, which became a living, million-fibered integument that bound me to the past, not only of my own life, but of the very earth from which I came, so that nothing in the end escaped from its inrooted and all-feeling explorativeness" (701). The "giant web" that George describes no doubt is that of the melancholic subject whose detachment from the world around him comes from the need to cling to an "inheritance," an "integument that bound [him] to the past" in a way that made "home" into a form that could only compel fear—fear of a Southern past that he was not only clinging to but that also seemed familiar in an "American" present.

For this reason, the end of Wolfe's novel projects a different image of "America"—one that attempts to reject exceptionality by shirking the idea of "home" as an uncanny performative. Thus he asserts that "America" may indeed be "lost" but that its discovery "is before us. I think the true fulfillment of our spirit, of our people, of our mighty and immortal land is yet to come. _ think the true discovery of our own democracy is still before us. And I think that all these things are certain as the morning, as inevitable as noon. I think I speak for most men living when I say that our American is Here, is Now, and beckons on us, and that this glorious assurance in not only our living hope, but our dream to be accomplished" (702). While these finals lines seem blindly utopian, Wolfe's vision of America as a possibility and a fulfillment "yet to come" demonstrates the desire of the melancholic to find an new object-love, one not located in a haunted past, but in the "Here" and "Now." Before this moment, Wolfe's image of the United States was one whose own claims to exceptionality mirrored those of the South; they did not stand as an opposition. In this moment, Wolfe's vision of the United States as a possibility suggests a desire to shirk exceptionality as an entity performed by nations. In other words, to say "You can't go home again" does not mean that home does not exist, but instead that "home" must always remain in flux, if only to ensure that one never melancholically clings to it.

Wolfe's rejection of concrete ideas of home or nationhood sprung directly from his experiences with fascism, particularly Nazism, while traveling in Europe. For Wolfe, fascism itself was emblematic of accepting a partial fragment as complete truth. Critic Shawn Holliday paints such an image of Wolfe during the final years of his life when his writing became explicitly political. In particular, Wolfe's reaction to Francisco Franco's decision to arrange for tourism during Spain's Civil War led to a chiding response from Wolfe in a letter when he says he would like to "visit the various craters and ruined masonries throughout the town of Barcelona, paying particular attention to the subway entrance where a bomb exploded and killed 126 men, women, and children" (quoted in Holliday 77). Wolfe's sarcasm reflects a distaste for fascism, but its biting critique at the hands of Franco's desire to encourage foreign tourism seems particularly poignant for a man who was horrified at the commodification of his sleepy Southern Asheville, much as George is in *You Can't Go Home Again*. In other words, as Holliday has posited (77), Wolfe seemed to understand the importance of selling an image of a culture in trying to present a static image of it to the world. While Wolfe was by no means unique in his rejection of Francoist Spain (in this respect, he echoed many of the "Lost Generation" he chastised), he was particularly sensitive to the perils of accepting a tourist-driven image for a national whole. Thus his rejection of fascism was not just political, but very personal, as ability to demystify an exceptional South made him see that exceptionality was by no means a claim that was uniquely Southern.

Within Thomas Wolfe's acceptance of the "possibility" of America was a process in which he had to cope with his own anti-Semitism and racism. Robert Brinkmeyer Jr. follows Paschal Reeves's study of Wolfe in identifying his virulent anti-Semitism and indications of a eugenics-based image of race, which was common in the period. While Wolfe no doubt became more leftist and readily antifascist by the end of his career, his conceptions of race and ethnicity still provoke debate. Scholars like George Hovis see, by close-reading Wolfe's fiction, a writer who was not handicapped by his racism, but instead asserts that "the albatross of racism was the very thing that gave Wolfe the power to write so authentically and powerfully about racism in America" (98). While it is not my desire to engage directly the issue of Wolfe's racism, the debate at hand speaks to the manner that Wolfe's exile from the South, embracing of Germany, and abandonment of both were indeed the very elements that informed his images of nationhood as it related to his personal identity. The fact that his relationship to place and identity was fraught with struggle speaks to the potential inherent in the liminal space the exile possesses—the same space, I argue, that exists within the realm of performativity. The conscious role of exile, meanwhile, is one that Juan Goytisolo continues to play to this day, having left for Paris in 1956 and choosing to live in Marrakech to this day. Yet Goytisolo's desire to rid himself of Spain and its exceptionality is also one of struggle, as he admits, "In spite of all my efforts to remain in the margins of the problem of Spain, it was impossible to do so. Spain came back to haunt me in my most grave moments with its destructive force. I am referring to the resurgence of my indignation against all that official Spain represented, the same indignation of old, as if the only possible link between me and my country were, after all these years, that oppressive feeling of frustration, impotence, and rage of which I ingenuously thought myself cured and which, after having poisoned me since adolescence, threatened to escort me to my grave" (quoted in Ugarte 149). For Goytisolo, as well as his Álvaro Mendiola in *Señas de identidad*, remaining on the margins of Spain comes at a high cost, and his interest in the ways in which claims to national exceptionality fragment personal identity speaks to William Faulkner's influence on his work, who not only served as godfather to Goytisolo's stepdaughter but whose *The Sound and the Fury* was a major source of inspiration.[1] Yet most like Wolfe, it was tourist commodification that best epitomized the fragmentation of national exceptionality, and this experience famously ends his already fragmented voice in *Señas de identidad*.

The first in what is known as the Mendiola trilogy, *Señas* concerns an autobiographical main character who, coming from a prominent family who made their fortune in Cuba and having lost a parent in the Spanish Civil War, must reconcile his claims and losses to Spanish exceptionality, which Álvaro must do as he returns to Spain to make a documentary about domestic migrant workers. Through the fragmented perspective stemming from his own memory, his camera's eye, as well as his current observations, Goytisolo, through his character, manipulates the idea of "home" to such a degree that it becomes, in the same moment, nostalgic and grotesque, reflective and forward-thinking. In so doing, Goytisolo is able to take the idea of an "exceptional" home and extract it from any sense of a perceived "Spanishness." Or, as Randolph Pope has put it, "His novels are an unconditional search for *a truthful life*—not for a *truth* that could become institutionalized and be imposed as a dogma on others—and they drive away the reader who is not willing to examine his or her own cherished certainties" (93).

Álvaro's time in Spain, filming, remembering older films of the Civil War, and recalling his own experiences, produces a situation in which Álvaro, instead of being closer to his native country, remains melancholically detached from it. Genaro J. Pérez, in his book *Formalist Elements in the Novels of Juan Goytisolo*, points to the use of defamiliarization when he describes Álvaro's filming of a bullfight as he remembers scenes from the Civil War, specifically the massacre of locals at La Graya on May 29, 1936. The juxtaposition between the massacre of civilians by the Civil Guard and the killing of a bull illustrates to the reader Álvaro's place within Spanish national identity as he struggles to remember and says, "Rescata esta imagen del olvido: la

asamblea acecha la bocacalle en silencio y dos hombres apuntan por un za-
guán con una bandera roja.... Es el grito de la antigua y amorzada libertad,
del Viejo tiempo en que la esperanza de los tuyos se cifraba en su símbolo
elemental y hermoso. Tú asistías, alucinado, a su despliegue insólito al cabo
de tantos años sidos y no vividos, vacíos y privados de su sustancia con la
misma emoción con que en la cinemateca presenciaste los documentales
de Ivens y Karmen sobre la guerra civil" ["Rescue this image from forgetting. The crowd gathers silently in the street entrance and two men appear
with a red flag.... It's the shout of an ancient and stifling freedom, of an old
time when the hope of your countrymen was coded in their beautiful and
elemental symbol. You were there, hallucinated, at this unusual display after
so many years that have been and not been lived, empty and private of sub-
stance with the same emotion you had in the cinémathèque watching Ivens
and Karmen's documentaries on the Civil War"] (114). In Álvaro's attempt to
"rescue" his memory—an effort to reclaim the object-lost—his detachment
from an exceptional Spain becomes an allegory for the detachment of the
film's spectator who watches the "unusual" display of something that should
be quite familiar. Simultaneously, Goytisolo's hero is "hallucinated," haunted
by the familiarity of what he sees coupled with his own alienation from that
very image. In one moment Goytisolo has captured the very uncanniness
of "home" as he breaks that idea down not just into a ritual, but into an
image of that act that can be projected onto a screen. Thus "home," as in
Wolfe's novels, is deconstructed to a performative, and Álvaro's exile is the
only means by which he can understand it in relation to his own identity.

As Álvaro struggles to grapple with a conception of home that he has
lost, he continues to be more and more alienated from that concept, particularly as Spain becomes more and more attractive as a tourist destination.
Like Wolfe's character who shows scathing hatred of real-estate speculation
and tourism in the "sleepy mountain village" meant to represent Asheville,
Goytisolo paints a fairly negative picture of 1960s Francoist Spain, which
had just begun opening up to tourists. The novel ends with Álvaro in Barcelona, visiting the city among a group of tourists, remembering moments of
his past and seeing a monument to a group of fallen Nationalists, of which
his father was one. This moment in the novel is by far the most fragmented
as Goytisolo parodies the tourists' comments in bits of European languages:
"regarde comme c'est beau / c'est magnifique / mais ou c'est Chistophe Co-
lomb / it's so wonderful / qu'est-ce que c'est que ça / do you see the boat /
guarda il mare" (318).[2] As he depicts people overlooking the water in Barcelona—dressed in hackneyed print shirts and sandals (318)—he depicts the

tourist experience as not just inauthentic, but as a ritualized act, juxtaposing it with the two main lies of his childhood: his family's hiding the real death of his father and the arrival of a "relative" from Cuba who turns out to be a black man descended from his great-grandfather's freed slaves. Having been nourished with the image of Spanish nationalism—both in the context of the Civil War victory and imperial prosperity—Álvaro is truly left an exile, a tourist in his own country, as the "truths" of nationhood and selfhood become nothing more than images to soothe his melancholia. As he contemplates Spanish history, he finds himself "pensando en la historia de tu país tuya solamente a intermitencias / en su pasado que no era más que esto / pasado" ["thinking about the history of your country, yours only at moments / about a past that was nothing more than that / past"] (332). As Álvaro recalls a historical and a personal past, however, he reveals a hatred for both, which Michael Ugarte points to when he notes how intertextuality in *Señas* "remains subordinate to an existential problem, an all-encompassing issue that governs the structure of the work. The textual struggle is, in effect, a cultural and existential confrontation between the author and his world" (72). Indeed, the fragments of Spanish nationalist discourse throughout the novel become an effort to reconstruct the events of his life, and his failure to completely "reclaim" his marks of identity suggests a need to move away from history and toward discourse (Ugarte 73)—or toward a conception of the past that is nothing more than a collection of signs that can be molded, and performed, for individualized purposes.

With the move toward discourse, and with it performance, Goytisolo appears to follow Faulkner in asserting that one *can* always reclaim the past for personal reasons in a manner not at all unlike what Francoism and Jim Crow promoted. Yet what they suggest is actually closer to Wolfe's assertion: you really can't go home again. But this inability is not to suggest that the past remains unavailable to us but more that a concrete conception of "home" never existed to begin with—it was merely a performative. With this idea of "home" in mind, part of the reason this project has focused specifically on performance is that, as Diana Taylor notes, it "allows for alternative mappings, providing a set of strategies and conventions that allow scholars to see practices that narrative, poetry, or even drama as a scripted genre might occlude. Like other genres, performance encompasses a broad range of modes and categories" (1417). It allows us to engage in this process, furthermore, by uniting the various claims to exceptionality that seem to divide the field itself, that is, speech acts and ritual. Examining the various performances of Spanishness and Southernness within modernity and, even more, within Francoism and Jim Crow allows us see how discourse—words like "different," "pure," and "nation"—become enactments of identity that represent efforts to construct a memory of an identity perceived as lost. The melancholic response to that loss, furthermore, becomes a maniacal claim to authenticity that must be let go or that will uncannily haunt the individual. For this reason, Goytisolo describes a Spain that he cannot quite shake and why Southern writer Lilian Smith, as Robert Brinkmeyer Jr. has noted, identifies several ghosts of segregation in the South, noting, "Even its children know the South is in trouble" (quoted in Brinkmeyer 1). Thus in order for melancholia to be overcome, a coded Spain and South must be let go in order for the psyche to be free to simultaneously focus on a new, personal sense of identity while effectively remembering the old one.

In fact, one of the primary goals of this project has been to "let go" of Spain and the South if only to remember and examine these entities in new ways. The desire to study Spain and the South anew is by no means unique to this project, and, in fact, both Peninsular and Southern studies have undergone radical changes in the last twenty years as cultural studies and literary theory have informed us of the manner in which we, as scholars, construct history. As Jo Labanyi notes in the introduction to *Constructing Identity in Contemporary Spain*, "Histories of modern Spanish culture, and the individual critical studies that support them, tend to construct a seamless narrative which tells the story of the evolution of high-cultural tastes, given an appearance of continuity through the emphasis on influences" (3). Similarly, Tara McPhereson describes an analogous situation concerning scholarship on the South: "Though southern studies is by no means a unified or monolithic category, a tendency prevails within the field to *preserve* the South, that is, to focus on those elements that unify the region rather than to pursue it in relation to national or global contexts. Such an approach always runs the risk of fixing or freezing southern culture, often at its most stereotypical moments, even in work that seeks to overturn these very stereotypes" (9). Part of the reason that scholarship tends to "preserve" images of Spain and the South is the linguistic power of national identity. In saying, "I am a Spaniard/Southerner," one actually invokes an image of that identity that is hard to shake. My work, therefore, has been not to explore Spain and the South per se but their various performatives that extend beyond geographical boundaries to explore alternative representations of time, gender, and race that are contained in what seems Spanish or Southern.

While McPhereson makes it clear that the South is an imagined entity, she still insists that "if one is to understand the many versions of the South that circulate throughout U.S. history and culture, one has always to see them as fundamentally connected to, and defined in relation to, the non-South" (2). While my own work sees projections of Spanishness and Southernness as reliant upon—and a questioning of—a non-Spain and non-South, her assertion runs contrary to my desire to explore manifestations of Spanishness and Southernness beyond their own boundaries of Europe and the United States. Such has been the aim of, respectively, transatlantic studies within Peninsular and Latin American scholarship and studies into what critics in U.S. and Latin American letters refer to as the "global South." Within the field of transatlantic studies, examining the tensions and discontinuities between Europe and America has helped deconstruct the binaries that inform our knowledge of these spaces, particularly those of First World and Third World, colonial and postcolonial. That very move has caused contemporary U.S. scholarship at times to locate the South outside of its U.S. boundaries, seeing it, as scholar John Lowe does, at the northernmost point of the Caribbean. By locating the South within alternate geographies, there exists the ability to remap its particularities as pertaining to wider cultural and social phenomena.

Spain's and the South's alleged "exceptionality" was, and often continues to be, the driving force behind the study of each culture. While this project examines Spanish and Southern exceptionality, its primary goal has been to detach exceptionality from a specific space, like Spain or the South, and instead explore the construction, and performance, of exceptionality within modernity. Meanwhile, since the purpose of this project was to construct a narrative of exceptionality, then it seems reasonable to return to the question: why Spain and the South? Part of the reason is what Cohn and Smith point to as the South's "uncanny (*unheimlich*) hybridity" in that the South has served as both "self" and "other," or better, both a subject and object of postcolonial subjugation—a quality that Spain also shares. Thus within the context of regional or national exceptionality, Spain and the South are not concrete models of that phenomenon, but examples of its slippage. Both Spain and the South have served as others that have been "almost the same" as a "modern" U.S. or European "self" but not quite (Bhabha 86). In addition, the performativity inherent in each space's expression of coded identity is constructed around an ambivalence inherent in the desire to be both the same and different. It is that ambivalence, however, that allows a study of Spain or the South to disavow and deconstruct similarly essentialist ideas of a non-Spain and a non-South, for example, ideas that England or the northeast United States is more "progressive." Whether these assertions may or may not be true is irrelevant to the fact that they often rely on an image of these places as "other" in order to exist. Thus the process of "letting go" of Spain and the South involves abandoning the rigidity inherent in the relationship between self and other that informs our knowledge of these spaces. The result, furthermore, is a "lack" of stable identity, but it is one that, I argue, does not compel a melancholic self-identification with the past, but instead is a process by which memory and identity are fluid entities that come to signify not what we have lost as citizens and scholars, but everything that we have to gain.

NOTES

INTRODUCTION

1. Indeed, the monuments on the South Carolina statehouse grounds provide a detailed narrative of constructed memory that exists slightly outside the scope of this project. In addition to a gun from the USS *Maine*, there is a statue of a soldier in remembrance of South Carolina's participation in the Spanish-American War that, of course, asks us to "Remember the *Maine*." This monument, erected in 1941, stands to the direct left of the Civil War monument, famous for the Confederate flag controversy that still exists in South Carolina. The flag was removed from the statehouse on July 1, 2000, as part of a compromise in which a memorial to African American achievements in history was erected nearby. This controversy also includes an ongoing boycott by the National Association for the Advancement of Colored People (NAACP) in South Carolina.

2. All translations, except where otherwise noted, were made by the author.

CHAPTER 1

1. In his biography *Miguel de Unamuno: The Agony of Belief*, Martin Nozik describes the speech in detail (122) and cites several sources for it in his notes, above all, Louis Portillo's "Unamuno's Last Lecture," published in *Horizon* in 1953. Unamuno's comments are also described at length in Hugh Thomas's *The Spanish Civil War* (1961).

2. The accusation of "fascism" against the Fugitives and Agrarians stems from an editor at the *American Review* who both published and admired the Agrarian ideology but who also praised the efforts of Hitler and Mussolini. The Agrarians, particularly Ransom, staunchly refuted these accusations. Yet their connection to conservative thought of the period is fairly evident though it is both unfair and reductive to call it "fascist."

3. Mark Twain's disdain for chivalric tales in many ways dominated his work, evidenced by a novel like *A Connecticut Yankee in King Arthur's Court* and, more famously, his blaming Sir Walter Scott for the U.S. Civil War in *Life on the Mississippi*. In addition, his creation of the notably quixotic Tom Sawyer, who is influenced by tales of chivalry, appears most prominently as a juxtaposition with the pragmatic Huckleberry Finn, who contests one of his and Tom's "adventures" of looting diamonds from Arabs when all he sees is their wrecking havoc on a Sunday school picnic. Huck says, "I didn't see no diamonds, and I told Tom Sawyer so. He said there was loads of them there, anyway; and he said there was A-rabs there, too, and elephants and things. I said, why couldn't we see them, then? He

said if I warn't so ignorant, but had read a book called *Don Quixote*, I would know without asking" (25).

4. My discussion of *All the King's Men* comes from the reedited version of the novel in which Noel Polk recovered several of the novel's aspects that were removed by editors—the most notable of which is the change of Governor Willie Talos in the manuscript to Willie Stark in the 1946 final version.

CHAPTER 2

1. The lynching of black men, often for false allegations of rape of white women, was common during the Jim Crow period, and multiple photographs of public lynchings still exist. Similarly, Francoism saw as a major threat the order of the Free Masons, repressing the organization of which Franco's own brother was rumored to be a member. Instead of destroying the items collected from the Masons, however, Franco guarded them to study the group. Most of the items, including hoods and artifacts (not completely unlike those used in Ku Klux Klan ritual), can be seen in the Civil War Archives in Salamanca, Spain.

CHAPTER 3

1. While the name is the same, the assumption that Quentin Compson in *Absalom, Absalom!* is the same as the character in *The Sound and the Fury* is problematic, especially since we also find out later in the novel that Quentin Compson's niece also shares his name. Such playfulness with character and the fact that Faulkner often used the same name for different characters in his fiction suggests that we should see the two Quentin Compsons as different, despite the fact that they seem to be the same.

CHAPTER 4

1. Gregorio Maramón was a physician and philosopher noted for his work in endocrinology and sexual reform in early twentieth-century Spain. Hildegart Rodriguez, one of his students, was also famous in Spain for her work on sexual reform and eugenics, herself born to a mother who, unmarried, chose Hildegart's father for eugenesical reasons (his exact identity is still speculated) and later murdered her.

CHAPTER 5

1. Entzminger quotes an interview with Welty, who describes the character of Fay, "You could scratch the skin and there wouldn't be anything under it, the way she would see things. And to me, that is horrifying and evil, almost sinful" (136).

CHAPTER 6

1. While the essentialized "other" described in chapter 4 became a racial distinction, another image in the South—with its own racialized identity—is the Appalachian

hillbilly, a culture group of Scotch-Irish descent who are associated primarily with Virginia, Tennessee, and North Georgia. Because of the group's isolation (a consequence of their rural location), the stereotype of their being "inbred" has plagued images of the population, specifically following the film *Deliverance*. Yet at the same time, the group's unique speech and music give it a seemingly essential allure (in a manner not at all different from the depiction of African Americans in the South).

2. While the film as a whole has various moments of Old and New South differences clashing, the most prominent examples come from Lincoln Beach resident Eunice Stokes (Mary Alice) and her estranged daughter, Desiree (Angela Bassett), who has returned after a long absence from the town. Throughout the film, Desiree points out the various changes that have occurred since she has been gone, including her mother's warming up of Popeye's fried chicken in the microwave when she used to fry her own. In addition, when Francine Pinkney, bemoaning that she cannot invent a tradition to a local developer, says that she has booked a Seminole to attract tourists, the developer thinks she is referring to a Native American. She responds, "No, not the Seminoles, the *Seminoles*. . . . Of course, the football team. What would I want with a real Indian?"

CONCLUSION

1. While naming the alleged "influences" on Goytisolo's work seems somewhat ancillary, it is poignant to note that most critical studies of the author mention Faulkner as a major influence on Goytisolo's work. In addition, Kessel Scwartz's comprehensive study of the author lists, among the U.S. authors Goytisolo has mentioned, a notable array of Southerners. As Wade notes, "American novelists have left their mark on Goytisolo. He copied John Dos Passos in his slice of life technique, leading in and out of time stream in a lengthwise time direction. William Goyen's *The House of Breath*, Carson McCullers' *The Heart is a Lonely Hunter*, which was an 'astonishing revelation' for Goytisolo, along with *Reflections in a Golden Eye* and *The Member of the Wedding*, and Truman Capote's *Other Voices Other Rooms* and *The Grass Harp*, influenced Goytisolo. . . . He claimed that William Styron's *Lie Down in Darkness* would have made Flaubert grown [*sic*] pale with jealousy" (25).

2. The quote will be translated here with the specific languages in brackets: "look how beautiful [French] / it's magnificent [French] / of course it's Christopher Columbus [French] / it's so wonderful [English] / What's that over there [French] / Do you see the boat [English] / Look at the sea [Italian]." The slashes are used here to represent line breaks within the original text.

BIBLIOGRAPHY

Afinoguénova, Eugenia, and Jaume Martí-Olivella, eds. *Spain Is (Still) Different: Tourism and Discourse in Spanish Identity.* Lanham, Md.: Lexington Books, 2008.

Almodóvar, Pedro, dir. *Hable con ella.* 2002. Film.

———. *Todo sobre mi madre.* 1992. Film.

Allen, William Rodney. *Walker Percy: A Southern Wayfarer.* Jackson: University Press of Mississippi, 1986.

Anderson, Benedict. *Imagined Communities.* 1983. Reprint, New York: Verso, 1991.

Ashford Hodges, Gabrielle. *Franco: A Concise Biography.* New York: Thomas Dune Books, 2002.

Austin, J. L. *How to Do Things with Words.* 1962. Reprint, New York: Oxford University Press, 1965.

Baker, Houston A., Jr. "To Move without Moving: An Analysis of Creativity and Commerce in Ralph Ellison's Trueblood Episode." *Proceedings of the Modern Language Association* 98.5 (1983): 828–45.

Baroja, Pío. *El árbol de la ciencia.* 1911. Reprint, Madrid: Catedra, 2005.

Barriuso, Carlos. *Los discursos de la modernidad: Nación, imperio y estética en el fin de siglo español (1895–1924).* Madrid: Biblioteca Nueva, 2009.

Bhabha, Homi. "Of Mimicry and Man: The Ambivalence of Colonial Discourse." In *The Location of Culture*, 121–31. New York: Routledge, 1994.

Bial, Henry. "Introduction." In *The Performance Studies Reader*, ed. Henry Bial, 1–4. New York: Routledge, 2003.

"Blame It on New Orleans." *Designing Women.* Writ. Mark Alton Brown and Dee LaDuke. Dir. David Trainer. March 4, 1991. Television.

Blotner, Joseph. *Faulkner: A Biography.* New York: Random House, 1974.

Blotner, Joseph, and Frederick Gwynn. *Faulkner in the University: Class Conferences at the University of Virginia, 1957–58.* Charlottesville: University of Virginia Press, 1959.

Bone, Martyn. *The Postsouthern Sense of Place in Contemporary Fiction.* Baton Rouge: Louisiana State University Press, 2005.

Boorstin, Daniel. *The Image: A Guide to Pseudo-Events in America.* 1961. Reprint, New York: Atheneum, 1971.

Bowen, Wayne H. *Spain during World War II.* Columbia: University of Missouri Press, 2006.

Bravo, María-Elena. *Faulkner en España: Perspectivas de la narrativa de postguerra.* Barcelona: Ediciones Península, 1985.

———. "Los parientes faulknerianos de *Pascual Duarte*." *Nueva Estafeta* 50 (1983): 39–49.

Bretz, Mary Lee. *Encounters Across Borders: The Changing Visions of Spanish Modernism, 1890–1930*. Lewisburg, Me.: Bucknell University Press, 2001.

———. *La evolución novelística de Pío Baroja*. Madrid: J. Porrua Turanzas, 1979.

Brinkmeyer, Robert H., Jr. *The Art and Vision of Flannery O'Connor*. Baton Rouge: Louisiana State University Press, 1989.

———. *The Fourth Ghost: White Southern Writers and European Fascism, 1930–1950*. Baton Rouge: Louisiana State University Press, 2009.

———. "New Orleans, Mardi Gras, and Eudora Welty's *The Optimist's Daughter.*" *Mississippi Quarterly: The Journal of Southern Culture* 44.4 (1991): 429–41.

Brister, J. G. "*Absalom, Absalom!* and the Semiotic Other." *Faulkner Journal* 22.1–2 (Fall 2006–Spring 2007): 39–53.

Britt-Arredondo, Christopher. *Quixotism: The Imaginative Denial of Spain's Loss of Empire*. Albany: State University of New York Press, 2005.

Brooks, Cleanth. *William Faulkner: The Yoknapatawpha County*. 1963. Reprint, Baton Rouge: Louisiana State University Press, 1990.

Brown, Bertram Wyatt. *Southern Honor: Ethics and Behavior in the Old South*. New York: Oxford University Press, 1982.

Butler, Judith. *Gender Trouble: Feminism and the Subversion of Identity*. New York: Routledge, 1999.

———. "Performative Acts and Gender Constitution: An Essay in Phenomenology and Feminist Theory." In *The Performance Studies Reader*, ed. Henry Bial, 154–66. New York: Routledge, 2003.

Cabello, Gabriel. "Construyendo tiempo: Los ensayos cinematográficos de José Luis Guerín." *Ciberletras* 12 (2005). http://www.lehman.cuny.edu/ciberletras/v12/cabello.htm.

Carbonell, Jordi. "The Olympic Village, Ten Years On: Barcelona: The Legacy of the Games, 1992–2002." Centre d'Estudis Olímpics, 2002.

Cela, Camilo José. *La familia de Pascual Duarte*. Madrid: Ediciones Destino, 2003.

Cervantes y Saavedra, Miguel. *El Ingenioso Hidalgo Don Quijote de la Mancha*. Ed. Florencio Sevilla Arroyo. Madrid: Ludwig, 2004.

Charlebois, Lucile. *Understanding Camilo José Cela*. Columbia: University of South Carolina Press, 1998.

Clarke, John Henrik, ed. *William Styron's Nat Turner: Ten Black Writer's Respond*. Boston: Beacon Press, 1968.

Cobb, James C. *Away Down South: A History of Southern Identity*. New York: Oxford University Press, 2005.

Cohn, Deborah. *History and Memory in the Two Souths: Recent Southern and Spanish American Fiction*. Nashville, Tenn.: Vanderbilt University Press, 1999.

Cohn, Deborah, and Jon Smith. *Look Away! The U.S. South in New World Studies*. Durham, N.C.: Duke University Press, 2004.

Coles, Robert. *Flannery O'Connor's South*. Athens: University of Georgia Press, 1993.

Conkin, Paul K. *The Southern Agrarians*. Knoxville: University Press of Tennessee, 1988.

Cooper, William J., and Thomas E. Terrill. *The American South: A History*. New York: Knopf, 1990.

Cowan, Louise. *The Fugitive Group: A Literary History.* Baton Rouge: Louisiana State University Press, 1959.

Creel, Bryant L. *Don Quijote, Symbol of Culture in Crisis.* Valencia, Spain: Albatros Hispanofila, 1988.

Cubana, La. "Rams." *Teresines, S.A.* Televisió de Catalunya, 1992. Television.

Derrida, Jacques. "Signature Event Context." In *Limited Inc.*, 1–24. 1988. Reprint, Evanston, Ill.: Northwestern University Press, 2000.

Desmond, John F. *Risen Sons: Flannery O'Connor's Vision of History.* Athens: University of Georgia Press, 1987.

———. *Walker Percy's Search for Community.* Athens: University of Georgia Press, 2004.

Duck, Leigh Anne. "Haunting Yoknapatawpha: Faulkner and Traumatic Memory." In *Faulkner in the Twenty-first Century*, ed. Robert W. Hamblin and Ann J. Abadie, 89–102. Jackson: University Press of Mississippi, 2003.

Dupuy, Edward J. *Autobiography in Walker Percy: Repetition, Recovery, and Redemption.* Baton Rouge: Louisiana State University Press, 1996.

Dyer, Richard. *White.* New York: Routledge, 1997.

Eichelberger, Julia. *Prophets of Recognition: Ideology and the Individual in Novels by Ralph Ellison, Toni Morrison, Saul Bellow, and Eudora Welty.* Baton Rouge: Louisiana State University Press, 1999.

Ellison, Ralph. *Invisible Man.* 1947. Reprint, New York: Vintage, 1995.

Entzminger, Betina. *The Belle Gone Bad: White Southern Women Writers and the Dark Seductress.* Baton Rouge: Louisiana State University Press, 2002.

Fant, Joseph, and Robert Ashley. *Faulkner at West Point.* New York: Random House, 1964.

Faulkner, William. *Absalom, Absalom!* 1936. Reprint, New York: Vintage, 1990.

———. *Intruder in the Dust.* 1948. Reprint, New York: Vintage, 1991.

———. *Light in August.* 1932. Reprint, New York: Vintage, 1991.

———. *The Snopes Trilogy: The Hamlet, The Town, and The Mansion.* New York: Modern Library, 1994.

———. *The Sound and the Fury.* 1929. Reprint, New York: Vintage, 1984.

Flatley, Jonathan. *Affective Mapping: Melancholia and the Politics of Modernism.* Cambridge, Mass.: Harvard University Press, 2008.

Forter, Greg. "Against Melancholia: Contemporary Mourning Theory, Fitzgerald's *The Great Gatsby*, and the Politics of Unfinished Grief." *differences: A Journal of Feminist Cultural Studies* 14.2 (2003): 134–70.

Foucault, Michel. *The History of Sexuality.* New York: Pantheon Books, 1978.

Frese Witt, Mary Ann. *The Search for Modern Tragedy: Aesthetic Fascism in Italy and France.* Ithaca, N.Y.: Cornell University Press, 2001.

Freud, Sigmund. "Fetishism." In *The Standard Edition of the Complete Psychological Works of Sigmund Freud*, 21:152–57. London: Hogarth Press, 1961.

———. "Mourning and Melancholia." In *The Standard Edition of the Complete Psychological Works of Sigmund Freud*, 14:237–43. London: Hogarth Press, 1961.

———. "The Uncanny." In *The Standard Edition of the Complete Psychological Works of Sigmund Freud*, 17:219–56. London: Hogarth Press, 1961.

Fuchs, Barbara. *Passing for Spain: Cervantes and the Fictions of Identity.* Urbana: University of Illinois Press, 2003.

Galdós, Benito Pérez. *Doña Perfecta.* 1876. Reprint, Madrid: Catedra, 1997.

García Delgado, José Luis, ed. *Franquismo: El juicio de la historia.* Madrid: Temas de Hoy, 2000.

García Lorca, Federico. *Yerma.* 1934. Reprint, Buenos Aires: Editorial Losada, 1969.

Gautier, Théophile. *Voyage en Espagne.* 1845. Reprint, Paris: La Pallantine, 1982.

Geist, Anthony L., and José B. Monleón. *Modernism and Its Margins: Reinscribing Cultural Modernity from Spain and Latin America.* New York: Garland, 1999.

Gibson, Ian. *Camilo Jose Cela: El hombre que quiso ganar.* Doral, Fla.: Santillana, 2003.

Gilroy, Paul. *The Black Atlantic: Modernity and Double-Consciousness.* Cambridge, Mass.: Harvard University Press, 1993.

Ginés, Montserrat. "Intellectual Affinities: The Southern Fugitive-Agrarians and the Spanish Generation of '98." In *Nor Shall Diamond Die: American Studies in Honor of Javier Coy,* ed. Carme Manuel and Paul Scott Derrick, 179–88. Valencia: Universitat de Valencia, 2003.

———. *Southern Inheritors of Don Quixote.* Baton Rouge: Louisiana State University Press, 2001.

Girón Echevarria, Luis Gustavo. "Langston Hughes' Civil War Verse." *Anuario de Estudios Filológicos* 28 (2005): 91–101.

Gorfkle, Laura J. *Discovering the Comic in Don Quixote.* Chapel Hill: University of North Carolina Press, 1993.

Goytisolo, Juan. *Señas de Identidad.* Barcelona: Seix Barral, 1976.

Grandes, Almudena. *Las edades de Lulú.* 1989. Reprint, Barcelona, Spain: Fabula Tusquets, 1994.

Grant, Susan-Mary. *North Over South: Northern Nationalism and American Identity in the Antebellum Era.* Lawrence: University Press of Kansas, 2000.

Guerín, José Juis, dir. *En construcción.* [*Work in Progress.*] 2001. Film.

Gwynn, Frederick L., and Joseph L. Blotner. *Faulkner in the University.* 1959. Reprint, Charlottesville: University Press of Virginia, 1995.

Harrison, Jospeh. "Introduction: The Historical Background to the Crisis of 1898." In *Spain's 1898 Crisis: Regeneration, Modernism, Postcolonialism,* ed. Joseph Harrison and Alan Hoyle, 1–8. Manchester: Manchester University Press, 2000.

Hobsbawm, Eric, and Terrance Ranger. *The Invention of Tradition.* New York: Cambridge University Press, 1992.

Holguin, Sandie. *Creating Spaniards: Culture and National Identity in Republican Spain.* Madison: University of Wisconsin Press, 2002.

Holliday, Shawn. *Thomas Wolfe and the Politics of Modernism.* New York: Peter Lang, 2001.

Holthouse, David. "Shirley Q. Liquor, After Imus: A Black Face Comic Who Sings '12 Days of Kwanzaa.'" *Rolling Stone,* May 31, 2007. http://www.rollingstone.com/news/story/14474389/shirley_q_liquor_after_imus_a_black_face_comic_who_sings_12_days_of_kwanzaa.

Hughes, Langston. "Letter from Spain Addressed to Alabama." In *The New Anthology of American Poetry: Modernisms: 1900–1950,* ed. Camille Roman and Thomas J. Travisano, 190. New Brunswick, N.J.: Rutgers University Press, 2005.

Inman Fox, Edward. "Baroja and Schopenhauer: *El árbola de la ciencia*." *Littérature comparée* 38 (1963): 350–59.

Jerez-Farrán, Carlos. "Pascual Duarte y la susceptibilidad viril." *Hispania* 32.2 (1989): 47–63.

Jiménez, Juan Ramón. *Eternidades.* 1918. Reprint, Bilbao: Ediciones Beta III Milenio, 2007.

Johnson, Carroll B. *Don Quixote: The Quest for Modern Fiction.* Prospect Heights, Ill.: Waveland Press, 2000.

Johnson, Roberta. *Gender and Nation in the Spanish Modernist Novel.* Nashville, Tenn.: Vanderbilt University Press, 2003.

Kagan, Richard L., ed. *Spain in America: The Origins of Hispanism in the United States.* Chicago: University of Chicago Press, 2002.

Kamen, Henry. *Empire: How Spain Became a World Power 1492–1763.* New York: Harper Collins, 2003.

Kennedy, Todd. "Hitting the American Highway: The Ontology of the Hobo-Hero in Twentieth-Century American Culture." Unpublished manuscript in author's possession.

Kreiswirth, Martin. "Faulkner's Dark House: The Uncanny Inheritance of Race." In *Faulkner's Inheritance*, ed. Joseph Urgo and Ann Abadie, 126–40. Jackson: University Press of Mississippi, 2007.

Kreyling, Michael. *Inventing Southern Literature.* Jackson: University Press of Mississippi, 1998.

Kristeva, Julia. "Word, Dialogue, Novel." In *The Kristeva Reader*, ed. Toril Moi, 34–61. New York: Columbia University Press, 1986.

Kronik, John. "Pascual's Parole." *Review of Contemporary Fiction* 4.3 (1984): 111–18.

Labanyi, Jo, ed. *Constructing Identity in Contemporary Spain: Theoretical Debates and Cultural Practice.* Oxford: Oxford University Press, 2002.

———. *Myth and History in the Contemporary Spanish Novel.* New York: Cambridge University Press, 1989.

Laforet, Carmen. 1945. *Nada.* Reprint, Barcelona: Destino, 1996.

Lawson, Lewis, and Victor A. Kramer, eds. *More Conversations with Walker Percy.* Jackson: University Press of Mississippi, 1993.

Lima, Robert. *The Dramatic World of Valle-Inclán.* Suffolk, England: Tamesis Books, 2003.

Litvak, Lily. *A Dream of Arcadia: Anti-industrialism in Spanish Literature, 1898–1905.* Austin: University of Texas Press, 1975.

Lowe, John. "Richard Wright and Transnational Culture: *Pagan Spain*." *Southern Quarterly* 46.3 (2009): 69–99.

Loxham, Abigail. "Barcelona Under Construction: The Democratic Potential of Touch and Vision in City Cinema as Depicted in *En Construcción* (2001)." *Studies in Hispanic Cinemas* 3.1 (2006): 33–46.

MacCannell, Dean. *The Tourist: A New Theory of the Leisure Class.* 1976. Reprint, Berkeley: University of California Press, 1999.

MacKethan, Lucinda. *Daughters of Time: Creating Woman's Voice in Southern Story.* Athens: University of Georgia Press, 1990.

Magin, Alison. "Female Erotic in Post-Franco Spain: The Will to Disturb." *Ciberletras* 8 (2002). http://www.lehman.cuny.edu/ciberletras/.

Marsh, Steven. *Work in Progress. Senses of Cinema* 50 (2009). http://archive.sensesofcin
ema.com/contents/09/50/contents.html.

Mártin Gaite, Carmen. *El cuarto de atrás.* 1978. Reprint, Barcelona: Destino, 1981.

———. *Usos amorosos de la postguerra española.* 1987. Reprint, Madrid: Anagrama, 1994.

Martín-Santos, Luís. *Tiempo de Silencio.* 1961. Reprint, Barcelona: Seix Barral, 2001.

May, Robert. *The Southern Dream of a Caribbean Empire: 1854–1861.* Baton Rouge: Louisiana
State University Press, 1973.

McDermid, Paul. *Love, Desire, and Identity in the Theatre of García Lorca.* Rochester, N.Y.:
Tamesis, 2007.

McGowan, John. *Postmodernism and Its Critics.* Ithaca, N.Y.: Cornell University Press, 1991.

McKenzie, Jon. "The Liminal-Norm." In *The Performance Studies Reader,* ed. Henry Bial,
26–31. New York: Routledge, 2003.

McPhereson, Tara. *Reconstructing Dixie: Race, Gender, and Nostalgia in the Imagined South.*
Durham, N.C.: Duke University Press, 2003.

Merino, Eloy E. "La alegoría de la violencia falangista en *La familia de Pascual Duarte de
Cela.*" *Ojancano* 16 (1999): 3–28.

Monleón, José B. *Del Franquismo a la posmodernidad: Cultura española, 1975–1990.* Madrid:
Akal Editores, 1995.

Mullen, Edward. *Langston Hughes in the Hispanic World and Haiti.* Hamden, Conn.:
Archon Books, 1977.

Murcia Serrano, Inmaculada. *La razón sumergida.* Salamanca, Spain: Luso-Española de
Ediciones, 2009.

Neighbors, Jim. "Plunging (Outside of) History: Naming and Self-Possession in *Invisible
Man.*" *African American Review* 36.2 (2002): 227–42.

Newman, Harvey K. "Atlanta's Olympics and the Business of Tourism." In *Southern
Journeys: Tourism, History and Culture in the Modern South,* ed. Richard D. Starnes,
215–39. Tuscaloosa: University of Alabama Press, 2003.

Nozik, Martin. *Miguel de Unamuno: The Agony of Belief.* Princeton, N.J.: Princeton
University Press, 1992.

O'Connor, Flannery. *Collected Works.* New York: Library of America, 1988.

Oldfield, John. "Remembering the *Maine*: The United States, 1898 and Sectional
Reconciliation." In *The Crisis of 1898: Colonial Redistribution and Nationalist Mobilization,*
ed. Angel Smith and Emma Dávila-Cox, 45–64. New York: St. Martin's Press, 1999.

Ortega y Gasset, José. *La deshumanización del arte.* 1925. Reprint, Madrid: Alianza, 2002.

——— *España invertebrada.* 1921. Reprint, Madrid: Revista de Occidente, 1967.

———. *Meditaciones del Quijote: Ideas sobre la novela.* 1914. Reprint, Madrid: Espasa-Calpe,
1969.

Ownby, Ted. "Nobody Knows the Troubles I've Seen, but Does Anyone Want to Hear about
Them When They're on Vacation?" In *Southern Journeys: Tourism, History and Culture
in the Modern South,* ed. Richard D. Starnes, 240–50. Tuscaloosa: University of Alabama
Press, 2003.

Pack, Sasha. *Tourism and Dictatorship: Europe's Peaceful Invasion of Franco's Spain.* New
York: Palgrave, 2006.

Patt, Beatrice. *Pío Baroja*. New York: Twayne, 1971.

Peacock, James. *Segregation: The Inner Conflict in the South*. New York: Random House: 1956.

———. "The South in a Global World." *Virginia Quarterly Review* (Autumn 2002): 581–94.

Percy, Walker. *The Moviegoer*. 1961. Reprint, New York: Vintage International, 1998.

Pérez, Genaro J. *Formalist Elements in the Novels of Juan Goytisolo*. Potomac, Md.: J. Porrúa Terranzas, North American Division, 1979.

Pérez, Louis A., Jr. *The War of 1898: The United States and Cuba in History and Historiography*. Chapel Hill: University of North Carolina Press, 1998.

Pérez Firmat, Gustavo. "Carmen Laforet: The Dilemma of Artistic Vocation." In *Women Writers of Contemporary Spain: Exiles in the Homeland*, ed. Joan Lipman Brown, 26–41. Newark: University of Delaware Press, 1991.

Perrian, Chris, et al. *A New History of Spanish Writing, 1939 to the 1990s*. London: Oxford University Press, 2000.

Pinedo, Javier. "Ser otro sin dejar de ser uno mismo: España, identidad y modernidad en la Generación del 98." *Cuadernos Americanos* 2 (2000): 132–64.

Portillo, Louis. "Unamuno's Last Lecture." In *The Golden Horizon*, ed. Cyril Connoly, 397–409. London: Weidenfeld and Nicholson, 1953.

Pope, Randolph. *Understanding Juan Goytisolo*. Columbia: University of South Carolina Press, 1995.

Powell, Brittany R. "Don Quijote de Yoknapataphwa: Cervantine Comedy and the Bakhtinian Grotesque in William Faulkner's Snopes Trilogy." *Comparative Literature Studies* 43.4 (2006): 482–97.

Pratt, William, ed. *The Fugitive Poets: Modern Southern Poetry in Perspective*. Nashville, Tenn.: J. S. Sanders, 1991.

Preston, Paul. *Franco: A Biography*. New York: Basic Books, 1994.

Prown, Katherine. *Revising Flannery O'Connor: Southern Literary Culture and the Problem of Female Authorship*. Charlottesville: University Press of Virginia, 2001.

Quint, David. *Cervantes's' Novel of Modern Times: A New Reading of Don Quixote*. Princeton, N.J.: Princeton University Press, 2003.

Radford, Andrew. "The Invisible Music of Ralph Ellison." *Raritan: A Quarterly Review* 23.1 (2003): 39–62.

Ramon Resina, Joan. *Disremembering the Dictatorship: The Politics of Memory in the Spanish Transition to Democracy*. Amsterdam: Rodopi, 2000.

Richards, Michael. *A Time of Silence: Civil War and the Culture of Repression in Franco's Spain, 1936–1945*. New York: Cambridge University Press, 1998.

Roach, Joseph. *Cities of the Dead: Circum-Atlantic Performance*. New York: Columbia University Press, 1996.

Rosenfeld, Harvey. *Diary of a Dirty Little War: The Spanish-American War of 1898*. Westport, Conn.: Praeger, 2000.

Ross, Herbert, dir. *Steel Magnolias*. 1989. Film.

Sánchez, Antonio. "Barcelona's Magic Mirror: Narcissism or the Rediscovery of Public Space and Collective Identity?" In *Constructing Identity in Contemporary Spain:*

Theoretical Debates and Cultural Practice, ed. Jo Labanyi, 294–310. Oxford: Oxford University Press, 2002.

San Cornelio, Gemma. "Live Cities: Film and Media Approaches to European Cities." In *Shifting Landscapes: Film and Media in European Context*, ed. Miyase Christensen and Nezih Erdogan, 198–220. Newcastle: Cambridge Scholars Publishing, 2008.

Sayles, John, dir. *Sunshine State*. 2002. Film.

Scarlett, Elizabeth A. *Under Construction: The Body in Spanish Novels*. Charlottesville: University Press of Virginia, 1994.

Schwartz, Kessel. *Juan Goytisolo*. New York: Twayne, 1970.

Shank, Barry. "Bliss, of Blackface Sentiment." *Boundary 2: An International Journal of Literature and Culture* 30.2 (2003): 47–64.

Shaw, Donald. "The Concept of *Atarxia* in the Later Novels of Baroja." *Bulletin of Hispanic Studies* 34 (1957): 29–36.

Shinn, Christopher A. "Masquerade, Magic, and Carnival in Ralph Ellison's *Invisible Man*." *African American Review* 36.2 (2002): 243–61.

Sieburth, Stephanie. *Inventing High and Low: Literature, Mass Culture, and Uneven Modernity in Spain*. Durham, N.C.: Duke University Press, 1994.

Silber, Nina. *The Romance of Reunion: Northerners and the South, 1865–1900*. Chapel Hill: University of North Carolina Press, 1993.

Singal, Daniel. *Faulkner: The Making of a Modernist*. Chapel Hill: University of North Carolina Press, 1997.

Smith, Paul Julian. *The Theatre of García Lorca: Text, Performance, Psychoanalysis*. New York: Cambridge University Press, 1998.

Soufas, C. Christopher. *Audience and Authority in the Modernist Theater of Federico García Lorca*. Tuscaloosa: University of Alabama Press, 1996.

———. *The Subject in Question: Early Contemporary Spanish Literature and Modernism*. Washington, D.C.: Catholic University Press, 2007.

Styron, William. *The Confessions of Nat Turner*. 1967. Reprint, New York: Vintage, 1992.

Subirats, Eduardo. *Después de la lluvia: Sobre la ambigua modernidad española*. Madrid: Ediciones temas de hoy, 1993.

Taylor, Diana. "Performance and/as History." *TDR: The Drama Review* 50.1 (2006): 67–86.

———. "Remapping Genre through Performance: From 'American' to 'Hemispheric' Studies." *PMLA* 122.5 (2007): 1416–30.

Townsend, June. *William Faulkner y Luis Martín Santos*. Madrid: Editorial Pliegos, 2000.

Trueba Mira, Virginia. "Lulú: El *extraño* personaje de *El árbol de la ciencia* de Pío Baroja." *Anales de la literatura española contemporánea* 28.1 (2003): 183–202.

Twain, Mark. *Adventures of Huckleberry Finn*. 1884. Reprint, New York: Norton, 1999.

Twelve Southerners. *I'll Take My Stand: The South and the Agrarian Tradition*. 1930. Reprint, Baton Rouge: Louisiana State University Press, 1997.

Ugarte, Michael. *Trilogy of Treason: An Intertextual Study of Juan Goytisolo*. Columbia: University of Missouri Press, 1982.

Unamuno, Miguel de. *Niebla*. 1914. Reprint, Madrid: Catedra, 1988.

———. *Del sentimiento trágico de la vida*. 1913. In *Obras Completas*, 106–302. Madrid: Escelier, 1966.

———. *En torno al casticismo.* 1895. In *Obras Completas,* 775–856. Madrid: Escelier, 1966.

Valls, Fernando. *La realidad inventada: Análisis crítico de la novela española actual.* Barcelona: Crítica, 2003.

Vázquez Montalbán, Manuel. *Barcelonas.* Barcelona: Editorial Empúries, 1987.

Warren, Robert Penn. *All the King's Men.* 1946. Ed. Noel Polk. Reprint, New York: Harcourt, 2001.

———. *Segregation: The Inner Conflict in the South.* New York: Random House, 1956.

Welty, Eudora. *The Optimist's Daughter.* New York: Random House, 1972.

Williamson, Edwin. *Cervantes and the Modernists: The Question of Influence.* London: Tamesis, 1994.

Wilson, Charles Reagan. *Baptized in Blood: The Religion of the Lost Cause, 1865–1920.* Athens: University of Georgia Press, 1980.

Wolfe, Thomas. *Look Homeward, Angel.* 1929. Reprint, New York: Scribner, 2006.

———. *You Can't Go Home Again.* 1940. Reprint, New York: Harper, 1998.

Woodward, C. Vann. *The Burden of Southern History.* 1960. Reprint, Baton Rouge: Louisiana State University Press, 1968.

Wright, Richard. *Pagan Spain.* 1955. Reprint, New York: Harper Perennial, 2008.

Yates, James. *Mississippi to Madrid.* New York: Shamal Books, 1986.

INDEX

CPSIA information can be obtained at www.ICGtesting.com
Printed in the USA
BVOW05*1609220115

384416BV00002B/2/P

9 781628 461978